MUCH ALIVE
AT NINETY-FIVE

MUCH ALIVE AT NINETY-FIVE

How God answered my Prayer of Dominant Desire

PHILIP L. GREEN

iUniverse LLC
Bloomington

MUCH ALIVE AT NINETY-FIVE
How God answered my Prayer of Dominant Desire

iUniverse books may be ordered through booksellers or by contacting:

iUniverse LLC
1663 Liberty Drive
Bloomington, IN 47403
www.iuniverse.com
1-800-Authors (1-800-288-4677)

ISBN: 978-1-4759-9622-7 (sc)
ISBN: 978-1-4759-9627-2 (hc)
ISBN: 978-1-4759-9626-5 (ebk)

Printed in the United States of America

iUniverse rev. date: 08/29/2013

CONTENTS

THIS BOOK IS DEDICATED TO

My three children:
Marcia Helen Thompson
Philip Lambeth (Elsie) Green, Jr.
Miriam Louise (Bruce) Salimi

My eight grandchildren:
Allen Scott Thompson (deceased)
Kathryn Suzanne Nowicki
James Arthur (Sherrie) Thompson
David Lee (Carrie) Thompson
Jennifer Lynn Salimi
Carolyn Sue (Neal) Newman
Cynthia Lynn Green
Christine Joy (Jon) Crowe

My twelve great-grandchildren:
Jamie Lynn Thompson-Gregory
Jessica Jane (Donald) Siefert
Patrick David Nowicki (Kristin Lewis)
Lisa Marie (Jonathon) Thompson-Jimenez
Jacquelyn Mae Thompson-Murphy
Victoria Rae Thompson
Erik Ross Thompson
Joshua Philip Green Newman
Matthew Alexander Newman
Eleanore Grace Newman
Thomas Jon Crowe
Michael Christopher Crowe

My thirteen great-great grandchildren:
Timothy Jon Gregory
Allison Jade Gregory
Austin Michael Siefert
Julia Elizabeth Siefert
Blake Charles Siefert
Kassidy Lynn Nowicki
Kody Lee Nowicki
Alexa Laraine Nowicki
Jonathon Allen Scott Jimenez
Elijah Felix Rayne Jimenez
Noah Austin Mart Jimenez
Ethan Owen Murphy
Peyton Jonathon Joseph Murphy

FOREWORD

Rev. O. Gerald Trigg, PhD

It occurred during a Methodist Council of Bishop's meeting in the early 1960s. Bishop Gerald Kennedy, then the youngest bishop, was elected President of the Council, and wished to honor Matthew Welch, then the oldest bishop, just celebrating his 95th birthday. Bishop Kennedy, obviously touched, with misty eyes and quaking voice, turned to the elder bishop and said:

"Bishop Welch, I just hope to be around when you celebrate your hundredth," (never suspecting that the old man might make it). Bishop Welch, not missing a beat, jumped to his feet and replied,

"You look fit; you might make it." And nine years later, at 104, Bishop Welch, with sparkling eyes and vibrant voice, was still attending the General Board of Social Concern's annual session.

For almost three decades, I have been privileged to know, work with, learn from, and marvel at Philip Lambeth Green, son and father of Methodist preachers. From a distinguished career as an Air Force chaplain, ecumenical leader, author, and faithful husband, father, grandfather, great grandfather, and great-great grandfather, he here brings together lessons from his "prayer of dominant desire." He has answered many a call from church and community, with a humble: "Here am I, send me."

Those of us who have journeyed life's road with Phil have not imagined any target year for his departure; rather we have celebrated the arrival of his latest of a series of achievements, his opus magnum: *Much Alive at Ninety-five.*

Augustine once described the Bible as understandable enough for a lamb to wade and deep enough for an elephant to swim. Readers will discover that the faith of Philip Green is like true Christianity: it is "deep and wide." And rather than suffering a "brown-out" with age, he stays forever "Green." Though he writes as a 95-year-old astute observer of life, there are universal truths recorded here.

I cannot think of anyone, regardless of age or station, who will not be enlightened and inspired by reading this book. I am honored to recommend it.

THEIR-WORD

By Marcia (73), Philip L. Jr. (72), and Miriam (64)
(Philip's three children)

There are not many books written by a 95-year-old man using two forefingers on a computer. Our father has written this book while looking in his life's rear-view mirror. He has lovingly given the written word of his wonderful life to us, his three children, his eight grand-children, his twelve great-grandchildren and his thirteen great-great grandchildren and to his many adoring friends everywhere. It is a legacy we will each cherish for the rest of our lives.

Dad has given us meaningful and important reminiscences and insights into his very unique life. Through them we see a rich tapestry of a life lived with the *joie de vivre* of a man who has faced life and its challenges with a simple, yet powerful, devotion to God, to whom he has looked at every turn to guide his path. Many of his reflections are very familiar to us, but we never tire of them; they are an integral part of us. We have always enjoyed our times together when we looked back and played "don't cha remember . . ." This book will help us always remember.

In an often humorous and light-hearted style, he shares his myriad life stories, not in any particular order, taking us here and there, highlighting the memories that were so important to him. What leaves an impression are the experiences of a man with an underlying happy heart, ever glad to be of service to God and others.

There are so many of life's lessons on our father's full life: love, commitment, humor, friendships, dedication, integrity, responsibility, devotion and love of music. His is truly an exemplary life, one of which we are so very proud to be a part.

"Dad, while you were on duty as an Air Force chaplain for twenty years, you moved us around a lot. With every change of residence, as we drove to our new destination, you taught us to sing,

'We've come a long way together, but we still have a long way to go!'

We give you hearty thanks, Dad, for staying with this book, and through it, sharing your very special life memories with us. Throughout our lives you have always been there when we needed you."

MY-WORD

By the author

Most of my friends who are still alive have been wondering about why I wrote this book entitled, *Much Alive at Ninety-five.* I once heard it said that, "Old preachers never die. They just go out to *pastor*." But not me! After 46 years as a pastor (6 in churches, 20 as an Air Force chaplain, 17 as the associate in a 6,000-member congregation), I chose to spend the remaining retirement years in ministries, writings and activities that have kept me up and going.

I wrote this book at my age because I felt led to do so. I have had nearly a life-long "prayer of dominant desire." Such a prayer is one that you really want God to answer, so much so that you put yourself on the line to help Him answer it. As a youth, I found a well-used copy of a book in my father's library entitled, *The Meaning of Prayer,* by H.E. Fosdick. I inherited it and have read it many times. It is priceless.

During my early years as a pastor, I began developing my own prayer of dominant desire. In the beginning it was simply, "Lord, use me." Later I added, "Lord, use me whenever, however and wherever you may wish." After finishing the manuscript for this book, I added, "Lord, use me as long ever as you may wish."

When I was impressed, or led, to write this book, I quibbled a bit with God, saying, "Lord, I am an old man. It's a bit much to do this."

His thoughts to me were, "Philip, you helped your two wives to the end of their lives at age 81 and 94. You have learned to live meaningfully and happily to age 95. You can do it, and I will help you."

He made good on that promise. Others helped me, too.

A young couple in one of my first churches (1936-'40), wrote a letter to us eight years after I had left that appointment. Included in the letter were these words:

"We know that what you did for our church, God did through you."

This book has much to say about what God has done through me. That's another reason I have written it.

The story of how I managed to go from one stage of life to another and another, and how I survived all health and career challenges for more than nine decades, just might help other readers.

ACKNOWLEDGEMENTS

The authenticity of the dates quoted are substantiated by the earlier writings of the author; Time Almanac; my personal journal, copies of 50 years of Christmas letters sent to 150 or more cherished friends and loved ones, and personal correspondence across many decades abroad and in the USA.

In my Christmas letter of 2008, I included more than 20 possible chapter titles for the book I was writing entitled, *Being Young at Ninety-four*. Because I was tardy getting it finished at that age I renamed it to *Much Alive at Ninety-five*. From many of those who received that Christmas letter I received many appreciated ideas and suggestions as to chapter title changes, additions and content. Many of them are included in this book. Thank you to all of you for your suggestions.

I received many helpful suggestions from Rev. Dr. Charles Whittle, *Beliefs Have Consequences,* and *Obey the Holy Spirit,* from Ellie Williams, Joyce Drew, Jennifer Salimi, Ruth Vayhinger (who went all out with suggestions); Harold Ritter, Peggy Iwagoshi, Jo Corbin, Elvira Zenisek and many, many others whose names have been misplaced.

Some of the corrections to my two-finger printing on the computer have been helped by Karen Benberg Agre, Mary Phillips, Jackie Thompson, Victor Snodgrass and my three children, who have proofread all or parts of the manuscript. And to Thomas Walker for helping with some content.

I am especially indebted to Kelly Dennis for stepping into something she had no idea would be such a project and becoming editor of a book. Thank you for sticking with it and taking it through the publishing process. And to iUniverse, Inc. for being so supportive through the whole process.

Finally, my family. They have stood by me and supported me through this book. I can't thank my daughter, Marcia Thompson, enough! Thank you, thank you, thank you! I couldn't have done this without you.

ACKNOWLEDGEMENTS

SECTION I

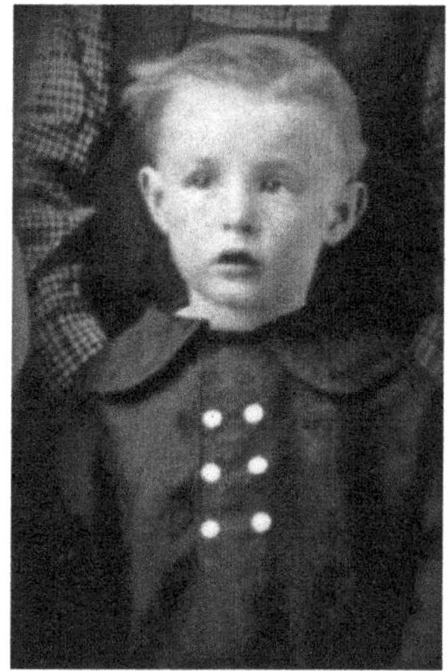

Philip L. Green, age 3

The fears of childhood were mixed with many fun experiences and at little or no cost. I was rich in relationships—poor in earthly possessions.

The life stories of most of the elderly with whom I was acquainted were of interest. My own Grandmother Green was left a widow with five boys and two girls. The oldest was my father. Grandma passed on to them her vibrant faith in God and in a good life. Three of the boys became ordained United Methodist ministers.

On the fourth Monday of each month I meet for lunch with other retired clergy and their spouses. At a recent luncheon, I gained their attention and told them I was grateful for their friendship and that their continuing friendship helped keep me wanting to stay alive at ninety-five.

Everyone I know likes to be chosen (wanted, needed, and asked for). In my own life I took several difficult tasks because some person, or situation, needed me.

The most help and guidance and motivation came from models I admired and wanted to act like and be like. To speak the truth, the nearest I came to breaking one of the Ten Commandments was the one that said, "Thou shalt not covet." I have often wished to be able to preach like many of the preachers I have heard. It was impossible to imitate any of them, but they showed me how to improve my sermons.

1

GROWING UP, A MIXED BAG

Home-life and School for a Preacher's Kid

Mealtime together was a requirement in my home. We were always ready for the next meal because the last one was hardly adequate to last until the next. Food for a family of seven growing children often stretched my mother's ingenuity to the limit. Meat was a commodity available not more than twice a week, but meat derivatives (or leftovers) appeared the next day(s) in food extenders like meatloaf and soup. To kill and prepare one of mother's pullets, or one of her fat hens, was an occasion of happiness, for its meat and juices flavored rice and potatoes for days. Chicken gravy was delicious over a fresh open-faced biscuit.

Gathering us together to eat was never a problem. Getting us quiet and keeping us from snitching morsels of food before "the blessing," or table grace, was a special challenge for mother when father was away. Retaining us at the table, after gobbling up our portions, when we wanted to be off fast to play or follow our own private desires, was another issue. Coming home after school, hungry as bears, we often found the cupboard with hardly more than a crusty piece of stale cornbread. Then, when suppertime came, we would not dare to be absent, though some of us would be guilty of disobedience or infractions of family rules deserving a thump on the head by a tired mother who in that way reminded us that the thump was well deserved. So, frequently, elbows went up to ward off the mild punishment, as she circled the table with platters of food.

There were times when food was so scarce that the meal consisted of nothing more than a glass of milk and freshly baked cornbread. On those evenings we had what we called evening "crumble-in"—meaning we'd crumble the cornbread into the milk and spoon it out. Later in life I saw and heard a commercial that advertised a brand of soup that "ate like a meal." That's what we had for supper—"crumble-in that filled in for a meal."

Hog killing time in the fall was a time of great interest and abundant meat. The hams were hung up, covered with salt and other seasonings to be eaten during long winter months. But the other parts needed to be eaten quickly while they were still fresh. We had no refrigerator when I was little, so neighbors were the beneficiaries of whatever we couldn't cook and eat right away. A delicacy was "chitterlings" made from the inner linings of the hog's small intestines. They lasted for days.

Later, when I was a college student, an evangelist by the name of Rev. Hezekiah Ham came to Greensboro, NC, and introduced himself to his first congregations by saying, "Just think of the best part of a hog and you'll know my name." He told us in one city, a woman of color shook his hand after the service and said, "I sure did enjoy your sermon, Mr. Chitterling."

Unless my memory is faulty, a young man by the name of Billy Graham was converted in one of Rev. Ham's meetings.

A Fearful Childhood

Several things contributed to a fearful childhood. The absence of a male head of the household when my father was away in evangelistic meetings made for reliance on my mother—who herself had a fearful disposition. During severe electrical storms, she huddled us together away from electrical drop cords and appliances (a wise decision, but it made us more afraid of being struck by lightening than we needed to be). To make the country home more "safe," all the doors had to be locked in communities where most people left their doors open day and night.

We were exposed to imagined dangers of a literal hell, preached by some evangelist in which an angry God held an avenging sword over sinful and disobedient people, ready to sweep them away at the Day of Judgment, if not before. The concept of God's "all-seeing eye" was something to fear.

Scary ghost stories and yarns about preternatural happenings, told after supper on a dark porch by the elders, made going to bed a frightful experience. Our bedroom was dark, and going up and down the stairs was in darkness. Reason said there was nothing to fear, but darkness after such stories made for uncertainties. There were some gruesome events that happened in the community to add some authenticity to what was untrue, like the man who cut his throat while hanging himself.

My mother had premonitions of deaths in the family and among close friends. These came in the form of an unexplained "knocking"—a knocking in the house that came spaced a few seconds apart. These seemed never to come when Papa was at home. We children were party to these knockings that came in an otherwise peaceful night, and one night in the midst of a powerful electrical storm, we were frightened spit-less, wondering who among our relatives (or ourselves) the knockings were for.

One Sunday, as a lad of ten, I had gone with Papa to a service in one of his seven churches. Several neighbors were invited to eat in one of the homes. At the table the conversation covered many subjects. We had fish in the meat dish, and was it ever delicious! My young ears pricked up when someone said that one should never eat fish and drink milk at the same meal—that she knew of a man who had died after eating that combination. Imagine how I felt. I had just drunk two glasses of milk with my fish. Immediately after the meal, I made my way into a cornfield away from the adults, and there made my peace with God, and waited to die. It never happened, thank God, but I was very frightened!

Nightly Prayer—Time at the Parsonage

Always when my father was at home, and nearly always when he was away, we gathered around what devout people called "the family circle." The Scriptures were read, after which we'd all kneel at our chairs while Papa prayed. When he was absent, Mama would gather us and ask us to quote Bible verses. It was a race to get to say the shortest ones, like "Jesus wept," or "God is love." One night my sister Lois, two years younger than I, had memorized a much longer verse. It was, "Come unto me, all ye who are weary and heavy-laden, and I will give you rest." She was the nervous type so, when it finally became her turn, she blurted out, "Come unto me, all ye who are weary and heavy-laden, and I will give you trouble." That ended the session in much hilarity.

I never saw my father pray a silent prayer. Whether at church or camp meeting, or yet in the privacy of his bedroom, his prayers could be heard. He prayed for causes and for people by name. His bedroom was next to mine, so I heard his prayers for those on his heart. I often heard my name being lifted up to God. It was a "warm fuzzy" to know that he thought enough of me to pray for me. That made up somewhat for the fact that he never told me he loved me.

Mama's First (and Last) Driving Lesson

One day several members of the family were out riding with our parents. It was a lovely day and the top cover of the car was folded down. Papa kept asking Mama to take a turn behind the steering wheel. Finally she gave in and drove us a short distance. Nervously she kept asking Papa to take the wheel again. She didn't know how to stop the car and make Papa take over, so she guided the car off to the side, right up a bank. The car turned over on its side, and we all spilled out like peas from a pod. In retrospect, I wondered how many of us would have been badly hurt or killed if the car had turned all the way over, but the car on the side was bad enough. Papa looked over the situation, and I could tell he was worried. The best I could do was to cry out, "Papa, Papa, get a man, get a hundred mans." Other motorists stopped, and several men put the car on its wheels again. That was Mama's first and last drive, and that was the last time Papa invited her to "take the wheel."

Youthful Chores

Slopping the hogs was a job I reluctantly performed. It was a necessity in order to be ready for "hog-killing" time in the fall. That meant meat all winter. So often it was my responsibility to see that their food was mixed with water and poured into their trough. I knew when it was time to feed them, for their squeals were insistent at mealtime.

I learned to milk a cow when quite young but preferred to "let" older siblings do the milking. In the summer, when grass was green, the cow had to be moved from one spot to another—that is, when she was not in a pasture.

Chopping kindling to start fires in the kitchen stove, and gathering dried bark and twigs for the same, was a perpetual necessity—no fire in the kitchen stove meant no hot cornbread or biscuits or hot meal. Mama would not stand still for that. Not having a fire in the stove would have made her feel like the children of Israel in Egyptian bondage, when they had to make bricks without straw. When I was a teenager, Papa was gone to preach in revival meetings for several weeks at a time. Often this meant that we'd run short of firewood for the house during cold weather, as well as "decent" dry wood for the kitchen stove. When he did have a break in those duties, he'd come home, take one look at the wood pile, grab the crosscut saw, and say, "Philip, let's go out and cut some wood for your mother."

That meant sawing down a large tree and working it up into useable lengths and splitting the pieces into stove wood for Mama. I wasn't nearly the man at the other end of the crosscut saw I wished I were. Papa was a 200 pound man, and my poor back ached as I tried not to let him know that I was too tired to pull the saw through the wood one more time.

I didn't mind gathering the eggs. The hens hid their nests around the barn and yard in a variety of places. They cackled after laying an egg—but only after they had gotten off their nests. It was a game to find their nests, and sometimes difficult. It was necessary to find every one of them because a hen would sit on her eggs in an attempt to hatch them. Unless the eggs were gathered regularly, they were spoiled. The embryo of a chick would begin to form inside the shell. The rooster had seen to that. When we wanted chicks, we'd buy eggs of the variety of chickens we wanted and let a hen hatch them. Sometimes we'd buy the chicks already hatched.

The Ole Swimming Hole

Without a doubt, the swimming hole a half mile from our home in the town of Rutherford College was the source of much activity and happiness for me. It was a natural place in the creek east of our house where the water came over a solid formation of rock and carved out a good-sized pool deep enough for swimming. My first experience as a child was not the most pleasant one. My older brothers threw me in before I had learned to swim. I almost drowned before they pulled me out. Every summer it was a gathering place for the boys of the community. Girls were allowed with bathing suits, but so many boys had no swim suits that the girls were reluctant to come most of the time.

The water was cold and fresh from under South Mountain. It took a bit more than a little courage to plunge in, but that's what we did. Going into water that cold, a little at a time, was excruciating and only delayed the inevitable final plunge. No lifeguard stood near by because it wasn't a public place. You were on your own, and as far as I can remember, no one ever drowned there. We liked to have it available because it was three miles to the Yadkin River. That was too far to walk more than once or twice a month.

Camp Meetings

A great influence upon my young life was the midsummer 10-day evangelistic meetings at Camp Free, between the towns of Rutherford College and Connelly Springs. The latter town was on the main railway that ran east and west across the length of the state. In earlier years, a large hotel had been built there for people who would take the train to the mountains for extended vacations. My father was the founder of Camp Free (Camp Meeting) a mile west. Using funds from a powerful revival in Thomasville, NC, he purchased land and, with the influence and help of like-minded clergy and laity he built, organized and scheduled it annually—usually in late July through early August. A look at the tabernacle showed no walls on three sides, admitting everyone. The north end had a wall behind the participating speakers, musicians and special guests. The wall helped augment the sound system, when we had one, and the voices of the speakers.

At the time of the first camp meeting in 1921, I was only seven. Year after year I took an increasing part in helping get the camp set up—washing off the many very dusty 15-foot homemade wooden benches, removing last year's dried out sawdust, hauling in fresh sawdust and scattering it over the dirt floor, opening and readying the dining room and kitchen for use, preparing cottages for those who had built them for the camp meeting dates, and many other chores.

The older youth enjoyed piling the fresh sawdust in the middle of the tabernacle where, before scattering it all over, we would climb up into the rafters above the pile and drop from there to the top of the sawdust pile. What fun! I could hardly wait until I was big enough and brave enough to do that myself.

The year finally came when I decided to try it. I needed to try, in order to prove I could do it. So, with older youth watching, I climbed up and over to the drop-point and let myself down arms-length. Then I made a mistake. In fright, I hesitated. The others egged me on. I looked down and measured the distance to the top of the pile. I had never heard the expression, "He who hesitates is lost." I decided finally that it was not the year for me and tried to climb back up the 2" x 8" rafter to safety. My strength and skill were not equal to that awkward task. What to do?

I yelled loud enough to attract the attention of my father who was working nearby. I did not have the sympathy of the other kids, who wanted to see me drop. Sizing up the situation quickly, Papa piled benches crossways and climbed up. He could almost reach me and said, "Philip, turn loose."

I hesitated again because I decided that, if he missed me, I'd be in real trouble. Papa said, "Don't worry, I will catch you." I cried, "Oh no, Papa, if you missed me I'd be hurt bad on those hard benches."

Finally, I could hold on no longer and my young fingers slipped from the rafter. It was great to feel the strong arms of a 200-pound caring father enfold me and lift me to safety. There's a sermon in that incident that I'll save until later. It could be summed up in the oft-quoted expression, "Man's extremity is God's opportunity."

Earliest Memories

To confirm my earliest memories, I could go no further back than age three. My father was pastor of the Candler Circuit in Buncombe County, southwest of Asheville, NC, for a year beginning November 1917. The square two-story parsonage sitting uphill across a road from a naturally formed swimming hole was forever engraved on my mind.

Water flowed over a huge rock in the creek and hollowed out a basin where my two older brothers had many swims.

One day as I watched in anguished disbelief, James, the oldest, began vigorously kicking the water as though he were struggling for his life. He was holding onto a large rock on the edge of the pool so I yelled out the best advice a nearly 4-year-old brother could give, "Hold to the rock, James, hold to the rock!" I was undeceived only when he calmly released his grasp on the rock and swam across to the other side—all of that ruckus for my anxious benefit.

Further down the creek there was a mill pond that froze over in the cold mountain winters. I remembered the sad incident of a boy who skated out too far toward the middle where the ice was thin, broke through, and was drowned.

Up the creek from the parsonage, a curve around a high hill was necessary for a road beside the creek. It was fenced with two strands of barbed wire to prevent cattle from falling from the cliff. Everyone was saddened to learn that a part of the fence was broken down and a cow had fallen to her death in the road below.

Farmers with wagons were frequent passers-by. The tail end of the "coupling pole," protruding from the rear of the wagon, was an attractive temptation to a boy hankering for a free ride for a few yards. One day a farmer stopped for a brief visit with my pastor father. That first "free ride" was costly. My father had never mentioned that riding someone else's coupling pole was forbidden. I found out when he spanked me and hustled me up the bank to the yard of the parsonage. That was the last of any free rides.

More than fifty years later, my wife and I passed the town of Candler on a modern highway. I had an overwhelming urge to find that parsonage, if it still existed, and find out whether or not my memories had any basis in fact—or were they perpetuated by my parent's verbalized stories? I pulled off the highway and stopped at a country store below the road. The merchant was interested enough to tell me that there was a creek behind his store and that the bridge across it led to an unpaved road. He said that I might follow it up the creek and locate the spot where I might have lived so long ago. It was only a short distance until "there it was," and much as I had remembered it. No one lived there now, so I checked the swimming hole and continued around the curve where the cow had fallen. An old two-storied country store was there. It looked largely unused but I stopped anyway. The door to the store was locked, but I climbed the exterior staircase to the second floor and knocked, on the outside chance that someone might live there.

The door was answered by an elderly man, old enough to be able to know more about the community. He told me that the house in question was indeed a former Methodist parsonage, and that the swimming hole had been there since nature first carved it out, and that he remembered the child who had been drowned in the mill-pond. He had not heard about the unfortunate cow that had fallen to her death from the unguarded precipice.

It was an immense satisfaction to have my earliest memories authenticated. As a matter of interest, I did not remember having gone to church with Papa that year. In all likelihood, my father left my sister Lois, two, my sister Ruth, then an infant, and me at home with my mother. Ruth was the last of ten children my mother birthed. Three of them had died before the age of two (Ossie Clementine, Van and Andrew).

In November 1918, we moved to Lincolnton, NC, where our parents and all seven of the rest of us faced the deadly Spanish flu epidemic. Thanks to a merciful God, and the care of loving neighbors, we all survived. The epidemic kept church and other meetings to practically zero, so Papa was at home and got a taste of what it meant for Mama to be left at home with such a large responsibility while he was away "in meetings."

Bath-time Life at The Parsonage

Whether in a parsonage or in our home in the town of Rutherford College, the weekly bath was inevitable. In summers, the boys could take soap to the river (when there was one nearby) and bathe there on Saturday. We all had to be clean for Sunday—behind our ears all the way to our toes. In winter, the three of us who were from four to eight years old, much younger than the others, had our own baths. There were no bathtubs as we know them today. A clothes washing tub was big enough for our needs. The big question was, who gets the first tub of fresh water? The reason for that question was that all three of us had to bathe in the same water—water that had to be heated by hot bricks. We had no hot water tanks, and the tubs were too large to be heated on the kitchen cook stove. There was always a struggle remembering whose time it was to go first. I don't remember under what conditions the four older siblings (two boys and two girls) took their baths.

My next oldest brother, Kilgo, was four years older than I. Since my two younger sisters were girls, I preferred relating to him. My legs were shorter than his, but I tried to keep up. One day as I was entering the path across our yard after school, I noticed a water hose in the branches above the path. When I reached the "right spot," water filled my face. Kilgo was waiting to turn on the water at the connection beside the house. That was one time I wished my legs had been longer, but I could never catch up to him. We had fun times together playing tag in the sugar maple trees in our yard. It's a miracle that neither of us ever fell while trying to escape being tagged in the tree limbs.

The banes of my existence were poison oak and poison ivy. I seemed annually to come in contact with their innocent looking vines before their spring foliage appeared and they were more readily identifiable. I was allergic and broke out wherever contact was made. The worst experience I ever had was getting in the smoke when someone was burning the vines. It was saturation coverage. Why did the growth appear among the grape hyacinths that I loved to pick? I picked them in early spring and always broke out with the "hidden poison."

Cost-Free Games, Almost

Most children I knew lived in families of modest means. Store-bought toys and sporting equipment, including clothes, were rare among us. In clothing, hand-me-downs were more the rule than otherwise. In amusements, the imagination was a powerful tool. I remember talking car-race-language to a piece of wood sawed thin at the front and rising to four inches at the rear—like a race car—only there were no wheels. The cost was nothing. It came from the remains of a carpentry job on our new home. But it was a racer. My imagination made it so.

Much later as an older teenager, I couldn't afford a golf club, even though I had collected many golf balls lost at a nearby golf course. What did I do? I made myself one—not a pretty one—but one that sent the golf balls streaking into a cornfield across the road from our front yard. How did I make it? I found a healthy sprout in the forest, dug it out by the roots, shaped the hitting surface to my liking, leveled the bottom, trimmed twigs from the handle, and I was in business. The cost was some personal effort and limited skill.

Most everyone possessed a rubber ball or a worn out tennis ball. A small group of kids could play "hat-ball." All that was needed was a rubber ball and a hat, or cap, or even a paper bag when nothing else was available. Whoever was "it" would drop the ball and call a name. If your name was called, you had only a few seconds to pick up the ball and throw it at the closest person dashing away. If you missed that one, you had to be "it." Everyone knew that it was best to be near the hat when the ball was dropped. Otherwise, all the others had time to get out of range. Because formal ball games were "out" for Sunday afternoon, hat-ball was a good substitute form of fun. Hardly any cost at all.

An old broomstick would do for the game of "peg" (not mumble peg, for that was played with a pocketknife), but a small sapling cut fresh from the forest and trimmed up into a slender bat was best. The rest of the equipment cost nothing either. A "peg" about ten inches long was sharpened slightly at one end and placed on a "riser," or sharp edged rock driven into the ground. With the bat a player had three "pecks" to get a good whirling rise of the peg so that the player could knock it some distance away. If missed, the batter was out until his next turn. After the peg was hit at some distance, the hitter had an estimate call to make. He needed to judge the distance from the riser to the peg and call a number. The number should be just short of what a straddle jumper could jump it. If the estimate was off, and the jumper made it within the number assessed, he got that many points toward the 100-point game. Otherwise, the astute player collected those points toward game. My cousin, Glenn Stokes, had the longest straddle jumps of all and threatened every estimate call within reason. Because it was not a disapproved ball game for Sunday afternoon, it had the blessing of the "old folks."

When no game was wanted, or the number of youth was limited, we spent many afternoons (Saturday or Sunday) walking through the forests, looking for wild grapevines high in lofty oak trees, or gathering the aromatic bulbs of sweet shrubs. Sometimes we "raided" someone's watermelon patch, or fed ravenous appetites on wild "rusty coat" apples that needed to be peeled because the skin of the apple was like brown sandpaper.

The worst thing that could happen was to have no one to play or walk with me. Those Sunday afternoons were indeed lonely and accentuated the usual loneliness of teen years. I sometimes filled the hours by going through a field of rye and picking long fresh stems. With a sharp knife, I'd cut them off at the right place and cut a gash near the stem and blow for a musical note. By experimenting with the length of the cut or stem, I found it possible to blow three of them together and get a pleasing harmony.

Swings were where you found them, or made them. A grapevine swing was one where the vine grew high up in a mighty oak tree on a hillside in the forest. By cutting the large vine near the ground, one would have a means to swing out over the downside slope or ravine and get a thrill. The vine always brought you back to the base of the tree. Once I swung out over a ravine on a vine that had been cut the year before. Suddenly, while out over the highest part of the ravine, the anchor in the limbs above gave way, and I fell many feet to the ground below. Luckily, the soil below, made marshy from a spring of water, made the landing less than brutal. Other kids helped me out, and there were no broken bones.

In winter, sometimes there were snow-covered hillsides where kids, and adults, had fun with sleds. Those who had no sled were given rides behind those who did. But what about the summertime and when there was no snow? We learned to put together three old barrel staves, scrape the bottoms with broken pieces of glass for slickness, and go scooting down beneath pine trees and, on those pine needles, get to the bottom of the hill. The speed was exciting, and the sled was not guidable. The name of the game was to avoid slamming into one of the many pine trees. Many bruises resulted from not being able to guide the "sled."

Going fishing in a nearby river, or lake, gave opportunity for a swim as well as catching a string of fish, when one had a good day for fishing. We found a tree that had limbs extending over the water of the Yadkin River. Someone had installed a rope so that those who had the nerve could swing out over the water and drop into the stream. Someone always seemed to have a boat to play around. One day I dived into the water and came up under the boat. How on earth can someone get trapped under the bottom of a boat? But I did. I kept trying without success to find the narrow part of the boat, grab the edge, and pull myself out. In my youthful confusion, fright and frustration, I almost drowned. Thanks to my playmates, I didn't.

So the fears of childhood and youth were tempered with many fun experiences at little or no financial cost. We were rich and poor—rich in relationships—poor only in earthl*y* possessions.

2

THE INTERESTING ELDERLY

I was the guest speaker after being gone for 60 years from Big Sandy Church on the Sandy Circuit. Standing next to me is Charlie Wells. He got out of sick-bed just to come to hear me preach again. He died a few months later.

As Minister of Pastoral Care in a mega-church of more than 6,000 members for twelve years, it was one of my duties to provide a workable caring system for some 230 shut-ins in homes, nursing homes, and hospitals in the greater Colorado Springs area. Shortly after beginning this task, I discovered that a number of people who should have been receiving care were not getting it. The big question was, why not? One of the reasons was that different organizations in the church took on responsibility in part for certain categories of people. For example, the United Methodist Women gave special care to the women in the various circles. Women not affiliated with a circle, or not picked up by a circle, did not receive care. What about men? They were not the responsibility of the women in the UMW. What about people in the periphery of church membership and church life? What about persons of every age in need of special care, sometimes for only a short time? What about the very elderly who did not want to be considered in need of special care, but who—with little or no warning—could cross the narrow line into a condition of the need for special care?

The new Special Care Council was brought into existence for the purpose of giving overall coverage to everyone under the umbrella of our church. We recruited, trained and directed 30 to 40 volunteers who dedicated themselves to the care of these people. Miss Etta Brummett was for many years the "captain" of that team. A roster of all persons was formed from every separate list and was consolidated into one master roster so that hopefully no one would be overlooked or fall through the cracks. The lay volunteers were the heroes (often unsung) of this prodigious ministry. Members of the ministerial staff and lay staff joined me in an effort to make the system work. It was a challenge to keep this roster and the caregivers up-to-date, but each monthly meeting gave opportunity to do this.

To communicate to the shut-ins that the lay visitors did indeed represent the caring heart of our great church was a continuing challenge. One time a shut-in complained of being neglected by the church. I checked on who had visited her during the year and found on the records that there had been ten lay visits, two which I had made. When I visited her next, I kindly pointed out that Mrs. Jackson had visited her ten times, had taken her a poinsettia at Christmas and a lily at Easter, and had given her an Upper Room devotional booklet every two months. She apostrophized that Mrs. Jackson was her friend. Somewhere along the line she had not considered *that* lay visitor as a visitor from the church.

One morning I visited the home of an 89-year-old member whose wife was already in a nursing home. In the late morning, he seemed a bit out of breath, so I asked him if he had been gardening.

"No," he replied, "I've been bowling."

"Bowling?" I asked in surprise. "What is your average score, Ed?"

One hundred forty-six was his reply. I knew that many frames had to be more than 200 to reach such an average so I congratulated him on such an excellent score.

"How did you get to the bowling alley, Ed?" I asked.

"Oh, I still drive my car," he replied. Then I asked what he planned to do in the afternoon.

He said, "Well, my friend Paul Amber is coming over and together we're going to Sunnyrest where my wife is and sing for the old folks."

I always admired shut-ins who demonstrated an ability to round up their own caregivers. The one of whom I write was such a person. Everything she needed was given faithfully by a number of loving visitors. She lived in the only upper room in the house which was reached by an exterior staircase. Because she was bedfast (or chair-fast), she left her door unlocked. On one of my morning visits, I knocked but there was no answer. I could hear her loud TV, so I pushed the door open cautiously and entered. She and one of her caregivers had their eyes glued to the soap opera on the screen. Without interrupting, I stood and watched as a reconciled husband planted a rapturous kiss on the lips of his wife. My shut-in cried out in great joy, "O, praise the Lord!" It was then time for me to let my presence be known.

Evelyn Cook was not a shut-in when I first came to know her. She often came out the door to which I was assigned to greet worshipers as they departed the church. Almost invariably she shook my hand and said, "Hello, I'm Evelyn Cook." This day she surprised me by saying,

"Phil Green, I've come out your door I don't know how many times, and I'll bet you don't even remember my name."

I didn't, because she always told me. She told me one more time. I promised her,

"Evelyn Cook, if you should come out this door again, or if I should meet you anywhere in the church or downtown, and I can't call you by name, I'll give you five dollars." I never had to pay her.

One of our members was hospitalized and later transferred to a hospital in Denver—65 miles north. When I entered her room, she took one look and realized I had come all the way from Colorado Springs to visit her. She exploded, "My Lord, am I that sick?"

While the late Rev. Dr. Ben F. Lehmberg was still the senior minister, he did most of the hospital calls. One day he broke his habit of "doing it all" by turning to me and saying,

"Phil, I've goofed on one of our members in Penrose Hospital. The man was not in the same room where I visited last, and I assumed he had gone home. He had been transferred to intensive care, and I made no calls there. His wife is very angry at me. Would you visit them in their home and explain that I did not intend to neglect him, and why I did?"

This elderly couple was offended but accepted Dr. Lehmberg's apology. He died shortly thereafter. I was glad to say that I was able to reconcile them with the senior minister before he died.

I learned never, I mean never, to undervalue the importance of each person, regardless of what the ravages of age had brought to them. Bedraggled they might be now, wrinkled or maimed or blind or speechless as they often were. During better days they had very interesting and useful lives—lives worthy of remembering. Many of them had been active leaders and supporters of the church and, for no other reason, remembered and were thankful for those years.

Sadly, there were some who were no longer in a choir, a Sunday school class, or other ongoing activity. They'd been gone so long that no one followed up on them in their time of need.

I visited one home several times where the husband was ill. When he died, his wife told me that the neighbors wanted to bring food for a meal the day of the funeral. She told them that "her church" would do that. But there was no group planning to do that. Quickly, I assigned that duty to members of the Special Care Council.

A son in the family later helped me develop a "post hospital" committee to make sure that every member who had been in a hospital was followed up to see whether or not they needed continued care. "Red" Moldenhauer and his committee kept me informed so that no one went to another hospital, or home to die, or for a long convalescence without my knowledge. Our new neighborhood plan ensured that there was a geographical awareness of those on, or needing to be on, the special care list.

Most shut-ins were removed from the special care list by death. That is when the minister needed to count on some group to express special care for the surviving spouse, if any, or local family members. During many years, it was my privilege to be involved in 75 to 90 grief situations each year (alone or with other staff ministers). I sought to meet with every family member or associate known to the deceased. Whether he had been rich or poor, surrounded by family members and friends, or living alone at the Union Printer's Home. Now and then it was with a home visitation nurse, or an attorney, or even a caring neighbor with whom I learned enough about the deceased to include something on the tape of the service. I gave or sent the tape to a loved one somewhere who was too old, poor, or unable to travel to the service.

I helped to bury many nonmembers and "informal members," and a few who made no claim to faith in God. I made it a firm practice to bring the assurance of God's love and compassion to every grieving person and conducted the funeral/memorial service with dignity. Through prayers, Scriptures and poetry, I conveyed the biblical perspective of the God who cares what happens to us.

Whatever Happened to "You Know Who?"

Our Christmas letter list was lost in 1993 when I left my complete mailing list in a rent-a-car in San Diego, CA. It has been reconstructed from Christmas letters from those who regularly write at Christmas. But we hadn't heard from the Stouts of Chicago in a while. They were our faithful members of the American congregation in Madrid, Spain (1954-1957). We had kept in touch regularly across the decades. Now our addresses were lost. After a while, the question was, what has happened to the Stouts?

Forrest Stout was one of the architects who built the twin towers in Chicago. In Madrid, he was one of the architects and engineers drawing plans for USAF Bases in Madrid, Seville, and Zaragoza. His wife had been the principal scribe that kept us full of their family's activities.

We were glad, and sad, to hear from their married daughter from Rock Hill, SC, on May 8, 1994. Enclosed in *her* letter, was a copy of the Christmas letter her mother had written to be sent out. Her sudden death prevented its posting, so her daughter sent it to the family mailing list. I quote only the daughter's letter:

> *Dear Family and Friends:*
>
> *I am taking this opportunity to write to you on behalf of my parents, Forrest and Kelley Stout, in order to inform you of what happened this past year. My father had a stroke in April of 1990, shortly after their 50th wedding anniversary celebration which left him with impairment of his speech,*

some physical weakness and very limited eyesight. They left the Chicago area in early February 1991 and moved into a retirement apartment here in Rock Hill, SC. The family home in Illinois, which had been extensively remodeled, was put up for sale and did sell in June of 1992. My sister also moved down to this area in the summer of 1991, and is working and living in North Carolina.

We had nine happy months after their move, attending concerts, organizing their apartment, making new friends, etc. Dad got additional therapy, had an operation on his eyes (which allowed him to open them, eliminating the necessity of taping them open) and was making some progress. Unfortunately, in October [of 1991], *mother died. It was very sudden and very unexpected. She apparently, also had a stroke, followed almost immediately by a heart attack. From the beginning to the end was about three hours. Dad was devastated. He had a very difficult time adjusting. We felt that it was necessary to give up the apartment and to put him in an assisted living situation since he could not care for himself and did not wish to move in with any of us.*

Initially, we placed him in the nursing facility within the retirement complex where they had lived while searching for a facility which we felt was more appropriate to his needs. In early February 1992, we were able to find him a place in such a facility and moved him to a care center. His mental and physical state had been deteriorating while in the nursing facility since there was little stimulation for him there. Things improved after the move. He had a second operation on his eyes in January which improved things even more but, unfortunately, still did not allow him clear vision. We all had great hope that the second operation would eliminate the double vision or improve it to the point that prismatic lenses could be used to achieve normal vision. That was not the case, and he became very discouraged. He told the eye doctor that he found life without vision to be not worth living. His mind remained sharp to the end, but he had no will to live with the combined blows of his disappointment over his vision and the loss of a wife. Dad died in June. He simply fell asleep in a chair in the living room (which he was prone to do) and never woke up. We buried Dad in the small cemetery in Nebraska near his ranch home, after a small service in Woodriver. We also interred mother's ashes along with him as had been her wish.

I am sorry to have to bring such sad tidings, but I felt you, as their friends, would like to know. I hope that all is well with you and your families and that you will take great pleasure in each other as our time together is, sometimes, so much briefer than we expect. (Names omitted)

3

THE THERAPY OF FRIENDSHIPS

I'm seated here with other retired chaplains that attended the luncheon for the 50th Anniversary of the Retired Officers Association in 2010.

Friendship is a life-extender. The more friends you have, the longer your life—unless there are health factors that militate otherwise. One can expect a pastor to accumulate more friends as he or she moves from congregation to congregation. There are restrictions to this fact, as follows; (1) In my denomination, and others, a minister is advised to leave members of that congregation to the pastoral care of the following pastor. A departing pastor must not interrupt the establishment of the pastor/parish relationship between the parishioner and the new pastor. (2) There is a limit to the time and expense of the departing pastor, to accumulate too many friends in the years ahead.

There is such a thing as 'inherited friends.' Between 1910 and 1914, my father was the circuit-riding pastor of ten churches in a northern section of Buncombe County near Asheville. With horse and saddlebags to hold his Bible and other necessities, he made the rounds. Four years was as long as a pastor could fill one appointment. In those years, he was so much loved and by so many people that, when I became pastor of six of those same churches in 1936, there were many families who wanted to be the friends of "Brother Jim's" preacher son. I relished Papa's friends and basked in their heart-warming affection. I have outlived them all.

A career-long friendship was formed in Big Sandy Methodist Church, one of six on the Sandy Circuit I had served from 1936-'40. I became acquainted with a young adult member, Reeves H. Wells. His parents were well known by my father who served this church and nine others as a circuit rider 1910-'14. Reeves' mother 'adopted' me right away. Her profane husband was gloriously converted while Papa was there

Reeves had communicated with me through many decades. When I was back in North Carolina in 1999, he saw to it that I was invited to preach at Big Sandy, his original home church. Think of that! I preached my first sermon there in 1936, twenty-two years after Papa's last sermon. I stayed there for four years. How soon it is long ago! I still get a charge from those memories.

I want to tell you about another couple there, Bob and Lottie Reeves (last name is just coincidentally same as first name above). My first official board meeting was a shocker. I thought I had prepared for anything and everything. The last person to arrive was a very tall mountaineer who seemed to tower above my slim 6' frame. With a serious look on his face, he fairly crushed my slender fingers in a powerful grip, as he greeted me with these uncomfortable words:

"I don't know whether I'm going to like you or not!"

It was an embarrassing moment for a twenty-two-year-old novice to face his first challenge. I had hoped to ride in on Papa's popularity. But here I was at my wit's end, facing a hostile board member. The room had grown very quiet, all of a sudden, as the other board members waited for what came next. I managed to ask him why he said that. He replied,

"When your father was pastor here, he got me into a lot of trouble!"

I had a flashback at that very moment, my father had often recounted to the family some of the good times and difficult times during his circuit-riding days. One incident occurred during an afternoon service at one of his churches. In the middle of his sermon, two inebriates came in, sat down in the rear, and began talking out loud to one another. My father paused in his sermon enough for them to know they were disrupting the service. They continued to talk and disturb. Papa went back to them and asked for their names. They jumped up and one said, "My name is hell!" He drew a knife.

The congregation scattered, leaving only one member to handle the drunks. In the fray, my father was cut through the shoulder. A court scene ensued.

All this flashed through my mind. I wondered whether or not this man in front of me now might have been a part of that incident, so I asked him how my father had gotten him in trouble. With a huge smile he said, "He married me!"

That was Bob Reeves. He and Lottie became our best friends during the next four years. He was the mail carrier for most of our church members and was invaluable in letting his pastor know when someone was ill, in trouble, or in need. We had many tasteful meals in their home. He loaned us the funds for Lois to pay off her college debt. Her credits needed to be released so that she could become a teacher in the state high school. Actually, the last year there, she taught in Sandy High School, near Big Sandy church.

On Feb. 20, 1988, Bob surprised and pleased me by writing the following letter:

Dear Rev. Green:

I still want to call you Philip. I was delighted when Edith Wells called me and later mailed me your personal history statement. I have made a copy of the statement and will return the original to her. It does not seem to me that a half a century has passed since you were at Big Sandy! Your record during these 50 years is really fantastic. There are not enough adjectives to properly describe your record.

I vividly remember one Sunday afternoon the two of us were asked to speak in our church. It was my first experience and I recall that I used Micah 6:8.

I have slowed down my law practice. I am now a certified lay speaker in the Asheville District of the Western NC Conference of the U. Meth. Church and have, for the last 10-12 years speaking on average at one worship service per month. There are 92 Methodist churches in the Asheville District and I have spoken in 46 of these churches.

If our health remains good we just may undertake another trip—but if you plan a trip this way, please let us know for we would like for you to spend some time with us.

Bob Reeves

Many years later, I was on my way back to military duty in South Georgia where I was a chaplain. Bob heard I was in North Carolina. He phoned me, and told me that Lottie was dying in a hospital down state. He begged me to go and visit her. I would have been absent without leave (AWOL) if I stayed to make the visit. I could even yet have kicked myself, you know where, for not going and taking the consequences. I hope he understood my dilemma. Their faces are in that great cloud of witnesses. Knowing how they loved me, I'm sure they are rooting for me to have a reunion in heaven.

Earliest church friends, Lottie and Bob Reeves 1936-'40

Fred I. Ross came to Spence Field, Moultrie, Georgia, as a student-pilot at the Hawthorne School of Aeronautics in 1951 where I was the chaplain 1951-'52. My office secretary was Kit (her last name escapes me), a beautiful and talented young woman. Fred was required, as were all military personnel, to clear through the chaplain's office for interview. That's how they met. Before he left my office, he said to himself, "I'm going to marry that woman!"

After months of courtship, I was asked to perform the ceremony in the refurbished World War II chapel. When he was graduated from flying school, he was transferred to Japan, having to leave behind his beautiful wife. Shortly after arriving in Japan, I received this letter,

> *Dear Chaplain Green;*
>
> *At long last I'm getting a letter off to you. The fact that I haven't written has no bearing as a register of my esteem, for you, having been a major contributing factor to some of the finest experiences in my life, are often in my thoughts. You played a large part in my meeting the girl who to me is the greatest, most beautiful thing that ever happened to me. You officiated in my memorable marriage to that girl. Another inescapable point where you have left a mark in my life is that you—in your winning personality and departure from a staid, sour-visaged, self-righteous propensity of the banal clergy—have struck a hot spark of interest in the Christian religion into me, an interest that has surprised me. I would say that, in this case, you have done your work well. I can never find words to thank you properly for the good you have done me and the kindness you have shown my beloved wife. I can only say "thanks," and hope you'll sense the intense feeling with which I use the word. Fred.*

Thus began a lifelong friendship. I performed the wedding ceremony of their daughter in the USAF Academy chapel years later. And they happened to be visiting with me May 22, 1988, as we entered the room at the care facility where my own beloved Lois had just taken her last breath. Some years after that, Fred died, and I lost track of where Kit was. I hope Fred is "up there" waiting for me.

Another friend was the first full-time national executive director of The Military Chaplains Association, Chaplain Karl B. Justus. I first knew of him when he was a student at Asbury College, Wilmore, Kentucky, in 1931. I was a junior in high school and often watched

Karl play guard on the college basketball team. I didn't know my wife, Lois Ritter, at that time, but she was a classmate of Karl. The MCA was composed of chaplains of all military ranks (from Lieutenant through Major General), and religious affiliations of the Air Force, Army, Navy and Veterans Administration. Karl wrote a beautiful letter about my work as chairman of the national host committee for MCA's 1968 Convention in Colorado Springs to Bishop R. Marvin Stuart. In it he wrote:

> *Dear Bishop Stuart:*
>
> *In April of this year {1968}, the National Convention of this Association was held in Colorado Springs. By all odds the general program, the banquets, the professional workshops, and the entire organization of the convention was the best we ever had. The General Chairman of the Convention was the Rev. Philip Green, a retired Air Force chaplain, now serving on the staff of First United Methodist Church in Colorado Springs. I have known Phil for many years, but this was the first opportunity to work with him. I wish to highly commend him and say you must feel fortunate to have such an outstanding man in your conference. His intelligent approach, organizational ability, inspiration and cordial spirit, his dedication to the task, and his zeal and devotion "beyond the call of duty," helped to spell success to our convention. Sincerely, Dr. Karl B. Justus, Executive Director.*

In the years following that event, Karl and I became staunch friends. Because of the success in 1968, two years later my colleagues elected me their national president (1970-'72). When the association came again in 1978 and 1988, I had the honor of doing the same thing. When Karl retired from being Executive Director, I helped him go out with flying colors. We continued to correspond through the decades until his home-going. Ruth, his wife, and son John continue to receive a copy of my Christmas letter and a phone call now and then. What a true friend Karl was!

Glen Shaffer entered my life at first unwelcome. At the time, I was selected to be the chaplain of the reconstituted eighth Air Force that had made such a record in World War II. It was being put together at MacDill Field, Tampa, Florida in 1946. The plan was to counter Russia's push to take over all of Western Europe. But the plan was scrapped when diplomatic intelligence caused the war department to call it off. In the meantime a major was assigned to that unit. That meant that I had been removed as its chaplain. And that Major was none other than Glen Shaffer. I didn't know him but I didn't like him taking my spot.

The scene soon changed. The chaplains in Western Europe were finishing their leftover time after the War and were coming home. To replace them, there were twenty-six chaplains on orders for occupation duty in West Germany. Chaplain Shaffer and I were among them. He was sent to Camp Lindsey in Wiesbaden, and I was sent to the 831st Aviation Engineer Battalion nearby. My outfit was to remodel what had been a zeppelin balloon facility into a modern air force base. It became Rhein-Main Air Force Base in Frankfurt.

I was not pleased to be with "dirt-movers" instead of "fly-boys." My commander was not one to back up his chaplain. In short order, he began to low-rate me. The efficiency rate he gave me at the end of three months was much below what previous commanders thought of me. I took my story to Glen Shaffer who was close to the USAFE command chaplain, who erased that ER from my records. The commander, because of gross misconduct, was relieved of his command and returned to the USA.

Happily, three months later I was reassigned to Hoersching Air Force Base in Linz, Austria. Whee! Now, I was back with Air Force pilots! Glen Shaffer began to be both my rescuer and my friend. Back from Europe in 1949, I was sent to Vance AFB in Enid, Oklahoma. I had hardly gotten started when, guess what? You guessed it. Glen Shaffer arrived to be the senior chaplain. This time I didn't mind because he had proved to be my friend. Eighteen months later he put the following letter in my 201-file:

> *"As I relinquish my duties as Wing Chaplain, I desire to acknowledge your energy, initiative, loyalty, and fidelity to duty in the accomplishment of the many projects assigned to you. You accepted all assignments cheerfully and rendered far*

> *more service than was expected. Under your direction a most outstanding musical organization, the Chancel Choir, was developed and trained for Sunday and weekday presentations. Your vision and planning found fruition in the well-integrated Sunday school program to meet the needs of all ages. Of particular merit was the manner in which you expedited the Vacation Bible School, and the Chapel Annex activities. Your personal services through the ministry of correspondence, has merited the attention of higher headquarters due to its unique and effective contribution to the spiritual phases of morale."*

As he left with a promotion to lieutenant colonel and duty in the office of the Chief of Air Force Chaplains in Washington, D.C., I left as a major to be the only chaplain at Spence Field, Moultrie, Georgia. Shortly after arriving, I received word that the Centenary College Choir of Shreveport, Louisiana, would be arriving at Spence Field for a Concert of Sacred and Classical numbers on June 4, 1951, under the auspices of the Chief of Air Force Chaplains. Who do you think would accompany that choir to our base, and others? You're right again, Chaplain Glen Shaffer. It was a huge success, and I benefitted from that success by receiving high praise from my commander and from the Chief of Chaplains.

In 1952, Chaplain Shaffer had become the command chaplain of Parks Air Force Base near San Francisco. There were fifteen chaplains needed for that induction center for raw recruits coming into the US Air Force. Quite late in the year, I received a telephone call from Glen Shaffer. He wanted to know whether or not I would join his staff as his deputy. This was like moving from Mr. Big in a small one-chaplain lake, to being a not-so-big fish in a huge lake. What a challenge! And for one of my best friends! He wanted me to join him if I had no other plans. After talking it over with Lois, my answer was "yes!"

While I was at Parks AFB one day, I entered Glen's office at headquarters and found him hovering over a book in Spanish. Much surprised, I asked him why such a sudden interest in Spanish? He said,

"Phil, haven't you heard? The Air Force is opening some bases in Spain."

I replied, "Glen, you know that the military wouldn't send someone there who knew Spanish."

A year later in Madrid, Spain, I received a letter from Glen who was now the senior chaplain at Lackland AFB in San Antonio, Texas,—the largest Air Force base in the USA. In the letter he said,

"Phil, I still remember what you said about the Air Force not sending someone to Spain who already knew Spanish. Well you didn't crack a book of Spanish and there you are in Madrid, and here I am at Lackland."

What a friend Glen was! He not only made my day. He also made my military career!

Joanie Bainbridge Norris was the daughter-in-law of Rev. Dr. Warren Bainbridge who served churches and a district in the Rocky Mountain Annual Conference. Joanie was married to Robert Bainbridge, the principal of South Junior High School in Colorado Springs. He was a member of First United Methodist Church. While he was still comparatively young, he became ill and died. As I did for many others who died while I was the associate pastor, I brought consolation to Joanie and their two sons. Across the years, I had grave-side services for members of the family, including her father-in-law.

Joanie was a public school teacher. After Robert died, she married again, this time to Al Norris, a veteran of World War II. When Dr. Lloyd Nichols and I began a fellowship on the North-west side of the city, the fourth Sunday of October 1984, she and Al joined and became staunch members of the congregation. It later became Wilson UMC. They were a great help during the early months of that fledgling group. They were hit on the highway near Denver by a drunken driver and were almost killed. They survived after a long convalescence, however, and resumed places of leadership in the new church-in-the-making. Russ and Marian Wolfe gave us a place for worship in a small church built for the guests of their Flying W Ranch.

We were friends and colleagues at Parks Air Force Base, California in 1953-'54. Of the more than fifteen chaplains on duty there, I was closer to only one other chaplain, Glen Shaffer, but Tom Shaddox and I became spiritual buddies. He was open-minded and openhearted. The fact that he was a Baptist and I a Methodist mattered not at all to our friendship. In fact, in many assignments in the US Air Force, those of the Baptist faith were my most helpful supporters. One day, after a brief discussion of the dissimilarities between his denomination and mine, Tom smiled, patted me on the back and said,

"Well, Phil, you go ahead and worship God your way, and I'll worship him in His!" Such a friendship was a tonic to my soul.

In 1940-'43, I was the pastor of a circuit of six churches. In Snow Hill Methodist Church, there was a young couple with children. Often I was invited into that home for meals. Once, during a week of revival services, they invited me to stay overnight in their home. Josephine, a preteen daughter, gave her heart to Jesus Christ and joined the church. A few years ago, after more than a half a century, she learned of my address and reestablished a friendship. She shared with me photographs of herself, her deceased parents and grandparents and filled in the gaps of her life after I left there in 1943 to become a military chaplain. She sent me a copy of her baptismal certificate that showed my very own signature. Shortly before my ninety-fourth birthday, I received a card. Her note said,

> *"and remembering how blessed we were at Snow Hill to have you as pastor (1940-'43)—Thinking of how many lives you have touched though the years! Thank you, again, for leading me to the Lord as a child! Love, from both of us!!"*
>
> *Jo and Bob Corbin*

This was enough, and how it warmed the cockles of my aging heart!

Russ Wolfe is a friend worth having. He had married Marian, one of the two daughters of Don Wilson. Together they had initiated a most successful entertainment business known as the Flying W Ranch in northwest Colorado Springs. To look at Russ' scrawny body, you'd never guess he was a millionaire. But he planned and stayed on top of his business to the extent that he had between 1,000 and 1,500 dinner guests to feed and his Flying W Wranglers to entertain—seven days a week all summer long. In winter he had an indoor steakhouse for smaller crowds.

Russ and Marian and his in-laws wanted a Methodist Church up their valley in northwest Colorado Springs. In the early fall of each year, for many years, he invited the members of First Church, a church with more than 6,000 members to be his guests at a much reduced cost per person. Then, he gave the total sum back to his downtown church. I was in charge of that event for many years.

For his dining guests, Russ had a rustic country church erected at his ranch similar to one he grew up in somewhere in Kansas. It seated about one hundred people. He began having Sunday afternoon services at 4:00 p.m. so that early guests who came to wander through his concessions could pause for a brief worship service. I was among the several ministers who volunteered to lead and speak there. Shortly after the church was built, Russ wanted it to be dedicated to the glory of God. I helped him to get Rev. Calvin D. McConnell of his downtown church to do that. After my 1983 retirement from the Rocky Mountain Annual Conference, I continued in ministries that included fulfilling the wish of many people to begin a Methodist Fellowship in Russ and Marian's little church.

Because we were friends, I responded to his wish, and that of many people in the Pikes Peak Sub-District, including his wife and the Wilson family, by advertising and conducting an 11:00 a.m. worship service in the little church on the fourth Sunday of October 1984. The retired Rev. Dr. Lloyd Nichols and I were the founding ministers. The Fellowship was chartered as "Wilson United Methodist Church" in 1987 and has grown to around three hundred members. In 2007, I attended, with other ministers who had followed me, the 20th anniversary of the chartering of the church. They gave each former pastor a new Bible. In my copy Russ Wolfe wrote these words in his own handwriting:

"Because of you, Phil, and the Lord, we are still on our way."

During that first winter of 1984, Russ came every Sunday and built a fire in the large pot-bellied stove until he decided to purchase and install a heating system. He sat at worship on those hard benches until he decided to purchase cushions to sit on. Later on Russ and Marian gave the land for a church. Recently the second phase of the worship site was completed. A few years ago, Marian died. Russ still attends alone and helps with the ushering. What a Friend!

From childhood I have heard the comforting words of the hymn, originally written as a poem in 1855 by Joseph M. Scriven,:

What a Friend We Have in Jesus

What a friend we have in Jesus,
all our sins and griefs to bear!
What a privilege to carry
everything to God in prayer!

O what peace we often forfeit,
O what needless pain we bear,
all because we do not carry
everything to God in prayer.

Have we trials and temptations?
Is there trouble anywhere?
We should never be discouraged;
take it to the Lord in prayer.

Can we find a friend so faithful
who will all our sorrows share?
Jesus knows our every weakness;
take it to the Lord in prayer.

Jesus must be a friend of many, many people because I looked through the church hymn book and found more than three hundred hymns about Him. Whatever happened in the 1800s? Eighty percent of those songs were written in that century. The Protestant Reformation under Martin Luther and others occurred in the centuries just prior to the 1800s. Bibles were written in the King James Version and were widely distributed and read. People discovered that they didn't need a clergy person to divide it up and dish it out as ecclesiastical authorities decided. Happily, they could now read the scriptures and fall in love with the most Precious Friend ever.

On 11-9-2008, I received in the mail a letter from a friend—a friend who introduced me to the "New Life/Key Event Ministry" in 1979—more than thirty years ago. The orientation was in a Denver area United Methodist church. A number of other pastors attended this event. The teacher from the Board of Evangelism in Nashville, Tennessee, was H. Eddie Fox. It was a plan to help churches and districts to size up the condition of a church more intentionally and plan and organize in a better way to help the church reach out and grow. I was impressed with both the teacher and the program.

In 1977, Eddie had included me and some thirty-five other pastors to go with him to Africa for a month—some to Liberia, West Africa, and the others to East Africa. It was a spiritual odyssey whose details are included elsewhere in this book. I went on to become a member of the National Association of United Methodist Evangelists. He grew in leadership in our denomination to become the Royce and Jane Reynolds Director of World Evangelism of the World Methodist Church. So he has gone up and up and up, and because he has been a long-time friend, it pleased me to hear from him and about the prestigious ministry of that organization.

He calls me Phil, and I call him Eddie instead of Rev. Dr. Fox, Mr. World Director. I know that, across nearly three decades, we have had access to each other. I am glad that he has given me an opportunity to add my little bit to help make Jesus known around the world. The World Methodist Evangelism office has recently moved to Hermitage, TN, near Nashville. It warms my aging heart to remember Eddie's cherished friendship.

New friends can become old friends. Rev. Lonnie Eakle was a new friend when he was a young pastor at Aldersgate United Methodist Church. Some years later, when I was elected to chair the board of control at Templed Hills Conference Camp near Woodland Park, he volunteered to be the secretary of that board. I can't remember any secretary who had more fun while serving in that capacity, and who created more enjoyment for those who were at the board meetings, including those who read his minutes. Whoever heard of minutes being fun to transcribe and to read? He made my task much easier, and the business of the board moved along happily and with good cheer.

Lonnie went on to other appointments, gradually transforming churches wherever he went. Then he was appointed the Superintendent of the Sunshine District in Pueblo. At age seventy-four I had been appointed to the Avondale UMC in his district. That meant that he was now more than my friend—he was my District Superintendent as well. I will never forget the Sunday morning in August when he showed up for one of my "Cowboy Church" services. Right after that service in the church parking lot where a few horses and riders stood behind people sitting in chairs, he came up front smiling to greet me. His comment about the sermon was, "Phil, your words about the 'halter rail' needed more emphasis."

Through more than three decades, I never failed to get notes from him and his wife Terry, for my birthday, Christmas and other holidays. We had many get-togethers from time to time at church conferences. One of the bits of humor was about "How to stop a charging tiger." We still get ready to smile when we meet. He wants to know if I remember how to do that. I do:

To stop a charging tiger, you must (1) look him straight in the eye. If that fails, (2) show him a blade of metal, like a knife. (3) If that doesn't stop him, rub some manure on his nose. If you're wondering where to get the manure, just reach behind you.

It's not one that can be told in mixed company. However, it continues to bring two friends closer together. Lonnie drove more than a hundred miles for my 90th birthday party. What a friend!

James O. Frankowsky was a lost friend for forty-nine years. When I arrived in Madrid, Spain, as the only Protestant chaplain there, I was loaded with Protestant Sunday School literature. Why? Because the Chief of Air Force Chaplains, Maj. Gen. Charles I. Carpenter, had been alerted by the Catholic chaplain in Madrid to the fact that there was none available in Spain. The entire Protestant Chapel Program needed to start from scratch—worship site, furniture, ecclesiastical supplies, first worship service, first Sunday school, first adult and youth choirs—first everything. In organizing the Sunday school, someone wanted to know why I had chosen a Catholic colonel as the superintendent of the school. My answer was, "Colonel Frankowsky volunteered to be the superintendent, just as everyone else was asked to do. And besides, he is not a Catholic. He is a Lutheran!"

He and his wife, Alice, came to discuss with me whether or not he should fill the role for which he had volunteered. He had attended the class for adults in which the lesson was about the consumption of alcoholic drinks. Most of those in the class felt that religious leaders should abstain from such. Jim didn't want me to be in a position to be criticized if he became the school's superintendent. He said that he drank only at social occasions and then not to excess. Being a teetotaler, I had to make a difficult decision. I will always be glad that I turned down his tender of resignation.

Colonel James Frankowsky

He turned out to be the best leader I had ever had. He organized classes and departments for all ages, kindergarten through adults. He recruited teachers for each class as well as back-up teachers for each teacher. He was so well organized in this capacity that few business meetings were needed. Often, following each Sunday sessions, he'd phone me about a problem or concern. We'd discuss it briefly and decide the best next step to take. The last year we were there, the average attendance was more than four hundred.

We struggled with a problem families faced while abroad in the military. How could the cord be strengthened between their churches in the USA and their members scattered throughout the world, and particularly those in Madrid? We wanted them to be aware of their need to maintain loyalty and contact with home churches. With the youth, we went a step further. We organized "Church Membership Classes" for a number of mainline denominations. Eighth through twelfth graders were invited to take the instructions for membership in a church of choice in the USA. We wrote to the individual pastors of the churches involved and told them what we were doing and who among us of their denomination would be giving the instructions. We asked the pastors to give their consent to receiving the instructions. In every case the pastor admitted into their church's membership those who completed the instructions. There were no negative vibes.

After two years, Jim and his family rotated back to the United States. Before leaving us he sold me his car. My daughter Marcia married and returned to the States after one year. She and Phil Jr. both graduated from the American Dependents School. It was from Phil that I learned where Jim was, through one of his daughters. It was a happy day when we were personally in contact after nearly a half a century. He had retired as a major general, settled in Virginia, and was attending and busy working in a Lutheran church. His dear wife, Alice, had died two years earlier. We both were happy to be friends reunited.

Beverly Howard was the founder and president of the Hawthorne School of Aeronautics, Spence Air Base, Moultrie, Georgia. In World War II he was an ace pilot. Following the war he founded five flying schools—in Charleston and Columbia, SC, Greensboro, NC, Jacksonville, FL, and the Hawthorne School in Moultrie, Georgia. He was well known among flyers as a stunt pilot. He could fly upside down and, with his tail-fin, cut a string between two upright poles. I saw him do it in 1952, a feat that challenged blood distribution to and from the head.

"Bevo," as he was affectionately known, gave training to young officers in how to fly. In addition to USAF lieutenants, there were young officers from the Military Defense Assistance Partners in western European countries included in this training. At Spence Air Base we had French, Danish, Italian and other. Spence had been in moth balls for several years after the war. The Spence military community consisted of some 600 officers and enlisted personnel. That was not more than a squadron, but was looked upon as a military base.

So, when I was assigned there in 1951-'53, there was only one chaplain, a secretary and, later a sergeant on duty. The Air Force paid a nearby priest to take charge of Catholic services and other duties, in addition to his own church duties. For the few Jewish personnel, I was able to have the help of a local Jewish layman by the name of Aaron Heller.

Bevo Howard was the president of the training school and worked cooperatively with the base commander, Lt. Col. Steve Crosby, a survivor of the Bataan Death March in WW II. My job was to establish the Chaplains Six-Point Program in a chapel that needed a complete overhaul-heating system, pew pad, ceiling to floor drapes for behind the altar, pulpit Bible, Communion set, hymn books, chapel annex for Sunday School classes and vacation Bible school—you name it, we needed it.

Six hundred military personnel were assigned, some of whom were married and had young families on base. Bevo also had civilian staff and employees, some who attended religious and social affairs on base. Colquitt County people in Moultrie and environs often were invited to events at the base. The chaplain had major responsibilities only for military people, but quickly there was a mixture of anybody and everybody who sought attendance and involvement with what was "going on out there at the base."

When we had one of our quarterly musical concerts by a mixture of male student pilots and an equal number of young women from Moultrie, both military and civilian people were invited. When we had a chapel-sponsored Easter egg-hunt, any children living near the base were included in the invitation. On December 17, 1952, I received the following letter from Bevo, who said,

> *Dear Phil;*
>
> *I would like to take this opportunity to again congratulate and thank you for the wonderful Christmas party that was held at the Base Saturday, December 13. You certainly did a grand job and all the kids, including the parents, had a wonderful time at the Christmas party and, of course, this was because of you even more than Santa Claus.*
>
> *I would also like to congratulate you on the fine Glee Club program when the concert of Christmas music was held on December 11 in the chapel. Functions of this kind contribute more than you know to the success of our mission and particularly to the fine support among all personnel connected with the base.—Bevo, President*

To have a friend like Bevo Howard was an elixir to my soul. Even after I had been gone to my next assignment in California, my commander, Lt. Col. Mortimer Yates, forwarded the following letter from Bevo:

> *Dear Mort,*
>
> *The purpose of this letter is to express to you our appreciation of the fine service that Chaplain (Major) Green rendered while he was stationed at Spence Air Base. While he was stationed here, he formulated and put into effect a well-rounded program that affected not only the military personnel on the base, but had excellent results with all our civilian employees, their families, and many of the citizens of Moultrie and Colquitt County. He always fostered a feeling of friendship between Air Force personnel and others, and his efforts in this direction had a marked effect on the morale on all persons at Spence Air Base. In the Allied training program he originated "Southern Hospitality," which was quite successful in assisting the Allied trainees in their training and attitude toward this country, as well as contributing to the improvement of community relations. There are many other important ways that Chaplain Green assisted in the success of this base as he was generally active in all functions that took place.*
>
> *It is my feeling that Chaplain Green is one of the finest, if not the finest, chaplain in the Air Force today. It gives me a great deal of pleasure to be able to write this letter of thanks for the thoughtful and unselfish efforts on his part while stationed here. Sincerely, Beverly Howard, President*

A word about Rev. Dr. A. Purcell Bailey

On April 29, 1998, I received a letter from Beth A. Richardson, one of his four daughters. Because he was having surgery on his neck on May 6, the family wanted to collect a "Book of Letters" from his friends. I was happy to send the following letter to them for their book of letters:

While on active duty as a United Methodist Chaplain, A. Purcell Bailey was my mentor and denominational supervisor. During that time he was the Executive Director of the United Methodist Commission on Chaplains in Washington, D.C. Those who chose him for the challenging position did well, because he filled that position with efficiency and "heart." Chaplains in the field looked upon him as I did—as a "friend in court." I found it easy to open my heart to him, feeling that he understood and that I need not fear being misrepresented. The many hundreds of United Methodist chaplains throughout the world were fortunate to have someone who affirmed their ministries, and who fought to promote their best interests. Without a doubt there were a few "difficult" chaplains whose ecclesiastical endorsements had to be withdrawn, but never until every effort had been extended in their behalf.

He continued to touch my life after my military retirement in 1963, at which time I became Minister of Outreach at First United Methodist Church in Colorado Springs, Colorado. He kept in touch with me, and with many other retired chaplains. He did this through correspondence, newsletter, and by visits to our Annual Conference where he had us stand to be presented, and at which times he shared a meal with us. More than once, when he could not come personally, he entrusted me with the task of representing him and the Commission on Chaplains.

In the early 1970s, he did something very meaningful, caring and typical. It was when I was the first US Air Force chaplain to be elected national president of the Military Chaplains Association. At the convention where I was to give the "President's Message" he came in, sat with me, put his arm around my shoulder and whispered, "Phil, I'm with you!" When I rose to speak minutes later, I stood a few inches taller, and felt ever so much more confident.

For at least a quarter of a century we have exchanged Christmas letters or cards. In our senior years we both lost faithful, loving life companions. Each has been doubly blessed by finding someone to share our loneliness and inspire us "to keep on keeping on" doing the God-ordained tasks committed to our hands.

Well, here I am wishing him a belated happy 80th birthday, as I rapidly approach my 84th this September. Sometime ago I heard someone say, "Age is a matter of mind, if you don't mind, it doesn't matter!" Knowing Purcell Bailey, he will be comfortable with thoughts of his mortality, worry not at all about the "muffled oar," or the "brush of angel wings." There's too much yet to be done, and too little time left in which to do it. There are more Daily Bread articles to submit, more books to write in benefit of those in prison. Life is too rich in relationships with family and with a myriad of friends throughout the whole wide world, to hang up the robe, discard the pen and go—that is, until God shall say, "That's enough, Purcell Bailey, come on home!"

In closing, I salute the man who has gone farther, done more, been a greater blessing than most, and whose incalculable influence radiates down the corridor of decades the love of God and God's people. Helen and I are happy, yet exceedingly glad to call him friend!

Philip L. Green

Well, eight years later, I got a letter from Purcell's daughter. She said that he had gone to his heavenly reward. Earth is now poorer and heaven is richer for the exchange. I hope to see him beside the river of life where all is well, now and forever.

4

YOU WERE CHOSEN

Before you were chosen, you were created. You belong to your Creator. You are His! It is possible that you do not agree with what I have just said. For now, I hope you will choose to stand on neutral ground—between you and your Creator. If you believe your life has come through millions of years from a living cell, though ever-enlarging dimensions of that cell, no one will quibble about it. It could be true. Today, the geology of matter registers how ancient the stones are and how old are the skeletons preserved in them. Still unanswered is who made the first living cell, with all its limitless capabilities.

I went to a different school, to one that believes in an intelligent, all-knowing, almighty Creator who looked out one celestial day and saw nothing but an immense empty space and decided to fill it. Because he was almighty, he had the power to put there whatever he wished; all he needed to do was to say the word and substance appeared out of nothing visible. Hebrews 11:3 says,

> *". . . . for by faith we understand that the universe was formed at God's command, so that what is seen was not made of what was visible."*

That is more believable than anything else that I have heard. It fits into the "Big Bang" theory. Some astronomers believe the universe continues to enlarge. As time-without-limit passed by, the Creator observed a small planet whirling around one of his stars—our sun—and decided to make it an example of all the possibilities of his ingenuity. He created a master plan and ordered the law of gravitation to stabilize the planets in a right relationship with the sun, the earth and with each other—our solar system. He gave each piece direction and gravity commensurate with its size and weight. He brought order out of chaos, separated the water from the land and made life as we know it possible. He measured out on that planet enough light, heat and sustenance for all living things to thrive and multiply. There seemed no limit to the number and variety of animals, plants, birds, fish and the like. The speed-of-light was too slow for him to keep up with his expanding universe, so he invented the speed-of-thought so that he could tell himself to go from one end of the universe to the other in a flash.

As time-without-limit passed by, the Creator observed a small planet whirling around one of his stars, our sun, and decided to make it an example of all the possibilities of his ingenuity. He ordered the law of gravitation to stabilize the earth's relationship to the sun and the other planets in our solar system and began creating a master plan. In that beginning he brought order out of chaos, separated the water from the land, and made life possible—with enough light and heat and sustenance for all the living things to thrive and multiply. There seemed no limit to the number and variety of animals, plants, birds, fish and the like. Then he created a garden, a very special kind of place, and made it a place he himself would enjoy. It came to be called "the Garden of Eden."

He already had angels and archangels, cherubim and seraphim, who were made to obey without question all his desires. Then came a crowning statement, *"Let us make man and woman!"*

So he made Adam and Eve to fellowship with him in his favorite garden. But he didn't want them to "have to" obey his every wish, like the angels. So he breathed into each of them a living independent soul, with the gift of choice. It was a dangerous choice because there was the possibility that the time would come when they might choose to disobey and displease him. But he took that breathtaking chance—later to learn that the serpent, "a snake-in-the-grass," talked them into disobeying him. They ate of the forbidden fruit that was declared off limits, and awoke with new knowledge, that they were naked. The human body was a beautiful creation and meant to multiply. Alas! Now those human bodies were capable of misuse and degradation. Alienation and estrangement from the God who created them was a bitter pill. No longer could he trust them in the garden. So he put them out and cursed Satan for his dastardly act.

What to do now? Overlook the weakness of human flesh? Forget the whole thing? No. Sin had ended his dream forever. His heart was broken. In a search for a way of atonement that would erase the blemish on the character of sinful man, he came up with a plan—a plan that his only begotten Son would be called upon to execute. So Jesus became a human being as well as the Son of God. He took the punishment that was meant for us and carried it with him to the cross of Calvary. That's why he came—to reconcile the human race back to his Father.

So, you were created by God, redeemed by his Son, and chosen to again be included in the family of God. In his bestseller book, *The Purpose Driven Life,* author Rev. Rick Warren reveals "what on earth you are here for." His book will help you to know God's purpose for your life. He goes on to say,

"Having this perspective will reduce your stress, simplify your decisions, increase your satisfaction, and, most important, prepare you for eternity."

Good or bad, worthy or unworthy, you have been bought with a price—the blood shed by the Good Shepherd who is not willing that anyone should perish but that all could come to repentance. Claim what has been purchased for you. You've been chosen. You are an heir. You are royalty. You are a citizen of heaven.

> *"Your outlook goes beyond this present world to the hopeful expectation of the Savior, who will come from heaven. He will transfigure the bodies belonging to our humble estate so that they resemble his own glorious body, by that power of his that makes him the master of everything that is." (Phil. 3:20-21, my translation)*

Yes, in this world you were chosen—but chosen for a purpose. You are an ambassador with a message. The message you carry is not yours but your master's. His message is that of good news. The good news is that the door is now open for anybody and everybody who wishes may draw near to God and claim son-ship—a member of his family. Members of his family know what his purpose is. They get busy carrying the good news of God's open heart and door. They know that there is rejoicing in heaven over one lost stray and maverick that comes home.

One of the satisfying things of life is to be chosen by others. I have had the good fortune to be chosen (selected, wanted, asked for) for a wide variety of assignments and duty by bishops, commanders and friends. The Chief of Air Force Chaplains chose me to go to a semi-diplomatic assignment as the only Protestant chaplain in Madrid, Spain, for three years. My friend, Chaplain Glen Shaffer, invited me to be his deputy at a large 15-chaplain base at Parks AFB, California.

Dr. Ben. F. Lehmberg invited me to be his associate pastor of the largest Methodist Church in the Western Jurisdiction. Bishop R. Marvin Stuart and Bishop Melvin E. Wheatley kept me on that staff for seventeen years. In all my assignments, the one I most wanted to please was Jesus Christ who continually answered my prayer of dominant desire, "Lord use me—whenever, however and wherever you may wish."

When, at his feet, I wrote seventy-four *Prayers Jesus Might Have Prayed,* I placed number one at the beginning because it was the one He might have prayed before coming into the world. I struggled for five years with that topic. It intrigued me and challenged me. I didn't want to be considered a newborn fool for having the audacity to put words, especially prayers, in the mouth of my Savior. I finally agreed with myself to begin writing—but only after setting some strict ground rules. The most important one was that I would not write a single prayer Jesus might have prayed without a distinct urge by the Holy Spirit. Here's the first prayer:

> *Father, I am ready to go on the divine mission we have planned. People on earth need to know what you are really like, that you are a provident heavenly Father, and that you wish to lavish upon your children many good gifts beyond their ability to comprehend.*
>
> *It is now time to bruise the serpent's head, replace his domination, and counter his claim to the earth's ownership. His work of description no doubt continues because he makes his temptations almost irresistible. But I want to show people that your way is the best way. I know it will not be a friendly world, but it is your world. I want to redeem it. The divine image in people has been tarnished and I want to restore it to what you intended it to be.*
>
> *The prophets have laid the groundwork for my appearance. I will build your kingdom on love and not obedience to man-made understandings of what you require.*

Isaiah revealed that what I do will be costly—that I will be a man of sorrow and acquainted with grief. He also saw that my sacrifice will be effective in bringing multitudes into the Kingdom of God. With your help, Father, it can change the world.

I do not yet know what it will be like to be your divine Son in a human body. What I do know is that it will take that event to reconcile the world back to you. I want to do it for your sake. So, send me now, when you wish. Amen.

5

CHOOSING THE BEST MODELS

Those I have chosen to emulate as models have had a remarkable influence for success and happiness, thus a longer life. I have a two-page typewritten list of the many who have been important to me.

One of those models is the Rev. Dr. Harry Emerson Fosdick. He wrote a number of books that helped to bring me out of a more provincial view of life and ministry. One of those books he wrote in 1915 titled *The Meaning of Prayer,* which had inspired me to establish and hold onto my own prayer of dominant desire: *Lord, use me whenever, wherever, however and as long ever as you may wish.* The book I am now writing, at age ninety-five, is about how wonderfully God has answered that prayer. Chapter 49 of this book is a more in depth writing of my prayer of dominant desire.

Another of those models is Dr. Ben F. Lehmberg.

Alan Walker, in his book, *A Ringing Call to Missions,* says, "In the communication of truth, nothing is so powerful as a human personality incandescent with the love and power of God."

Ben F. Lehmberg was such a person. He was full of loving concern. People young and old, responded to the warmth of his personality. In his ministry, the proclamation of the Word held a place second to no other part of public worship. His preaching combined an unusual ability to speak without reference to notes, to place in Christian perspective the events of the historical present, to focus attention upon the ancient truths of Scripture in such a way as to bring them into contemporary usefulness, and to restore attractiveness to the Christian way of living.

He was a masterful teller of stories. He spoke with the direct force of his winsome yet challenging personality, which was backed up by careful and arduous study and a photographic memory. Many a person has been heard to say, "I have never met him, but I have heard him preach and I feel I know him." Few preachers have had the gift of communication of spirit and thought in similar degree.

He had a flair for the dramatic, for the emotional, for the humorous. But these did not extend to sensationalism or cheap sentimentality.

Nowhere in his ministry was the impact of his personality so forcefully felt as in his beloved pulpit. From it, with consummate ease and skill, he could deliver a sermon, welcome member and visitor to the ritual of friendship, sing a solo, or invite people to discipleship.

What were his basic beliefs? Bishop R. Marvin Stuart, in summarizing them at Dr. Lehmberg's funeral said,

"Belief that at the heart of the universe is good and not evil; belief in Jesus Christ which led to the life of devotion and dedication to the Kingdom of God about which he so often spoke; a strong conviction that the church is to be the instrument through which God's purposes may be realized here on earth; a growing optimism in the face of a pessimistic society—an optimist based on a firm faith in God; a conviction that God had called him to be a minister of Jesus Christ . . . ."

He believed in thinking big and planning big. The genius of his pastoral and preaching leadership resulted in the growth of a congregation with some 3,000 members to 6,237 within fifteen years—the largest within the Western Jurisdiction—and that in a city whose population had not reached 190,000. More than 2,000 worshipers heard him Sunday by Sunday for many years. And he made his church big, not in membership alone, but in friendliness, generosity, evangelism, and allegiance to Jesus Christ.

Dr. Ben, as he was affectionately known, loved people. This included his family in unusual degree, but extended to the congregation and to all anywhere who needed him. There was no more typical pose than of him beaming at a baby held aloft at the baptismal font. People felt his love as he dealt with them in groups or as individuals. His radiant faith in this life, and faith in life everlasting, was contagious. People were caught up in the spirit of his love of life and were strengthened and healed by it. His funeral was a paean of victory, which culminated in the singing of *The Hallelujah Chorus* by Handel.

One readily sees in the biographical data that Dr. Ben was a man of wide interests. He was involved in leadership activities of the church at all echelons, from the local congregation to the General Conference. He expressed his civic-mindedness in a variety of ways throughout the city, state and nation.

He was unabashedly patriotic. In 1965, at the request of the Chief of Air Force Chaplains, he flew to Europe to conduct four preaching missions for Armed Forces personnel there. He always came back after such trips full of new ideas for a more faithful and effective ministry. He was never afraid of trying out new ideas or of giving them up when they did not work for him. What an indefatigable worker he was and in what disdain he held the indolent!

The love of his congregation for him was best expressed in the words of a plaque presented to him at the opening ceremony of a magnificent new educational wing on September 18, 1966. It read, "*On this day, the 95th anniversary of First Methodist Church, Colorado Springs, CO, in recognition of fifteen years of devoted and outstanding pastoral leadership, we the people of the congregation unite in presenting this symbol of our lasting appreciation to Dr. Ben F. Lehmberg, whose life and ministry prompt us to pledge anew our allegiance to Jesus Christ and his Church.*"

More than 2,000 worshipers heard him Sunday by Sunday for many years. And he made his church big, not in membership alone, but in friendliness, generosity, evangelism, and allegiance to Jesus Christ. In the contrails of his return to God, may the people called Methodists ever see the greatness of one personality who was wholly devoted to Jesus Christ and to the will of God.

It may seem audacious for me to say that I have chosen Jesus Christ as my chief role model. As a child I came to love him. Even in my wayward period as a teenager, I came to him again and again for a new start. I learned that solid joys and lasting pleasures were lost without his smile of forgiveness. I regret those lapses when my guilt separated us. As a pastor, it was my happy privilege to introduce many people to him. I studied him and tried to be like him. Along the road of my ministry, I sought his guidance and help.

Jesus faced danger and trouble head on, forthrightly. As he and his disciples were leaving Cesaera Phillippi, where the clear Jordan River flowed from under a high mountain, he told them he was now on his way to Jerusalem. They tried in vain to keep him from going there. They knew, and Jesus also knew, that there were enemies who wanted to kill him. Jesus was not deterred. He knew what he had to do. In fact he told his disciples that he must suffer and die in that city. He knew he had to go there. It was to be the culmination of his mission on earth. As he approached that city, friends warned him not to go into it. They felt sorry for what he was about to face. He turned them away and said sadly,

"*Weep for yourselves*," for he knew that in a few short years, Jerusalem would be sacked and the people killed and scattered. He made his way to the Garden of Gethsemane where he prayed for deliverance, but he didn't ask his Father to send a legion of angels to do that. Rather, he got up, faced what he had come to do, and said, "*It is time to go now*."

What courage! The agony of his prayer moves us to tears. His cherished followers had fallen asleep. But Jesus knew what he had to do. It was already fixed in his mind and heart—the thirty-nine skin-breaking lashes, the crown of thorns upon his head, the betrayal by Judas, the denial by Peter, the false accusers before Pilate.

As I reread the scene in the Bible, in preparation for writing the poem below, my heart broke within me, and I wept, and wept and wept. My Savior—dying for my sins—the sinless one, dying for the sins of the whole world! But he knew what he was doing. On the way to the finish line He healed the ear of a guard that Peter had severed and ushered into paradise a penitent thief on one of the crosses. Now, here is the poem I tearfully wrote on April 28, 2008 a few months before my 94th birthday:

That's Why I Came

Jesus, my Lord! Why are you so silent,
When you have so much to say?
Your critics seek to trap and kill you.
Must you from day to day,
On each new day, seek a way, to rescue lost mavericks and strays?
He said, "That's why I came."

When you're like that they think it's true,
What they're saying about you.
They want you crucified right now, with no proof of guilt, somehow.

"I want the world to know the truth,
That no one took away my life.
I gave it. That's why I came."

Who are those you came to save?
"Tis my Father's wish and mine.
'Cause all have sinned, no other can save, only the sinless One.
Who could that be, except Me?
That's why I answer them not today.
I say again, that's why I came."

"The sin laid on me, was yours,
Not mine. For you the cup I drank.
Upturned in garden's lonely trist with evil's awful tank.
So all could know your sins forgiv'n,
My goodness, not yours, no shame,
I can but say, that's why I came."

The first verse of the twenty-third Psalm begins with 'The Lord Is My Shepherd.' That Psalm is the most beautiful poem one could ever find. It describes the heart of God in a most revealing way. That's one reason I have chosen the Good Shepherd as my model.

This 1947 photo reminds me every time of Jesus, the Good Shepherd, who knows and calls his sheep by name.

A model who taught me how to be a more caring pastor was Rev. Dr. Thomas Shipp. He was the founder and only pastor of Lover's Lane United Methodist Church, Dallas, Texas, until his death. He built it up from its beginning to more than 7,000 members. I knew him and about him before 1974—the year I began to plan a major "Conference on Ministerial Excellency" on pastoral care. To this event pastors and laity of very large churches of many denominations were invited. Tom Shipp was invited to this conference to speak on the topic, "The Caring Pulpit and the Caring Pew."

I had been impressed that his caring efforts were extended to several hundred alcoholics who found in him a pastor who went all-out in their behalf individually one by one. Most churches and pastors were making no great commitment to such a group of "losers," but who chose rather to leave alcoholics to Alcoholics Anonymous and other social agencies. He chose to get in the pit with them and—with the help of others as well as the help of recovering alcoholics—restore them to be redeemed members of society, and of his church. He made every effort to "be with" each person with whom he was relating as a counselor. There were plenty of times when he'd be very busy with other top priorities of his work, like giving a sermon, bringing comfort to a grieving family, performing a wedding, etc. In a pinch he'd say to the alcoholic in crisis, "Joe, I can't talk to you (or come to you) right now, but I'm sending Bill. I'll see you as soon as I can."

While at our conference in Colorado Springs, I put him up in a hotel overnight. When I paid his hotel bill, I noticed a telephone call to Dallas of two hours time during which, I assumed he was helping someone who couldn't wait for him to get back. That's the way he was. I wondered how such commitments to one-on-one counseling affected his performance in the pulpit. I later talked with the Rev. Dr. Harvey Potthoff, Dean of the Iliff School of Theology in Denver, about it.

Dr. Potthoff had done a workshop I attended in Lover's Lane Church. He told me that Dr. Shipp's sermons suffered at times for lack of preparation time, but that the congregation made no complaint because "they knew" he had been with someone in need of the caring that only he could give.

In his address at our conference in Colorado Springs, he told of an experience he had known. A pastor some distance from Dallas had invited him to preach a series of sermons to his congregation—a revival series during a week. He drove the distance Sunday afternoon after his sermon at Lover's Lane. Following the evening service, he and the pastor and others stood around the front of the church and talked about the week of services. A car drove up at 10:00 p.m. and stopped at the house just beyond the parsonage. A man got out and went in. Someone asked Dr. Shipp if he had noticed that. He had not. They told Dr. Shipp that the same man did that every night, seven days a week, and left at 4:00 a.m. Dr. Shipp saw nothing unusual about a man coming home from work every night. They told him that a widow lived in that house with a teenage daughter—that the teenage daughter was leaving the next morning for a city some distance away—and everyone "knew" why she was leaving—that she was no doubt pregnant.

Dr. Shipp asked the group if anyone had been to visit in that home. None had. The pastor said that his members would fire him if he visited in such a home. The next day, Dr. Shipp knocked on the door to that house and an overworked woman came to the door. When he told her he was the evangelist for the services at the church that week, she invited him in. He discovered the woman had a shut-in mother living with her and her daughter. Her mother had a serious affliction with her throat and breathing that required almost constant care around the clock every day. She said her daughter had gone to the city where she had a job that would help her mother pay the rent and living expenses. She also said that her brother, who lived some fifty miles away, came every night to care for her mother while she got six hours of sleep.

He invited her to come to the services. She said she would like nothing better but, now that her daughter had left, she would have no one to stay with her mother if she wanted to come. Dr. Shipp said he'd get someone to stay with her mother. None wanted to take on a job "in that family." He finally paid fifty dollars for a couple of hours for that duty. At the service that night, he introduced the woman to the congregation like this;

"Friends, I have a special introduction to make. Mrs. Abernathy lives in the second house from the church. When I visited in her home today, she told me that her daughter had left for a job in the city to help bolster the family income. I was surprised to discover that her afflicted shut-in mother lived with her because she needed constant care. Because she wanted to come to the service tonight, I found someone to stay with her mother. Every night her brother drives to take care of their mother from 10:00 p.m. until 4:00 a.m. so that his sister can get some sleep. Tonight, she is happy to be with us because it is the first time she has been able to get to church since she was a child—when her father was the pastor of this church!"

His membership had grown to one of the ten largest churches in Methodism and was in need of a larger sanctuary. The burden of his heart laid heavily upon him. One night, at a meeting of the building committee, everything was approved except the inclusion of some expensive windows in the sanctuary. He felt that they should be included, even at the expense of a larger sanctuary. During the discussion he put his head on his arms on the table and remained so. He was there in that position when a concerned group of men went to investigate. He had died on that spot. The committee reconvened later and approved the windows. Whoever said, *every worthwhile institution is but the elongated shadow of one man,* certainly had it right at Lover's Lane United Methodist Church in Dallas, Texas.

It has been my good fortune to have witnessed and heard many outstanding preachers, evangelists and expositors. It is not to my credit to admit that I have never been able to emulate them. Admire them? Yes. Learn from them? Yes. Be a better friend, person? I sincerely and prayerfully hope so.

SECTION II

My sixteen times crossing the Atlantic Ocean were mostly the transportation to and from duties in Germany, Austria, Spain and Liberia, West Africa. I saw with my own eyes the ash heaps inside a former Nazi concentration camp that spoke silently of the atrocities to millions of Jews and others that were considered undesirables. But I also saw the beauty of the Alpine countries of Switzerland, France, Italy, Germany and Austria. I even attended the once-every-ten-year Passion Play. Travel to the Bible Lands where the Apostle Paul was a missionary to the Gentiles and a Holy Land trip to Israel, Jordan and Egypt were occasions of pure enjoyment. I walked in the footsteps of Jesus and the Apostles.

I still remember when and where I learned to fish with stick-bait and being stopped at the border between Spain and Portugal where I arrived without a copy of my military orders. It was a truly challenging experience on a sweltering afternoon to try to reconstruct my orders and type them in French on a Portuguese typewriter.

Heaven's cheering section, composed of the faces of loved ones and cherished friends, and of the heroes of faith in the Old Testament, are all in that "great cloud of witnesses" spoken of in Hebrews 11 and 12, and ever keep me on the upward journey.

Without your body you might be a figment of your imagination. Your body houses your five senses, and maybe a sixth. It also houses your soul—the one the Creator gave you at birth. The way you treat your body indicates how you value both body and soul.

Music has been a lifelong health medicine for me. It has accompanied me from earliest childhood to age ninety-five. I awake many mornings with one of hundreds of tunes stored in my memory.

I've sung in an a cappella choir, in duets, trios, quartets (male and mixed), and in oratorios. I've even written several songs (words and music). I used to organize and direct choirs and congregations of up to seven hundred people. Most music reminds me of people, places and events.

6

TRAVEL, THE BROADENING VIEW

It has been my happy privilege to do many trips, both at home and abroad. Twenty years of it was while I was a military chaplain in the Army Air Corps and the United States Air Force. As a young pastor in the mountains of Western North Carolina I met a few people who had never been outside the county in which they were born. Often a much-traveled person like me wonders about the perspective of some who have only read about places elsewhere. It is possible to gain a limited view of the world from photos in books and the albums of loved ones and friends and from movies and television. But there is nothing equal to being able to say, "I've been there, I've seen that."

In all fairness I must admit that not every trip was a bed of roses, like a troop train ride across war-torn West Germany. I never want that experience again. It can't be forgotten for it is printed indelibly in my mind. It will always be there. To see city after city reduced to rubble by war was more vivid than any newspaper or magazine account. I can forget that I had a raging fever, a sore throat, icy feet, passengers riding on a third-rate train. But I cannot forget the urchins who flocked beside the train at each stop, holding out eager, begging hands for the smallest donation of chocolates, gum or even a cigarette butt to take home for an adult male in the family. I found out later that tobacco was illegal tender on the black market, and better to have than money.

German children 'entertaining' our troops by playing the accordion and hoping for a candy bar in return, near Bremerhaven 1936.

The two-day train trip to Furstenfeldbruck Army Air Corp Redistribution Center in Bavaria near Munich was an experience of its own. As indicated, I was ill. There were no medical personnel with us. The wooden bucket-type seats fit one's bottom but were totally unsuited for lying down. When you tried, half of your shoulder was not supported. The railcar in which I rode had a broken out window, allowing cold, damp air free access to all of us, and we had not been issued cold weather clothes. I was resourceful enough to put hot coffee in my metal canteen bottle to warm my icy feet. Meals were served, but when? One supper came at 11:00 p.m., followed by breakfast the next morning at 5:00. But it was not like marching with full packs the hundreds of miles to destination. Things were better at the distribution center. There we had warm rooms and something we did not have on the train, plenty of warm shower water.

What about money, the greenbacks we had brought from the USA? At the center we had to trade all of it for military "script"—paper money (no coins). It was against military law to possess American money while in Germany. Likewise, it was not legal for Germans to possess either greenbacks or script. We were cautioned about trading on the black market with tobacco or commissary food. Fraternization with the Germans was against the law. Already many servicemen who found German girls attractive were ignoring this wartime order. During my three years there I saw many blond German women. "Beautiful" blondes were rare.

The large high piles of ashes at the infamous extermination camp at Dachau were the remains of many thousands of Jews and political undesirables. I was among several of the new arrivals in Germany who took a guided tour of this death camp. What had taken place in Hitler's drive toward the genocide of the Jewish race was hidden from most of the German population. Here at Dachau before our very eyes was ample proof that this inconceivable cruel and intentional plan actually took place. Believe it or not, this barbaric plan occurred as German leaders took the beautiful strains of the Austrian Hymn by Haydn and made them the theme song of Hitler's Third Reich, "Deutschland, Deutschland, Uber Alles". In our hymn-books we continue to use the tune to the words, "Glorious Things of Thee Are Spoken".

The Iron Curtain Falls In Prague

We stopped in Nuremberg on the way to Czechoslovakia to see where the German war criminals were being tried for their atrocities. Adolph Hitler was the most guilty one of all, but he had committed suicide in the fall of Berlin. Others before the world tribunal needed to account for their heinous crimes against innocent people.

On the way to Prague, we had lunch in Karlovy Very (Karlsbad). I had a great thirst for water. When I asked the waiter for some, he asked what I wanted water for. I said I was thirsty. He gave me a quizzical look and I knew he must be thinking, "What's wrong with wine?" Most Europeans drink wine with their meals. At length he brought me a serving of bottled water. I opened and drank it and asked for more. An Englishwoman who asked to go with us got a large charge out of my effort to explain in German what I wanted water for. She was a civilian employee with the U.S. Forces. I learned later she was a spy.

We had no sooner arrived in downtown Prague than people on the street began to indicate we shouldn't be where we were. Our rider knew German well and explained that Russia was taking over the city that very day and that we might find ourselves in an uncomfortable situation if we didn't leave the city immediately. We did that very thing, but reluctantly. We wanted to tour the city, attend an opera, and eat one or more of their delicious meals. I remembered a World War II movie in which a coloratura sang the following haunting words about the sister city of Vienna;

"It was waltz time in Vienna, wine was flowing, hearts were gay. Broken is the wineglass, only memories live today. Vienna may be through, but Strauss and Schubert cannot die. Three things live forever; you, the waltz, and I."

We stopped at one of many fields of hops, an essential element in beer, and noticed how they grew tall on standing ten-foot poles. I never drank beer. Where I grew up, Christians, and especially ministers, did not drink alcoholic beverages. Another reason I didn't drink beer—I didn't like its odor. After tasting it once, I didn't like the taste either.

In January 1948 I was transferred to Wiesbaden Air Base where I helped convert a troop barracks building into a chapel for Protestant and Catholic worship. An additional duty was that of being responsible for the Post Sunday School at the community center located in the Eagle Club—the social center for the Post. Also, I was in charge of the music for the main community service at 11:00 a.m. This was at the request of Chaplain, Colonel, Charles Wesley "Dri" Marteney, USAFE command chaplain. I volunteered to relate to a Youth-for-Christ group of young service-men and women who met Sunday nights. They led their own services. Later, when there was a move to build a cultural bridge between the German community of the city and military personnel, I served as an interested chaplain representative. This was after the mandate of keeping the two cultures apart was changed to "occupation friendly."

The Russian Bear Shows His Claws

The only way from West Germany into the American, French and English Zones of West Berlin was a highway through the Russian Zone of East Germany. With little warning, Russia suddenly closed that road—the lifeline to two and a half million Germans and allied personnel assigned in West Berlin. It was a well-known fact that Stalin was not happy with the conference in Potsdam that kept Russia from having all of West Berlin. And it was generally understood that the West could not keep the Russian Bear from marching through West Germany and France to the Atlantic, if such were considered desirable.

The uneasiness with the situation was reflected in the establishment of a policy that gave Americans with dependents in Germany the choice of keeping them or returning them to the USA at government expense. Some dependents opted to return home. On the Saturday before Easter Sunday of 1948, bus loads of Sunday school children and parents formed at the Eagle Club and moved out to a park in another part of Wiesbaden for an Easter Egg Hunt. Fearful Germans were certain that the zero hour had come and that the Americans were shipping out for home.

The Berlin Airlift (Operation "Vittles")

This bold-faced confrontation of Russia with the western allies had to be met. How else could food, supplies and equipment reach West Berlin for the 2,500,000 people there? Would the western powers bow before Russia's challenge? Would there be war? Would the iron curtain surround all of Berlin with impunity? Could Russia be pressured into re-opening the highway from West Germany into West Berlin? With what? Diplomatic efforts failed. What next? The Germans waited with bated breath, as did the rest of the world. The American Forces in Europe were diminished to the extent that armed conflict with Russia was questionable. In such an atmosphere, the Berlin Airlift was born.

The beginning of the Berlin Airlift

Immediately, the United States, Great Britain and France began organizing to take on the unbelievable task of flying into West Berlin all that was needed to sustain the lives of everyone there. It remained to be seen whether it could successfully be done. General Lucius D. Clay, commander-in-chief of the European Command, thought the airlift was forced upon us and that we had the duty to demonstrate before the world that we could do it. The chief of staff of the USAF, General Hoyt S. Vandenberg, believed that we could fly "anything, anywhere, anytime," and pledged his support. Lieutenant General John J. Cannon, commander of the Berlin Airlift, believed that the essential unity of the Air Force, Navy and Army could make such an aerial bridge a reality. So, after Russia blockaded the land route to Berlin, on June 25th General Clay contacted General Curtis LeMay, USAF Commander in Wiesbaden and asked him to fly 45 tons of supplies to Berlin.

The very next day, 80 tons were delivered from Rhein-Main and Wiesbaden Air Bases. Shortly afterward, General LeMay appointed Brigadier General Joseph Smith his project officer for the American Lift.

On July 29th, Major General William H. Tunner, operations chief of the Military Air Transport Service (MATS), arrived at US Airlift Task Force Headquarters in Wiesbaden, bringing with him a staff of seasoned air cargo transport experts. Many who came had served under him while flying "the Hump,"—China's famous air supply line during WW II.

At the first, the C-47 Dakotas already in Europe were pressed into service. They were small and slow. But they were all there were. At Wiesbaden AFB, I took a winning photo of a long line of them waiting take-off time. They filled the gap until 100 C-54s could be assembled from all over the world. Later a few giant C-74 Globemasters came aboard but there were only 12 of them. How was the needed daily tonnage target met? The C-54s were standardized, achieving a greater utilization.

In all kinds of weather, day in and day out, week after week, and month after month a plane loaded to the "gills" landed on average every four minutes at Tempelhof Air Base and other allied fields in West Berlin. The winter of 1948 was predicted to be worse than other years. As it turned out, it was more wretched than all predictions—heavy fogs and socked-in airfields at both ends. Pilots had to take off and land on instruments alone. With that kind of heavy traffic, it was nothing less than a miracle that there were as few accidents as there were and that tonnage loads kept pace with needs.

My jeep at Y-80 Air Base, winter of 1948. It was terrible flying weather for the Berlin Airlift that landed a load of food, etc. for 2.5 million people in West Berlin, about one every four minutes, mostly flying blind on instruments.

When I thought about all the co-ordinations for supplies, the time schedule, and how materials had to be purchased from all over the USA, put into predictable pipelines for delivery in Germany, and assembled at the right air base, my hat came off to everyone involved. Who would have believed—certainly not Joseph Stalin!—that a city of two and a half million people could receive the necessities of life over such an air bridge?

The Russian Bear Thwarted

The Russians expected a failure by the inclement weather of early winter, a failure that would embarrass and belittle us. When November came and December followed, and the rest of that terrible winter passed, and the effort did not fail but turned into a fantastic success, our prestige was boosted to new heights. Morale in Western Europe was elevated to an all-time high, as people saw proof of our determination to keep them from falling into totalitarian hands again.

My Mission to Liberia, West Africa

February-March, 1977
Sponsored by the Evangelism Section, General Board
of Discipleship of the United Methodist Church

The Rev. Dr. Eddie Fox invited a large group of United Methodist pastors to go with him to Liberia and Kenya to observe and help train pastors in the New Life Mission technique of evangelism. Dr. Lacour recommended that I go and represent our congregation. I paid the way of my wife, Lois, so she could accompany me. I'm glad she went because I needed her when I was struck down by I knew not what.

Eddie Fox and Dr. Bevans briefed us in New York City. They laid the groundwork of understanding for the climate and culture shock to follow. Everyone's luggage but mine arrived when we deplaned at Roberts Field. Mine was four days late and I was wearing my Rocky Mountain winter-time clothes. Here I was in equatorial Africa, being royally welcomed by Bishop Bennie Warner and his host committee and I was holding everybody up while we searched and re-searched the plane for my luggage. It reminded me of the skipper of a submarine that had been under for weeks. One morning he cheerfully piped the crew to the briefing room and said, "I have some bad news and some good news. I'll give the bad new first. I've just received word that we are to stay less than three more weeks. Now, the good news, everyone gets a change of underwear today. Joe, you change with George. Bill, you change with Al, ..." That yellow shirt and those green pants will never be the same.

If I had not traveled a month in Liberia, West Africa, there are a few things might never have known about that country and its black people. It was a surprise to learn that the people in its capital spoke English as in America, and that their monetary system was like ours—in dollars. Before I went there I learned that one of our presidents, James Monroe (1817-1825) had befriended slaves, most of whom had been shanghaied in Africa and sold in America. He chartered a ship that transported freed slaves back to Liberia at no cost. That is how Liberia got its name and why the name of the capital is Monrovia.

A part of our group in Liberia had the rare privilege of going far inland near the eastern border to visit the mission center of Ganta. It was my great privilege to learn about Dr. George Harley, whose call to be a missionary resulted in his being sent to Liberia. He and his wife, Winifred, were from my home state of North Carolina. After four months of the study of tropical diseases in London, they landed in Monrovia. By early 1926 all his supplies had been pre-packed and shipped by motor launch up the St. Paul River to White Plains mission station. On January 29, the journey inland began. He had to change carriers every day and some days more than once. So the caravan and his very pregnant wife moved slowly over the next two weeks to reach Ganta. Ganta included a hospital, a church, and a leper colony.

Houses had to be built, furniture made, goats broken for milking and many other details to be taken care of. There was very little help during the first years. And tragedy struck rather suddenly. One day he glanced out the window of his clinic and saw his young son stagger and fall. The boy died of an over-dose of sugar-coated quinine.

On the way to the grave-site, the Harleys had the volunteer help of a native who carried his little casket. At the grave, with a breaking heart, he read some scriptures that he could not finish—he was so overcome with grief that he fell weeping beside the grave. The native ran back to the village crying, "White man, white man, he cry like us!"

During three previous years none of the natives had come to his services at the mission station. After that, the meeting-place was full every time. Such a memory as that I shall always cherish.

In 1921, Dr. Thomas S. Donohugh, African Secretary of the Board of Missions, visited Liberia and was shown this site in the hinterland as a possible expansion opportunity. Here's what happened as a result:

To be an observer at a Liberian Annual Conference was to witness God at work first hand. There was a feeling of spiritual warmth and renewal that seemed a close approach to first century fervor. It was interesting to observe Bishop Warner in action at the beginning of his second quadrennium. I witnessed his concern for the well-being of his ministers (most of whom do secular work for a livelihood); for the continuing upgrading of their education and competence in ministry; and for the spiritual dimensions of their ministry. God speaks through the English language in Liberia as well as through five tribal tongues. At the Annual Conference, a 60-voice choir from the Kru area sang—not an elaboration on Kum Bah Yah—but Handel's "Hallelujah Chorus," and that from memory and without an accompaniment. It was interesting that Bishop Warner only used the five interpreters when there were important matters that needed to be clearly communicated. One important fact was that pastors were to have only one wife. In a country where multiple wives were usual, some converts who became pastors had more than one wife. Only one could be number one wife, and her name was the one registered in conference records.

I sat at a Rotary International luncheon in the capital beside a doctor by the name of Dr. Cooper. He had one of the finest clinics in Monrovia. He said he was a Methodist. I asked him how he gained the education and motivation to become a doctor. As I looked into his thoughtful black face, he told me he had started in one of our mission schools. "There were no other schools," he said. "If it had not been for the Methodist Church, I would not be Dr. Cooper today."

The youngest bishop ever to have been elected to the United Methodist Episcopacy was Bishop Stephen Nagle, a native Liberian. While he was yet a young bishop, six years before our visit, he collapsed at a meeting of the Council of Bishops. After hospitalization in America, he was flown back to Liberia to spend his last days in a losing battle with cancer in the hospital at Ganta mission station. He was a deeply spiritual bishop, humble, open to everyone, and the one who had a wonderful gift of healing others. Before his death, multiple thousands wondered why God would let such a saint die in his middle years. He sent word that he did not know why God did not heal him—the healer of so many others. He went on to declare his faith in the fact, "*. . . . that God had a purpose in it.*"

The inspiration of his life and death, accented by his doctrine of *God Power* and *People Power* fanned the flames of new life in the Liberian churches. Bishop Nagle was buried in the center of the pathway immediately in front of the chapel at the White Plains Retreat Center. On the last day of the New Life Mission Training sessions, American Bishop Kenneth Goodson visited White Plains. He fell before that grave for a full thirty minutes of weeping and praying. It may be that among his prayers was one that many of us prayed, "O God, let a double portion of the grace and power that was upon Stephen Nagle be on me."

I became very ill at the training sessions for Liberian pastors and lay leaders at White Plains and was taken to ELWA hospital for a day and night. My doctor was probably in his 30's. I was impressed to hear him tell of his call to the mission field while in a well-established practice in the USA. He sold his practice and his buildings without a fear, he said, and answered the call to Liberia. In answer to my unspoken question he said, "You don't need to worry about the results when you obey God." The call letters of that hospital and of a powerful gospel radio station in Monrovia were ELWA. The letters took on significance when a young crippled boy in the hospital won the prize for suggesting that the letters stood for *Eternal Love Wins Africa. (ELWA)*

Afterwards Lois and I were moved from what was the equivalent to the Blair House in D.C. to a mission guesthouse in Monrovia. Bishop Warner, Dr. Fadely and others visited me there. My wife walked me to the beach nearby. It was like walking a sick horse so that I'd not "get down." The sound of the ocean breeze was so enticing to my fevered condition but it was a mirage of sound. The breeze was coming from the hot desert rather than from the Atlantic Ocean.

Upon the recommendation of Dr. Young of the ELWA hospital, we were "allowed" to leave by plane for London two days earlier than the others. In London, at the U.S. Embassy, Navy Dr. Colbert treated me. X-rays showed that I had pneumonia, which accounted for my sore rib-cage, cough, high fever and lingering weakness. Because of dehydration, I had lost 15 pounds. Just getting out of bed or up from a chair was a major challenge. But my poor appetite gradually improved once I was able to keep food down. We flew home ten days later, and I convalesced further.

In 2010, I remembered how many small children in Liberia were dying for the lack of good drinking water. I sent to the Methodist bishop there a gift of more than $3,000 for most needed wells in small villages. I had the money because I decided to give now, before my death, to good causes I had intended to give in my Will.

One of the wonderful things the people of First UMC did as I was leaving the staff as associate pastor, was a gift of tickets for my wife and me to travel abroad to Europe in 1980. It included attendance at the famous Passion Play at Oberammergau, Germany. That also included a bus tour of the Alpine countries of Switzerland, Austria, Germany, Italy and other beautiful scenic sights.

The photo below I took from a site that overlooked that town and its cathedral. It reminded me of my three years in Austria and Germany 1946-'49. We visited the town during our stay but the Passion Play did not take place until 1950 (every ten years). During that time I got a picture of a man making a crucifix of Christ on a cross in his shop. He was also growing a beard for a scene in the play coming up the next year. It was of interest to learn that the Passion Play did not occur during Adolph Hitler's reign of terror.

Scene of the famous Passion Play,
Oberammergau, Germany

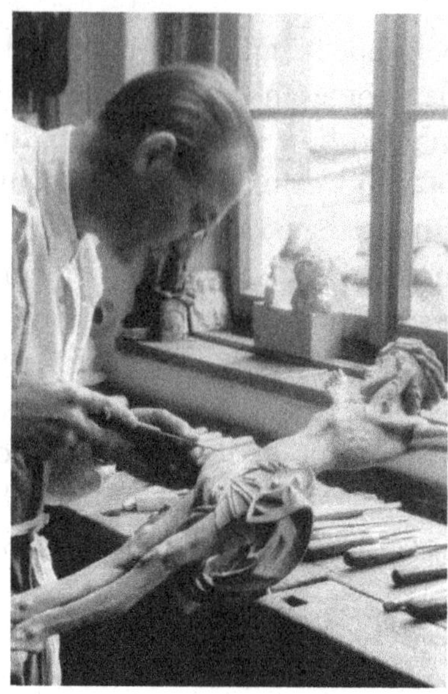

Making carvings to sell at the Passion Play

New Year's 1948

Had I not been in London on New Year's Eve in 1948, I would never have known, *the loneliest place on earth.*

Following the last of seven appearances of The Christmas Caravan (Bob Hope Show) during Bob's visit to the troops of the Berlin Airlift in Frankfurt, Wiesbaden, West Berlin, etc., I left Bob and his entourage—I had been with them for seven day. The last show was at Buttonwood Air Force Base in England, far from London. It would be another day before the flight back to West Germany. I was not close to any member of the cast with Bob. Alone, I caught a train to London. It was nearing midnight and London was getting ready for New Year's celebration.

I walked about downtown past several New Year's parties, already firing up to greet the New Year. I looked in on a couple of them. They were all strangers. I had not been invited to any of them. I was lonely. I missed Lois and my three children back in Wiesbaden, Germany. My duty as one of the escorts of the Christmas Caravan had taken me away from them for seven days. What a price to have to pay to accompany the show just to train and sing the refrain of Irving Berlin's new song, *Operation, Vittles.* I finally found a room in a hotel and went to bed. Then I felt it was indeed the loneliest place on earth.

One of Adolph Hitler's extermination camps, for Jews, and others he considered undesirable, was located at Dachau, near Furstenfeldbruck, Germany. In September of 1946, as I stood beside piles and piles of the ashes of multiple thousands of helpless people, I knew that what Hitler had done to millions of people in all his extermination camps, was literally true. When the horrors of World War II had dimmed from the consciousness of people five decades later, there were some who began putting out the falsehood that such was untrue, or very greatly exaggerated. But I saw with my own eyes the kilns in one of the camps in which trainload after trainload of people arrived but never left there. They were cremated.

I have a color photo of the safe spot that Hitler had established on top of a mountain in Bavaria. It could only be reached by a hidden elevator beneath the mountain. Thankfully, he never got to use it. One day I rode on Hitler's Rhine River yacht down that river with other chaplains and their spouses. Occupation forces had converted the yacht to the use of the Americans on duty there. I was able to capture many scenes of grapevines growing at steep angles on the sides of the river. I had clerks in my office in Linz, Austria, who had been displaced from their homeland in Czechoslovakia by Hitler's war to establish a super-race "uber alles."

Traveling in Athens, Greece, I stood at the spot where the Apostle Paul did—where one of the images of known gods had been added, "To the unknown god." The Apostle Paul then told them who the unknown god was—Jesus Christ. He had many converts as a result.

On board a ship we sailed to some of the Greek islands, one of which was the Isle of Patmos where the Apostle John wrote his scriptures. I noted that the ceiling of the cave had been blackened by a candle or lamp. Just imagine how I felt walking in the footsteps of two of Christ's chosen twelve.

Later, Lois and I were on a tour of The Holy Land—Jordan, Israel and Egypt. To walk in the footsteps of the Savior, and to sail by ship on the Sea of Galilee where he had quieted storms, was a humbling experience of enormous proportions. I even got to give communion to my group in a Jerusalem garden near his borrowed tomb. Now, in my daily walk with him, I feel him very near. Our mutual love entwines us and I try to see with my heart what he wants me to do next—like finishing this chapter of the book He's asked me to write.

During my lifetime, my travels have brought me across the Atlantic Ocean sixteen times. When my family and I were returning to the USA from three years in Madrid, Spain, in 1957, we sailed on a luxury liner, The SS Constitution. I was asked to conduct a Sunday worship service on the way across from Gibraltar. On the way also I learned about "the Law of the Sea." That law mandated that the nearest ship to a scene of disaster or a person in emergency need would sail to the scene immediately. The captain of our ship received a message from a Yugoslavian trawler on which a sailor had suffered a burst appendix. At that time the US did not have diplomatic ties with that country. Nevertheless, the Law of the Sea applied to our ship. The captain relayed the situation to the passengers over the speaker system, that he was redirecting our ship to the scene and that we would be a day late in arriving in New York.

I thought about what that would mean: (1) to the chef who would need to prepare three extra meals for some two thousand passengers plus the crew, (2) to the passengers who had loved ones and friends meeting them in New York City (Please come a day later or stay in your hotel).

Who would cover the extra expenses? None the less, very late that night, we found the two vessels nearing each other—with all the passengers standing on deck watching how a sick man got from a trawler (not too close to the large ship for fear that the turbulent waves might dash the vessel against the ship with disastrous results). I heard no grumbling while all were waiting and watching, and was very glad that a mighty shout of approval went up from the passengers when a man in need came safely aboard where we had a doctor who knew how to do an appendectomy. All that for just one man!

Every time I think about that event I remember a song written in 1868 by Elizabeth C. Clephane, 1830-1869, music by Ira David Sankey. The title of that beautiful song is *The Ninety and Nine*. I want to share it with you.

The Ninety and Nine

There were ninety and nine that safely lay
In the shelter of the fold.
But one was out on the hills away,
Far-off from the gates of gold.
Away on the mountains wild and bare,
Away from the tender Shepherd's care.

Lord, Thou hast here Thy ninety and nine;
Are they not enough for Thee?
But the Shepherd made answer,
This of Mine has wandered away from Me;
And although the road be rough and steep,
I go top the desert to find My sheep.

But none of the ransomed ever knew
How deep were the waters crossed;
Nor how dark was the night that the Lord passed thro',
He found His sheep that was lost.
Out in the desert He heard its cry—
Sick and helpless, and ready to die.

Lord, whence are those blood-drops all the way
That mark out the mountain's track?
They were shed for one who had gone astray
'Ere the Shepherd could bring him back.
Lord, whence are Thy hands so rent and torn?
They're pierced tonight by many a thorn.

And all through the mountains thunder riv'n
And up from the rocky steep,
There arose a glad cry to the gate of heav'n,
Rejoice! I have found my sheep!
And the angels echoed around the throne,
Rejoice, for the Lord brings back His own!

God cares for each individual. He knows the stars by name, the number of the hairs on our heads. He is like a father who grieves over one boy gone wrong. Saint Augustine believed that God loved every one as though there was but one of us to love.

It's a Small World

The bus ride I'll always remember was a happenstance of a lifetime. Getting back from an Air Force Spiritual Life Conference in Monterey, California, to my duty station at the USAF Academy, Colorado, should have been easier than it was. In 1961 it was easy for a serviceman to hop a flight from the west coast with little delay. However, on this weekend every space-available flight was going very far beyond Denver and Colorado Springs. I was anxious to get back to my family as soon as possible and found an immediate connection on a Greyhound bus to my liking and climbed aboard.

That Saturday afternoon, I took a spot three seats behind the bus driver by an open window. As the bus began to fill, I gained the pleasure of a seat-mate—a beautiful woman in her mid-sixties. She was neatly dressed and had tasteful makeup. Her nails were carefully manicured. As she approached my seat, I noticed that she walked with a stiff back. I learned later that it was caused by an accident. It was good to learn that she was a pleasant conversationalist. When she learned that I was an Air Force chaplain in his 40s, she conversed freely. Neither of us felt that an exchange of names was necessary.

I told her that I was on the way home to family and duty. I didn't ask, but she told me that she was on her way to Reno, Nevada, to "play the wheels" that night. She said she would catch the 3:00 a.m. bus back to California where she would rest a day before taking a job as manager of another apartment complex. I became more interested when she told me that, when she was in high school, she had been a voice student and was a soloist. I was even more interested when she said she had auditioned before world-renowned Madame Schumann-Heick during one of her tours to America from Germany. My seat-mate seemed proud to tell me that this famous artist had put her hands on her shoulders and declared, "You will be my replacement!"

I then asked about her musical career. Rather wistfully and sadly, she said that she had become restive with the strict discipline of the training imposed upon her by her parents who insisted that all her schooling should be private through high school and college. At age eighteen, she said she eloped with her fiancé, ending her dreams of musical greatness. She said that she had sung in a church choir and for weddings and funerals for many years.

Edith Crouse, my music teacher in 1933, had given me her unused ticket to a concert in Greensboro, NC, where I personally heard Madame Schumann-Heick. On this bus ride, I asked my seat-mate if she remembered who the pianist was that accompanied Schumann-Heick when she auditioned before her in California. She said he was a young German pianist by the name of Herr Muhlbauer.

With that, my mind did a quick flashback to my three years as a chaplain in Germany (1946-'49). My family joined me in 1947. Marcia and Phil needed a music teacher when we were in Bad Kissinger and later in Wiesbaden. The teacher we employed was none other than an elderly musician, you guessed it, Herr Muhlbauer. He had accompanied Madame Schumann-Heick earlier in his life. We had no idea he had such an illustrious musical career. I found that out fourteen years later on that bus ride in 1962, from my seat-mate who had auditioned before that renowned singer.

By traveling two weeks in Mexico in late November 1970, I had interesting experiences in that country. As long as Dr. Lehmberg, senior minister at First United Methodist Church, was alive, he was the front runner in relating to the church's ministry in the field of missions-outreach. The church asked me to join with thirty-seven United Methodist ministers in a "National Crusade of Evangelism in Mexico," under the leadership of the Rev. Dr. Roberto Escamilla, of the Board of Evangelism, Nashville, TN. This 14-day crusade took me to the village of Tepititla, a town of some 2,000 people, near San Martin Texmelucan, in the province of Tlaxcala, 60 miles southeast of Mexico City with its population of more than 7,000,000. The name of the small church was Templo Bethel.

I arrived in an overcrowded bus filled with people, chickens and farm and household purchases. Overflow passengers held onto the outside of the bus as best they could with very little footing. That Saturday I was met by the pastor, Rev. Noe Hernandez A.

The first service was to begin the next day. However, he had scheduled a service of preparation for the revival that night. I went to that service as a visitor, I thought. However, after the obvious opening songs, prayer and Scriptures, I heard him introducing me. I looked around uneasily for anyone who might look like an interpreter. There was none. Bishop Alejandro Ruiz had assumed erroneously that, since I had served in the Air Force in Madrid, Spain thirteen years earlier, I could get along without one. I still remembered some Spanish words and phrases, but all of a sudden I was caught in a situation where public address was expected. Besides, what little Spanish I had learned was Castillian, and not Mexican Spanish. They were similar but not identical.

So, I preached 7 of 11 times without an interpreter. I had to. I guess Bishop Ruiz figured I'd get along better than some of the 36 colleagues from the USA who knew no Spanish at all. It is absolutely amazing what a person can do with God's help. The people received me into their church, their homes and their hearts from that Saturday night on. They lovingly looked beyond the poor Spanish grammar, and the limited vocabulary, to the thoughts I had in my mind. What mind readers they were. When I grasped for a word, someone near the front always seemed to know what I intended to say, and gave it to me. After the service one night, I asked the pastor's oldest son, Julio, to tell me what I had said in an illustration. His reply was clear enough for me to know that he had understood, and so had the people. With that reassurance I no longer worried about not having an interpreter. But let me repeat, the Holy Spirit was never more consciously by my side than when struggling for the next sentence.

Most of the people in the USA have much to learn about our neighbors south of the border. We need to forget the false picture of the typical picture of the traditional Mexican—the one that shows him as lazy, untrustworthy with the opposite sex, always asleep beneath a sombrero under a tree or beside a wall. Dr. Gonzales Baez Comargo, a noted Methodist editor, author, and translator for the American Bible Society, says that there are five main traits—though common to some people everywhere—that might be especially descriptive of Mexicans. Here they are:

1. They are particularly sensitive to the dramatic side of life; to the tragic in the theater, to emotions that are dramatized and to the exclamatory style of speech.
2. They are very susceptible to the idea of beauty—to the aesthetic, to pageantry, to light and color, to literary beauty where sentences are well phrased and well finished.
3. They share in a common sense of inferiority that comes from a long history of being a subjugated people. For example, the Spanish ruled them for 300 years. They are great ones at imitation, at pretending, at trying to keep up with the Joneses. They are always wrestling with a sense of insecurity and the lack of a feeling of self worth.
4. They have an inner feeling of rebellion toward figures of authority—policemen, judges, bishops, any authority as such. They remember all too well that for so long Law was the imposition of the law of the "hacienda" on the people. Therefore, to be a he-man one must get away with something at the expense of the law and authority. When stopped by a cop they are likely to say, "*If you knew who I am, you wouldn't stop me.*" They are great for individualism. When asked to do something they are likely to say, "*It is not my royal whim.*" Alone with friends they are likely to say, "*Under my cloak I kill the king.*"
5. They are fatalistic. Whatever is to be will be. "It is the will of God." They feel they are victims of mere chance. They have good luck or bad luck. So be it. This destroys a feeling of responsibility. But this is changing some with secularism.

A vast majority of the people of Mexico are Roman Catholics, at least in name, who look upon "evangelicals" by comparison as some of us might look upon Jehovah's Witnesses, or snake-handlers. Our services were not molested in any way, but I was wary of walking alone through the village knowing most people were aware that I was a visiting evangelist. I remembered the long struggle for recognition the evangelicals had in a predominantly Roman Catholic country (and often brutally and intolerantly so) that had left scars and martyrs. For many decades now there had been a separation of church and state.

One day I visited a Presbyterian home in another village. The family was wealthy from all appearances. As I talked to the head of the family—a man in his 80s (though still vigorous)—told me that his father had disowned him, and had driven him out in 1903 because he had brought a New Testament into the home and was reading it. His father gave him the choice of staying if he would destroy the Testament. He now thanks God that he had the courage to leave home and take the consequences. He said he found food for his soul in the Scriptures. His life is an eloquent testimony to what God's Word does for anyone who will read it and take it seriously.

I wish I could introduce the congregation at Templo Bethel to First United Methodist Church. Though small, it existed in a tight little village of about 2,000 people—and one telephone for the whole village! Over it the traditional church towers as for centuries, yet these people seemed to know God in a first century way. How they could sing, and without an instrument! The little pump organ had a note that was stuck open, so it had to be abandoned for the services. But the walls rang with voices made glad by the love of a forgiving Savior. And how they could pray! If our congregation ever prayed like this group, people in Colorado Springs would sit up and take notice. Even the small children prayed in public and voluntarily. I know. I peeked when I thought I recognized the voice of the little six-year-old son of the pastor beginning to pray. His skill in prayer would put most of our adults to shame.

I am glad that our church has always been a missionary-minded one. Just two years after General Palmer's wife started the first Sunday school in Colorado Springs, the first Methodist missionaries were sent to Mexico. They celebrated their 100th anniversary in 1973. Ten thousand dollars was set aside at the General Conference of 1872 to open a work in Mexico. The first Methodist bishop arrived on December 4, 1874.

Following my short ministry at Templo Bethel in Tepititla that summer, some of the youth of our church went with the Rev. Josephat Curti on a work-trip to help do needed repairs on that church building.

And Jesus said to Peter, "Follow me and I will make you a fisher of men."

7

I REMEMBER

Fishing with Stick-Bait

I have always enjoyed going to our mailbox, or to the post office. Especially was this true in Franklin, NC. Many times I saw the friendly and eager face of a Postal employee by the name of George Malone. His mother was a member of the Iotla Methodist Church—one of six I served on the Franklin Circuit in Macon County, NC. Though he was not a member there, he considered me "his pastor." I liked the extended chats with him. His occasional check to the church on his mother's behalf was also welcomed.

Many times George talked of our taking off and going fishing in the Nantahala Mountains high up west of Franklin. A river meandered at times from lofty heights through upper meadows, beneath towering overarching evergreens, and plunging at other times down rapids and water falls. One day he called to tell me that he would not be working the next Saturday, and if I would get a can of earthworms, he'd show me his favorite fishing spots. My wife, Lois, fixed a basket lunch for the two of us, and we drove up, and up, and up a serpentine highway to the turn-off dirt road that led to his "secret" fishing area. The river at that spot was some thirty feet wide and fairly level there. It was shallow enough to wade in up to our knees. George had high rubber boots that kept his legs and feet dry and warm. We fished a couple of hours until we were hungry. Our luck with trout fishing had not been all that good. We had only four "keepers" on the string.

With renewed enthusiasm and on a full stomach, we walked farther down the stream to an area under magnificent conifers where George guaranteed that the fish would fairly jump for my worms and his fly-hook. A half an hour later we were doing well when, in an awkward moment of re-baiting my hook, I dropped the can with all the worms in the river. I grabbed for it in vain. How very disappointed I was in having "ruined" the first fishing trip with such a friend. Seeing my chagrin he said, "Don't worry, preacher. We can still fish with stick-bait."

I had never heard of that kind of bait and turned to George for an explanation. He smiled and reached down to the bottom of the shallow river and brought up two small sticks about an inch long that were stuck together. One stick was longer at one end and the other was longer at the other. They appeared to have been put together that way intentionally by some kind of intelligent being. They had been, in fact. George pulled the sticks apart. Where they were joined together, I saw the larvae of an insect. It was just big enough to cover the point of a small hook, but the trout had a taste for it. We caught our limit.

I often wondered what insect made the larvae. Fifty-four years later I learned the answer. I was back in Franklin in November 1996 to conduct the wedding of my niece, Rachel Green, to Jack Williams. After the wedding, several of us gathered for refreshments at a local café. As we sat there, I told the others about fishing with stick-bait more than a half century earlier. My daughter, Marcia, was all ears because it happened when she was six years old and she had been collecting many things during her childhood. The story intrigued her. At an adjoining table, a woman of that town overheard me as I wondered aloud about which of God's insects had made the larvae. She knew and was happy to tell us that it was the larva of a mayfly.

Only God could give that living creature the wisdom to bring two twigs no larger than match-sticks together in the same way every time and build a temporary metamorphic home and drop it into a mountain stream. Every two sticks were put together in the same way. I know. We had gathered many of them for the larvae we needed for our fishhooks in 1942. I believe that anyone who might go today to that river in springtime would find "stick-bait" made the same inimitable way. The instinct to select two nearly identical one-inch twigs and glue them together around a developing egg is strong proof of God's intentional plan.

Stopped at the Border

We were on our way from Madrid, Spain, to Portugal. I was tired, bone weary and eager to get far, far away from my solo responsibilities as the only Protestant chaplin in Madrid, Spain. Mine was the only English language chapel service in Madrid for the US Forces of the 16th

Air Force, the US Embassy, architects and engineers and construction companies building Torrejon Air Base. I say "solo" because, to get away for this and other vacations, I had to ask for a substitute chaplain from USAFE in Germany. I was not solo really, for I had some 150 volunteers who performed a multitude of ministries in the chapel program. Even so, a multiplication of lay volunteers meant expanded hours of supervision. Anyway, I hoped nothing, I mean nothing, would get in the way of this well-earned time away from it all.

Four hours out of Madrid we were at the final point in Spain, at the desk of an official who had only to stamp my orders and Lois' passport, and the three of us would be in Portugal. But wait! Where were my orders? Why were they not in my coat pocket where I had put them?

A search of the car proved no help. Finally, Lois asked, "Did you change coats before you left?" Yes, I had. The patient guard informed us that we could not pass without my orders. What to do? I could drive back to Madrid and lose an entire day of vacation. I decided to phone the office. Sgt. Gaertner promised to go to my house on the edge of that city of more than 2,000,000 people, stop at the gate or be eaten alive by our guard dog, Bobi, and hope that our maid would hear his call and search for my orders. That took an hour. He phoned me and began to read the orders and guess what? The particular line was one that had intermittent blank spots so that it took 45 minutes to get a coherent copy of the orders. Then they had to be typed in English. And wouldn't you know? The only typewriter available was a Portuguese model on which none of the letters of the alphabet were in familiar locations. My two-finger-job was a challenge. Finally, I made it. Whee! But wait, the orders had to be written also in French. It had been a couple of decades since Lois and I had been in French classes, but we muddled through what we thought was an acceptable translation. Our ten-year-old daughter, Mickey, seemed resigned to her daddy's dilemma. Late in that sweltering day, I finally took our joint efforts to the guard who asked, in Spanish, "How can I be sure these orders are authentic?"

Seeing what a sweat I'd been in all afternoon, he took the imperfect orders, stamped them and sent us on our way. Once an official stamped a document, it was good for the rest of our travels in Portugal. The beach beyond the capital was a welcome sight and we enjoyed the remainder of the trip.

Missing Passport

In Europe in 1977, any thing as important as a passport should have been guarded with an eagle eye and put in a safe inside pocket. I thought I had done both in London as Lois and I prepared to leave for the Pan American airline office. Ours had been a welcome visit to England after my collapse in Liberia, West Africa. We left there early by special permission of the president of that tropical country, aboard a British Caledonian airplane. What a difference there was at 33,000 feet in an air-conditioned situation. Upon reaching London, I applied to the US Embassy for medical help and found a US Navy doctor in charge of the small embassy medical center. Near the end of my stay at the American sponsored hotel, he said that I had been badly dehydrated with severe diarrhea and pneumonia. During that short illness in Liberia, I had lost 15 pounds. How glad I was that no *serious* disease of equatorial Africa had latched on to me! And I had by now begun to have an appetite and keep food down.

The Pan American Airlines office had confirmed our flight back to the USA, but we needed to go by there to pick up our tickets. I changed our English pounds to US dollars, got Lois, picked up our luggage and went to the cab-door of the hotel. Cabs were lined up 15-deep. We took the one at the head of the line. Upon arrival at the Pan American Airlines office, we found a check-in window where we could pick up our tickets and deposit our luggage. The agent asked for our passports. Mine was nowhere to be found. A quick call back to our hotel revealed that my passport had been inadvertently left where I had changed English money to US dollars. I got a cab back to the hotel, picked up the passport, and went to the same cab-door of the hotel. This will be hard to believe, but the very same cab driver was sitting there at the head of the line—the one that had taken us to the airlines office. When I told him where I wanted to go he said, "I just took you to that airlines office!" I explained, and he got me back in a hurry, just in time for us to board the Heathrow airport bus to a Pan American plane. As I reflect upon this happenstance, I have tried to calculate the odds of the same cab driver being at that door in line a second time, the same morning, at the right moment! The odds are incalculable!

Interview with Philip

Q. You are also the author of a little book called *Prayers Jesus might Have Prayed.* Now that is a very interesting book. Tell me how you happened to write that book.

A. Yes. Well, several years ago I said to some of my colleagues, 'Why doesn't someone write a book about prayers Jesus might have prayed.' No one paid any attention, so I got to thinking; "Why don't you write such a book?" But I thought, "Who wants to put words in the mouth of my Savior?" The thought wouldn't go away. I began setting down rules to go by. What rules should they be? Every writer has to discipline himself in some way. One of the rules I put down was 'write nothing that contradicts the Scriptures.' Another was, 'Write nothing not in keeping with the character of Jesus.' 'Write nothing without feeling the move or push of the Holy Spirit to write on a particular subject.' So I wrote down ten rules for myself before I would put one word in the mouth of the Savior. Then, after being at his feet for some years, still feeling unworthy, I started writing the book of 72 prayers. Dr. Jerry Trigg wrote one of the prayers that I added to the book. I had invited several people who received a test marketing copy of the book to consider submitting one for inclusion. Jerry sent the only one.

They are not in the book in the order I wrote them. I arranged them according to how I felt people would follow the life of Jesus. The firm in Nebraska that advertised itself as a publisher turned out to be only a printer. So I ended up with 5,000 copies and found myself in the publishing role. Barnes and Noble wouldn't distribute them because there was nothing on the spine. So I have been giving some of them away to non-profit organizations for just a receipt for income tax purposes. I recently received an email from a woman who said, "*Someone gave me a copy of your book and I just had to tell you that I started reading and couldn't put it down until I had finished it. It was wonderful.*"

I didn't recognize her name so I sent an email, thanking her for her comments about the book and ended by saying, "At nearly 90 I have been trying to remember where I met you, if I did." She replied, "No, we have never met. A woman at the Seminary in Jamaica gave me a copy of your book." Then I remembered having sent 960 gift-copies to the President of that Seminary to be distributed throughout the West

Indies. She doesn't know it, but hers was one of those I had sent. What a joy to know that this precious addition to devotional literature is already being a blessing.

Edison-Leader United Methodist Church

On 1-19-2009, I picked up my ears when I saw an article in the Gazette Telegraph newspaper about a new school at Edison. My mind flashed back to 1964-'67 when I was asked to do an additional duty. My main job was associate pastor of a very large church in Colorado Springs. The District Superintendent, Rev. Hugh Critchett, asked Dr. Lehmberg if he could spare me on Sunday nights to be the pastor of Edison-Leader United Methodist Church. It was located 56 miles out on the plains in the extreme southeast corner of El Paso County.

That church had been served by ministers from churches in Colorado Springs, Pueblo, and other churches on the prairie. I wasn't needed very much on Sunday nights, so I was appointed the pastor of that little 35-member church. We had worship services Sunday nights. At least a fourth of the members were nonresident in Colorado Springs and beyond. But there were young families with children who needed a Sunday school and worship opportunities. Compared to the six-thousand member church in Colorado Springs, it was almost nothing at all. Yet, I took that responsibility seriously. How to help a church, so isolated, to grow was a challenge. In those three years I helped it to grow 11%, or to 39 members.

In an effort to fulfill my obligation as their pastor, I used Sunday afternoons to visit families in that community. Included in those visits were people who were considered to be interested in that church, whether members or not. I visited them, too. Everyone seemed glad for me to make a personal visit in their homes. At the church I scheduled a pastor's class for youth and adults who were possible prospects for membership. I put no pressure on anyone to do more than attend the classes—they could attend a few or many of the sessions. To motivate my congregation to reach out to nonmembers, I asked their help in making a map of the area around the church that included fifteen miles in all directions. On an area county map, I asked them to put a number for all the dwellings in the area. Some of the buildings were empty, but many had people. I felt that the entire area was my responsibility.

The dry-landers on the plains had a club called "The Dry-Lander's Club." I was invited to be a member of that club. A requirement for membership was that a prospective member must fry an egg on burning cow-chips! Fortunately, they waived that responsibility for me. At a banquet of "dry-landers", one of the speakers included the following bit of humor:

A farmer called the veterinarian about his sick cat and what to do to help the cat get well. The vet said "Buy a pint of castor oil and give it to your calf." A few weeks later, the vet saw the farmer and asked "How is your calf?" "Calf!" exclaimed the farmer. "It was not a calf, it was a cat!"

The vet asked, "Do you mean to say you gave your cat all that castor oil? What happened after that?"

The farmer said, "The last I saw of the cat, there were nine other cats; three were digging, three were covering up and three were looking for new territory."

The church building sat alone, with only a "house out back" with no running water for the toilet. It was two miles from the nearest house. The house that had been the parsonage had been sold and moved to Colorado Springs. In the earlier days there were two churches, one in the Edison school and the other, called Leader, ten miles further south. The name of the church was Edison-Leader, but there was no longer a congregation at the Edison school when I was there.

The last year I was the pastor, the secretary and I wrote the fifty-year history of that little church. After the children in those families grew up, they moved away to other types of jobs than farming. The few living adults joined other nearby churches, and the church closed.

It is interesting to remember that, during my seventeen years as associate pastor of the huge church in Colorado Springs, while I served Edison-Leader, the senior minister had a heart attack and died. After his death, I was appointed interim senior minister. I suddenly found myself pastor of the largest church in the Rocky Mountain Conference and pastor of one of the smallest at the same time.

8

HEAVEN'S CHEERING SECTION

The greatest incentive to keep a Christian minister going is a vision of the end of the journey of faith. At my journey's final breath, there are great expectations with no uncertainties and no fear. At that time, I will gladly thank my Savior for helping me answer my "prayer of dominant desire," which has been so much a part of my life—"Lord Use Me." But along with that most important motivation for me has been a vision on earth of "that great cloud of witnesses" referred to in Hebrews 12:1-2, 7, and I quote:

> *"Therefore, since we are surrounded by such a great cloud of witnesses, let us throw off everything that hinders and the sin that so easily entangles, and let us run with perseverance the race marked out for us. Let us fix our eyes on Jesus, the author and perfector of our faith, who for the joy set before him endured the cross, scorning its shame, and sat down at the right hand of the throne of God." NIV*

The eleventh chapter immediately precedes these words. In it are found the names of a galaxy of the Old Testament heroes of faith. Like Abraham, they "believed God, and it was accounted unto him (them) for righteousness." They did not receive the fulfillment of the promises but—looking down the corridors of the future—they believed, and lived as though they were true.

As a young minister, this scripture made an indelible impression on me. It still does. For more than seventy years, I have labored in God's vineyard in the belief that there were present in that cloud of witnesses also the faces I had loved "long since and lost awhile." Through the years, I have believed there are myriads of saints scattered throughout church history whose faces are among those heroes of faith. Though they may, or may not, be rooting for me to make it successfully to the company of the "church triumphant," the very thought of their presence there is incentive enough to spur me on.

The knowledge of such an assembly of the faithful in such "an endless line of splendor," has caused me to stay on the upward journey and, when I have strayed, has kept me from becoming a maverick. The Elmer Gantry temptations have been plentiful and alluring along my pathway, but I could do no more than toy with them, because of so many faces in my "cheering section" up there. Any temptation to be proud has been tempered by the fact that everyone knows I am a preacher's kid from the mountains of western North Carolina. When I have become enamored by the thought of becoming a "who's who," the words of my sainted mother have reminded me of her adage, "Self brag is half scandal." I'm happy enough now to be a "who's he?"

I have always liked (too much, I expect) to be thought well of. It has pleased me to receive such words as were written by the editor of the Macon County weekly paper when I left to become a military chaplain in World War II. She said (and she was not one of my members):

"It can be safely said that no more beloved pastor ever served in our county."

As welcome to my heart as these are and many others received during long years of ministry, I would gladly lay them aside to hear my grandmother say, "Phip, you've been a good preacher." (she used to call me Phip!)

Most of all, I hope to hear these words from my Savior, Jesus Christ: "Well done, good and faithful servant. Enter into the joy of thy Lord."

My father was a sanctified and enthusiastic minister of the old school. His sermons, rich in illustrations, and warm from the heart, made me aware that he was constantly in touch with the source of his power—his God, in prayer. He always prayed aloud, in private as well as in public. Some years of my childhood found him in his bedroom next to mine. Most nights I was awake enough to hear him mention my name before my heavenly Father. How safe I felt and how quickly I fell asleep, even before he finished his prayers for others. He went to his reward in May 1955, while I was on duty as an Air Force chaplain in Madrid, Spain. No flight could get me across the Atlantic in time for his service. But on the day after it, I stood among the leftover fading flowers around his grave, beside my mother's, and pledged anew to meet them in heaven and in that great cloud of witnesses.

Please allow me to put another face in that host above. While I am doing so, you may wish to put a few faces there, also. Wilbur Cole was a senior in the same high school where I was a junior. We were both new students there in Kentucky. His father was a missionary in China. He had sent his son to Wilmore to finish high school and enter Asbury College. Since we were both new and lived near each other, we walked to school together and became good friends. Wilbur's mother was Chinese, and he had some Asian features, except for his eyes. I enjoyed hearing him tell of growing up in China. He liked for me to help him get accustomed to life in America.

I was so happy the morning he told me that he had confessed his faith in Christ the night before. This was a surprise to me because, since he was the son of a minister, I thought he was already a Christian. On weekends during the school year in 1930, we often walked down to the Kentucky River. It was fun for both of us to enter some of the many caves beside the river and see the stalagmites and stalactites that had formed in them. In June, my family moved back to North Carolina and Wilbur enrolled in college. We kept in touch with letters. When I fell two letters behind, I received a scorching letter addressed to me as Dr. Philip L. Green, D.D., LLD, PhD, and other pseudo titles. Inside was a very frosty,

> *Dear Sir,*
>
> *If you write I will reply. If you do not, the next time I see you, I will apply so much pressure to your Adam's apple that the hard cider, running down your throat there from, will produce within you a complete state of intoxication.*

He got a letter. Such was our friendship. The next year in 1932, Wilbur was drowned in a swimming accident. I long to see him again in God's great tomorrow in that great cloud of witnesses. I wouldn't miss it for anything. For now, I look up and think a greeting.

Apart from my parents, Grandmother Green had a most important and lasting influence on my young life. Her husband, James Tippit Green, a Civil War veteran, died some twelve years before I was born. She was left a widow with seven children—five boys and two girls. She was born Mary Jane Cook on May 1, 1865, and married when she was about fifteen years of age. She gave birth to ten children, seven of whom grew to adulthood; namely, James Henderson (my father), Joseph Marshall, Cora Lee, George Washington, John Henry, Cyrus Franklin, and Carrie Belle. I came to know them all in adulthood.

Grandma lived in a one-room log cabin with a lean-to side room on a small farm in the Great Smoky Mountains near Todd in Ashe County, NC. She was a devout Christian woman and filled with a great determination to raise those seven children in the "fear and admonition of the Lord." That was not to be easy. "Pap," as her husband was called, had taught the older children how to do farm work. She became a cook in a school in Boone ten miles from home. The whole family worked as one in making a living.

My father, the oldest, tested her resolution to be father and mother to the children—as I am sure the others did too. One day neighborhood guests arrived for a visit. She said,

"Jim, run down to the spring and fetch some fresh water for our guests." He made an important mistake—one he never forgot.

He said, "I'll not do it!"

In the chase that ensued, he ran up into the pasture to a large chestnut tree stump with huge sprouts, around which they "played" peek-a-boo. After working his way to the lower side he made a mad rush to the split-rail fence below. If he could make it across that fence he would "be safe" at least until later. He didn't make it. He only got one leg over the top rail when judgment day happened. His mother was a large and vigorous woman who proved that she was fully capable of holding her own with her seven children.

It is to her credit that three of her five sons became Methodist ministers—among which was my father. Joseph and John were the other two. Before she died in 1930, all her children pledged to meet her in heaven.

For many years, she lived in a large house on the north end of the town of Rutherford College. My father built a permanent home on the south side of town. Grandma shared her home with a widowed daughter, Cora Lee Stokes, and her two children, Glenn and Lessie.

The term "babysitting" was unknown at that time. However, she did it anyway. She "kept" me from time to time when mother's load of seven became too heavy. I enjoyed staying with her. She treated me, not as a child, but as someone special. At a very tender age I learned the value of a penny. Near her home was a small country store where, for a penny, a little boy could buy two pieces of candy shaped like huge peanuts and flavored with banana oil. Every penny was saved for that treat when I went to Grandma's house.

Other attractions were found there also. One could go blackberry picking, eat cherries, and pick up fallen June apples—the earliest of the season. Once when I was larger, Grandma and I were having supper alone. She had taken some biscuit dough and baked it into a pone. It looked and smelled delicious. She broke it open, gave me a piece and was very curious that I did not eat any of it. She tried her best to get me to tell her why. Finally, I broke down and, in great embarrassment, said

"Grandma, the bread has had a worm in it."

The dark brown hole that baking powder made in the pone of bread, looked exactly like a hole in a June-apple a worm had made. How she laughed! How her tummy bounced! And how relieved I was to learn the truth—no worm in Grandma's bread!

During my younger years, and up until she died at the end of my sophomore year in high school, I noted in what respect and care my uncles and aunts held their mother. That only added strength to my love for her as my grandmother. A few years later she moved from the north end of town to a house on the edge of Camp Free (a camp ground) at the south end of town, where she spent her declining years. In this modest home, my grandmother cooked and served meals in her home for several ministerial students of Rutherford College nearby.

In my older youthful visits I became more aware of the source of her spiritual strength and devotional depth. She read her Bible and meditated upon her readings. She sang the hymns of the church I came to love so well. I watched her one day as she looked out over a snowy landscape and sang one of her favorites, *Life's Railway to* Heaven also known by it's first line, *Life is like a Mountain Railroad;*

Life Is Like a Mountain Railroad

Life is like a mountain railroad,
With an engineer that's brave,
We must make the run successful,
From the cradle to the grave . . .

My youthful heart affirmed the hope that, if I ever got religion, it would be the kind Grandma Green had. The authenticity of her faith convinced me that her kind of faith in God was what I wanted. She kept in step with my yearnings and knew that I wanted to become a preacher. After all, wasn't I the only son who actually wanted to go with Papa to worship and revivals? I was the only one who committed to memory vast stretches of Scripture, wasn't I?—even in the third and fourth grades, didn't I?

So it was in the summer of 1930, just after the financial crash of 1929, that I found myself a part of her entire family of seven children and most of her grandchildren gathered around her sick bed. Three serious maladies, any one of which was bringing her to the grave, gave the doctors abundant problems in keeping her pain within bounds. For all of us, it was a summer of waiting.

In the midst of uncertainties, one day she asked her seven children to come to her room—all at the same time. As she lay there, she said, "Children, I'm going home one of these days." Thinking she was a bit disoriented and had forgotten she was in her own bed at home, they tried to reassure her. One of them said, "But mother, you are at home, and we're all here to take care of you." "I know," she replied, "but I mean my heavenly home! I have called all of you here to ask each of you to promise me that you will meet me there." Each promised to do that.

Before she died the next day, she asked all the grandchildren to come to her room. We were crowded but we all got in. She blessed us all and gave me a special blessing. As I knelt beside her bed, she placed a fevered hand upon my head and said, "Phip, make a good preacher." She was buried in a new cemetery near the southeast corner of Camp Free.

Eight years later, Bishop Claire Purcell laid his hands upon me and ordained me a Deacon in the Methodist Church. Both his and grandma's blessings have made me doubly humble and glad! I believe the face of Grandma Green has been in that 'great cloud of witnesses' across the decades—encouraging me to do my best to "be a good preacher."

There were many occasions for me to observe the faith dimensions of Grandma Green. She loved to sing the great hymns of the church, such as *Amazing Grace, The Old Rugged Cross, In the Garden,* and many others. I noticed at the annual midsummer camp meeting she did not shout, as some did. I would look at her and see tears of joy running down her face.

In 1999, at age 85, I visited her grave-site back in North Carolina. As I stood there, my heart yearned upward as I said, "Grandma, I'm still trying." And my heart knows she is still cheering me on.

I hope you added, or will add, a few dear faces to that illustrious host above. And I hope you will never forget that they form a part of those who yearn over us, pray for us, hope the best of us, and cheer us on. In that journey of faith yet before us, we might well remember the secret of success:

"Look unto Jesus who, for the joy that was set before him, endured the cross, despising the shame, and now sits at the right hand of the throne of God."

When my turn finally comes, and it will, in the contrails of my return to God, I probably will leave a Tarheel State message,

"Y'all come, you heah?"

This is why I keep looking ahead and pressing onward—to help God answer more of my prayer of dominant desire: "Lord, use me." He may need me for a few more years, I hope. I eagerly await his next message will be. What? Another book?

J. Lem Stokes married a college classmate, Alda Beaman at Asbury College, Kentucky. He was the oldest of four sons born on the mission field in Korea to Rev. and Mrs. Marion B. Stokes of Seoul. He and the others were educated by their mother and father on the mission field until college age. Each graduated from Asbury and went on to earn doctoral degrees. They all became ministers. Their parents had grown up in South Carolina but the sons joined the Western North Carolina Annual Conference. Charles, the youngest, went back and distinguished himself as a missionary in Korea. James was a pastor and later editor on the North Carolina Christian Advocate, covering both North Carolina Conferences. Mack taught at the Candler School of Theology in Atlanta. From there he was elected a bishop.

While I was pastor of the six churches of the Franklin Circuit, 1940-'43, Lem was appointed the pastor of a downtown church in Franklin. Lois had been a student at Asbury 1928-'32, at the time the Stokes boys were there. (Lois was a few years older than I.) As a junior high school kid in 1931, I often watched a couple of the Stokes brothers take top honors on the college tennis courts. So to Lem and Lois it was old home week (year). The friendship was genuine and lasted until Lem's death at the age of ninety-nine. I was glad to be able to create a choral group of seventeen singers that included Lem and Alda, Lois and the Presbyterian pastor, and others. Ten years down the track as an Air Force chaplain, Lem had gone on to accept the presidency of a Methodist college—Pfeiffer College. He wrote and invited me to consider becoming his vice president. But I had too many years toward military retirement to consider the change.

Alda Beaman-Stokes grew up in Troy, NC. My father and I were hosted in their home when I was just ten or twelve years of age, while my father conducted a revival meeting in that town that was sponsored by Mr. Beaman and others. Alda was a few years too old for me to be interested in her. But her younger brother, Charles, was just my age and willing for me to alternate rides down a hill in his little red wagon. Charles grew up to become a Methodist pastor.

Lem and Alda became engaged in college and were married. Following pastorates elsewhere, Lem was appointed to Franklin. We became close friends and remained so for life. We kept in touch by Christmas letters and occasional phone calls. Under Lem's leadership, Pfeiffer grew into a four-year college. Later, Lem took it into the NC University System in which he became an administrator. He was also an avid tennis player, and played until he was past ninety.

In 2002 I sent Lem and Alda a copy of *The Mountains Are Happy*, my autobiography. Shortly thereafter I received a phone call from him, thanking me for it, and saying excitedly, "Phil, I've read all 385 pages of your book, even the fine print. It's great!"

He declared that it inspired him to write his life story. Because he was ninety-four at that time, I suggested that he get started right away. I was surprised and pleased to later receive a copy of "Remembrances of a Nonagenarian." Lem died at age ninety nine. I will ever be grateful for the warmth of a friendship that covered more than sixty-five years. He made me want to keep on keeping on. He is up there in that cloud of witnesses, and is encouraging me on.

Samuel Onofrio Morreale sat at the end of the front pew of First United Methodist Church. I sat on the same pew, as did other retired clergy. Now I am the only one left on that pew. In 1999, Sam was ninety. That spring he had difficulty climbing the twenty steps to his bedroom. His doctor found him very anemic. After several blood transfusions, he was his old self again. He invited a few of his friends to his home on the edge of Colorado College. He asked me to purchase some refreshments and have them there in time. That was the least I could do. And you know what? He wouldn't let me get away without a full reimbursement—despite my strongest protestations. That was Sam! Before his birthday celebration, a few of us invited him to be our guest for lunch at Giuseppe's Restaurant. Against the protest of everyone, he picked up the check. For more than two years, he had prepared participatory Scriptural topics for that Monday morning group. We considered him the "dean" of our Bible studies.

In the fall of 1996, he promised to be the wintertime pastor of a small English-language Korean congregation where I was the preacher at the nine-thirty morning service. I had plans to be out of the state during those months. Before he could begin on his part of the agreed-upon duty, Sam fell in his bathroom and became wedged between the wall and the metal hot water heat register. He was stuck there for more than a day. The skin over his left kidney was badly burned. It took more than six months for it to heal.

Maybe I'd better swing back to more than a half century ago to when he and I were beginning chaplains in World War II. We were beginning chaplains in the Military Chaplains School at Harvard in the July-August Class of 1943. There were 443 ministers, priests and rabbis in that class alone. We didn't know at the time that we were classmates. Two weeks after graduation we were on our way to active duty. Soon after the end of the war, we both retired to Colorado Springs, Colorado. He served as the senior post chaplain at massive Fort Carson south of town, and I served at the United States Air Force Academy.

Thus began a friendship that lasted through the tragic death of his son, David, and his wife, Euphemia ("Feme") who died after a short illness. I was honored to be the one in charge of both services-of-remembrance. Sam and Feme and Lois and I were close friends across the decades. I lost Lois in May 1988, after nineteen months of near incapacitation in a care facility. Sam visited her many times and prayed for her each time—even though there was little to let him know that she was aware of his presence.

In military retirement we were both active in the Rocky Mountain Chapter of the Military Chaplains Association. In 1966, I was asked to chair the host committee of the national convention in Colorado

Springs. It was scheduled for April of 1968. During the two years of preparation, the Chapter needed to come up with a theme—a theme calculated to bring a maximum number of chaplains and guests from across America. Happily it turned out that more than four hundred registered. Sam Morreale came up with a perfect theme—ORDER. That was during the troublous years of the war in Vietnam when most young people rebelled against anything they saw as "the establishment." Out of Sam's cogent theme, my committee came up with five major sub-themes: *Order and the Law, Order and the Family, Order and the Church, Order and Education* and *Order and Public Opinion.*

The 1968 convention turned out to be the best one MCA had ever experienced. After it, I wrote Sam a letter to tell him that he had been instrumental in making it so, and that he deserved some of the credit that had come to me. As a splendid result, I continued for seventeen years on the staff of the largest United Methodist Church in the Western Jurisdiction. I told Sam later that the success of that convention resulted later in my election as national president of the Military Chaplains Association.

In 1998, I received word that Sam had suffered a relapse of his longtime bout with cancer of the prostate—and that he was at home, being cared for by Hospice. During my visit, he said,

"Oh, I'm all right. I made them take back the bed they sent so that I could sleep without climbing those twenty stairs."

The next thing I heard was that he had fallen down some of those stairs and was in St. Francis Hospital in Hospice. He was barely conscious during my visit and prayer. Helen and I took him a bouquet of fresh flowers, a card of concern, and the copy of a poem, entitled, *The Tenant.* His prognosis indicated that he'd be gone very soon. He died shortly thereafter and I helped Rev. Dr. O. Gerald Trigg with the service of remembrance. At the grave-side committal service, I silently said, "I'll see you soon, Sam." Is he cheering me on? You bet! I hope!

But here I am, 13 years later and in no hurry to meet him. His friendship and cordiality motivate me to continue going on till God has finished using me.

Then there are Bob and June Sparks. It was my great privilege to have had both as leaders in the chapel program in Madrid, Spain, 1954-'57. He was the teacher of the Adult Sunday School Class, and she earned merits by organizing and directing the Youth Choir. They were both loyal members of the Southern Baptist Church, and from Texas. Like most of our leaders, they were active in other aspects of the chapel ministries—like Women-of-the-Chapel and Men-of-the-Chapel. I never had more loyal helpers than they were. They worked faithfully to help build, from scratch, a Chapel Six-Point-Program that was the envy of most bases. It is of interest that a representative of the National Lutheran Council expressed the fear that Protestants in an all-Catholic country were apt to get less than the best in chapel worship, Sunday school, and other programs. A copy of the letter of reply to their anxiety from Maj. Gen. August W. Kistner, 16th Air Force Commander, made me very glad. It said,

Percentage-wise, we have one of the most active and growing Protestant programs anywhere in the Air Force.

In a country like Catholic Spain, there was only one place in all of Madrid that had a worship service in English. In addition to the military personnel and families, there were US Embassy personnel, architects and engineers at work drawing plans for four military bases and contractors with their families. Even Protestants attending Catholic churches was considered a threat to the United States primary mission in Spain. It was up to me to build a chapel program adequate for Protestant families and personnel.

The director of the youth choir and later President of United Chapel Women called my hand for announcing *Holy Communion* in the bulletin. She said Southern Baptists did not have Holy Communion. The next time I inserted *The Lord's Supper* in the bulletin. Smiles, again. Later, she took exception to *The Apostles Creed* in the bulletin for the same reason—"Baptists have no creeds," she said. I changed the entry next time to *The Affirmation of Faith* and all was sweetness and light once more. There was no rancor either time.

I thought the millennium had come when the Baptist teacher of the adult class said to the Mormon postmaster, "Bill, will you lead us in prayer this morning?" At another time he said to him, "Bill, I'll be working on the pipeline from Rota to Zaragoza next Sunday. Will you teach the class?" And this coming from a wonderful Christian whose provincialism was clear when he said to me one day, "Chaplain, I never take Communion anywhere except in my little hometown church in Texas." Navy Captain Bob Sparks and his wife, June, were and still are cherished friends even after forty years. I learned humility and adjustability from them. They were staunch supporters of the chapel program in Madrid. Serving Communion to such a diverse group of worshipers prompted me to preface the invitation with these words: *"Everyone is invited to partake of The Lord's Supper and place upon this act of worship whatever special meaning seems in keeping with your prior teaching."*

A Methodist Bishop Dies with His Chaplains

Leaving America in April 1943, Bishop Leonard arrived in England in time to take part in an open-air service in London's Hyde Park on Easter morning. After that he made the rounds of Camps and Hospitals, meeting high-ranking officers of the Army and Navy, British officials, and spending long hours visiting with our GI's. He preached extensively. He held retreats for chaplains and conducted discussion groups for other officers and enlisted men. He went to Ireland for more visitations and inspections, and more preaching and discussions. Then he took off for Iceland. Letting down through a dense fog, the Army plane in which he was traveling crashed and burned on May 3, 1943. In the wreckage died Bishop Leonard, General Frank M. Andrews, Commanding General of the European theater of Operations, and twelve other military personnel including Chaplain Frank L. Miller, a member of the Presbyterian Church, USA, and Chaplain Robert H. Humphrey, a member of the [Methodist] Virginia Conference, both of whom were accompanying Bishop Leonard as his military aides.

Bishop Leonard's death shocked the religious world. He had been a most faithful and vigorous leader of many causes, and was a soldier at heart. He had thought and prayed and worked for 'the boys' who had taken their places in the armies of freedom. They were far away on the seven seas and in battle lines that spread across islands and continents, but they were always in his heart. And he prayed and labored that the church at home would go with them wherever they went. No Christian soldier hated war and all it implies more intensely than did Bishop Leonard. He knew something of the temptations to which our boys, as he always affectionately referred to them, would be exposed in the camps. He envisioned the horrors of battle and heard the frenzied cries of men locked in the struggle of death. He knew that the Church's message of assurance and comfort could mean to them now more than ever; that the words of the chaplain in the Sacrament of the Lord's Supper would have a new significance for every serviceman and woman as the commemoration fell from his lips, "This is my body which is broken for you."

Following his death, a poem was found in Bishop Leonard's desk. Its author, S. Hall Young, also had been overtaken by sudden death, after he had written three full stanzas and the first lines of the fourth and fifth. The poem was completed by the late Rev. William K. Anderson. Because it is so descriptive of Bishop Leonard's spirit, it is made a part of his record.

Let Me Die Working

Let me die working.
Still tackling plans unfinished, tasks undone,
Clean to its end swift may my race be run;
No lagging steps, no faltering, no shirking.
Let me die working . . .

. . . (unable to use full poem)

(Added by me, Philip L Green, at age ninety-four)

Let me die remembering.
To whom I owe, for what I owe in four-score years & more,
In home and church, in school, in friendships all o'er;
Life's road adorned, beautified unending.
Let me die remembering.

9

YOUR BODY, A PRECIOUS GIFT

My daughter recently brought home a book entitled *Atlas of Medical Anatomy*. It was huge. The pages were twelve by twenty inches in size and it was an inch and a half thick. I thumbed through the first few pages and was intrigued, fascinated. To satisfy my curiosity I kept on until I had reviewed a complete section. As I looked further I found that there were pictures of all the body part—every bone, organ, muscle, blood vessel, arm, leg, and individual parts of the human body. What an eye-opener it was to discover such a book existed.

It occurred to me that there were, not just a few, but a thousand parts of a body to keep healthy, or about which to be concerned. Something awry in any part of the body could affect another part, or parts, of the body. Imagine how many things the Creator needed to consider in putting such a body together. Add functions such as seeing, feeling, emotions, needs and the like. The search for what is wrong in a person often confuses or mystifies medical authorities. As I looked, mentally I reviewed the multiplicity of things that my body had survived, and marveled at how I have come through it all alive and in one piece.

A human body is the house in which I live. It is also the dwelling place of the soul, and the temple of the Holy Spirit. What is the worth of a human body? It is of the "earth earthy," and subject to diseases, decay and ultimate death. On any market, except for transplantable organs, its value is quite small. But what is the worth of a human soul? In human values, since it is one of those realities not seen, it is not marketable. In the eyes of its Creator, its value is beyond any price. Jesus said that it is more valuable than all the riches of the earth.

If the soul is of such enormous value to the Creator, and the human body, its dwelling place, it follows that a primary duty for us is to keep our bodies healthy and free of things that destroy it. For some people, it is relatively easy to use tobacco, alcohol and illegal drugs. Can one live with a guilty conscience after "a night with Venus" and the threat of AIDS? But what about the things people eat that hasten the obesity that brings on a multitude of human ailments? What about those who sit long in an easy chair rather than take the exercises needed to make muscles strong, and the heart pumping multiple gallons of life-giving blood to all parts of the body? And what of the lungs that become blackened by the smoke of tobacco that predisposes one to cancer of the lungs?

While riding home on a school bus in 1932, one of the boys lit a cigarette. A girl turned upon him and yelled, "Don't you know that you're driving nails in your coffin?"

Fifty-five years later, I was making visits to a hospitalized woman of about forty years. She was dying of cancer of the lungs. When she saw me, she pleaded, "Oh, how I wish I could live to attend my daughter's graduation from high school." Sorry to say she didn't live that long.

The length of your time on planet earth depends upon how you care for your body. If your mother was like my mother, she helped you to eat right. I like the advertisement that says, "Don't worry mom, I'm eating right at ARBY's!"

She would probably smile and tell you that she could do better than Arby's fast food shop. Not only that, she would mix it with something a mother knows how to give—her unspoken and unadulterated love. There are a thousand ways you can mistreat your body. And nearly everyone could list the first five, beginning with tobacco, alcohol, drugs, illicit sex and fattening foods.

It is your body. But it is a gift. The late Frederick Lawrence Knowles, in an earlier century, wrote a poem that beautifully describes a body, entitled, *The Tenant.*

The Tenant by Frederick Lawrence Knowles (1869-1905)

This body is my house, it is not I;
Herein I sojourn till, in some far sky,
I lease a fairer dwelling, built to last
Till all the carpentry of time is past.
When from my high place viewing this lone star,
What shall I care where these poor timbers are?
What, though the crumbling walls turn dust and loam,
I shall have left them for a larger home.
What, though the rafters break, the stanchions rot,

When earth has dwindled to a glimmering spot!
When Thou, clay cottage, fallest, I'll immerse
My long-crampt spirit in the universe.
Through uncomputed silences of space
I shall yearn upward to the leaning Face.
The ancient heavens will roll aside for me,
As Moses monarch'd the dividing sea.
This body is my house, it is not I.
Triumphant in this faith I live, and die.

10

MUSIC'S MAGIC CHARM

Before there was music by radio or television, people got together Saturday nights and Sunday afternoons just to sing or play musical instruments. As a teenager, I produced harmony by cutting freshly-pulled rye straws different lengths and blowing through them at the same time.

That gave two and three-part harmony, in the absence of a musical instrument. I knew so many gospel songs by heart that I often found myself humming a tune, whistling one, or singing the tune with some of the words. The repetition of the gospel of good news in song augmented and stabilized my faith in God and made the good life attractive. Camp meeting singing often brought tears of joy as well as shouts of praises to our Lord Jesus Christ.

My second wife, Helen, during the last four years of her life, had developing dementia. When she could no longer remember that we were married, she could still remember many songs. Music seemed to inspire her. If ever she was upset and fretful, music helped to bring reality into focus and, with it, consolation.

In my life, and the life of many of my friends, music was good medicine. My dear mother died at age sixty-three of breast cancer spread to an armpit. I firmly believe she would have died sooner if she had stopped singing a hopeful song like, *There's a better day coming I know, I know—'twill not always, not always be so.* Bernard Vessey, the gospel songbird of the Rockies, was diminutive in body and had curvature of the spine, cramping his lung space. The doctor who did his autopsy, held his pitiful lungs in his hands and said to his assistant, "If Bernie had not used his lungs singing the gospel with such gusto, he'd have died years ago."

The chart of music entitled, *Music in Philip's Life*, a little further down, runs from my childhood to age ninety-five. I still sing, but my fingers are too stiff to play the piano. Some photos show some of the ways in which my musical bent has been used.

My childhood home was filled with music. We had a pump organ as well as a piano in what we called "the parlor." Two younger siblings and most of my older siblings played one or the other. We often gathered Saturday nights and Sunday afternoons to sing. Most of the music was church hymns and choruses. I still remember some of the words to songs we used to sing. They went something like this if I remember correctly;

Can a little child like me, thank the Father fittingly?
Yes, oh yes, be good and true, faithful, kind in all you do.
Love the Lord and do your part, learn to say with all your heart,
Father, we thank thee, Father, we thank thee,
Father, in heaven, we thank thee.

and

I washed my hands this morning, so very clean and white, and gave them up to Jesus, to work for him till night.
Little hands be careful all the whole day through, anything for Jesus, only let me do.

Songs remind me of places and people. The most beautiful song I had ever heard was *The Old Rugged Cross* which reminds me of my first Sunday school in the parlor of Mrs. June Bolick (1922). *There's A Better Day Coming I Know* was often sung at home by my mother who stayed home and cared for seven children while my father was away in evangelistic campaigns. Other kinds of music do the same.

One night on television there was a musical extravaganza from the esplanade in Boston, led by the Boston Pops Orchestra. At once, my mind flipped back 56 years to July 1943 when I sat on the grass in that same place and heard that world famous orchestra give a free concert. For a month I was at Harvard University taking military orientation with 443 other ministers, priests and rabbis who were being initiated into the armed forces of World War II.

The song, *Just As I Am* reminds me of Billy Graham. *The Love of God* reminds me of his bass soloist, George Beverly Shea. The hymns of Fannie J. Crosby remind me of my father who loved *To God Be The Glory, Jesus Keep Me Near The Cross, 'Pass Me Not, Oh Gentle Savior,' 'Blessed Assurance, Jesus Is Mine,' Close To Thee, 'I Am Thine, O Lord'* and *Rescue The Perishing. I Will Not Be Afraid* reminds me of E. Stanley Jones, founder of the United Christian Ashrams. *Since Jesus Came Into My Heart, Glory To His Name, 'Hallelujah, Praise Jehovah,' Softly And Tenderly, Almost Persuaded, My Mother's Prayers Have Followed Me, Why Not Now, Whosoever Will May Come, Beulah Land, Where He Leads Me I Will Follow,* and *I Surrender All,* remind me of camp meetings with the sawdust trail, and revival meetings in churches and brush arbors. *When We All Get To Heaven* brings to mind a pastor named A. Burgess. Anthems and certain hymns remind me of worship services in some churches with excellent choirs and musical talent as *How Beautiful Upon The Mountain, The Holy City, O Holy Night, How Great Thou Art, Joyful, Joyful, We Adore Thee, O My Soul, Bless Thou Jehovah, A Mighty Fortress Is Our God, Are Ye Able, Said The Master, Holy, Holy, Holy, Great Is Thy Faithfulness, All Hail The Power Of Jesus' Name* and *If With All Your Heart Ye Truly Seek Me.*

Patriotic songs remind me of my early school days as well as twenty years as an Air Force chaplain. Big bands stir my soul and my feet. I feast on stringed ensembles. In elementary schools I attended, we always sang *My country, 'Tis Of Thee* and then repeated the Pledge of Allegiance to the Flag. From the *Gray Book of Favorite Melodies,* we often sang a Stephen Foster song, or a marching melody. I still remember *Long, Long Ago,* and *In The Gloaming.* In my senior high school year, I sang in all mixed musical groups. On weekends I walked three miles each way to Valdese to sing in a male glee club that practiced on Saturday afternoons. Part of the motivation was that I was a lonely teenager in search of both musical participation and friendships.

Secular favorites: *You Light Up My Life, Beer Barrel Polka* (the music only); most of the classical and semi-classical—*Liebestraum,* Dvorak's *New World Symphony;* the big bands playing marching music; classical Viennese waltzes.

During the first three years of college, much of my limited musical talent was put to use in benefit of Peoples Bible College in Greensboro, NC. My father was the founder and, for twenty years, the president. I lived on that campus, but caught a bus to Guilford College nearby for a college education. In Greensboro, I was invited to be a member of various musical groups—quartet, trio and duet teams to go over the state to advertise the school.

A special enjoyment was a teacher, Lois D. Ritter, who had an outstanding contralto voice. My thin tenor voice sounded pretty good in a duet with her. I fell in love with her and, on January 5, 1936, my father married us. Together, we sang in the six churches of the Sandy Circuit and at other public gatherings.

In Greensboro, NC, we attended a small church on Sundays, as sweethearts. We were in charge of the youth choir that competed once a month with other youth choirs from churches in that District. I am glad to remember that we won a majority of those monthly events.

At Guilford College my senior year, I joined their outstanding A Capella Choir of 45 voices. To go on the spring tour, it was necessary for me to learn the second tenor part of twenty-nine numbers, some in Italian, Latin, Russian and French. Having to prove to Dr. Ezra H.F. Weis, Director, that I could do it, I sang my part alone without the other singers, while he had a pianist play the music. What a challenge! But I was on the tour bus.

We went up the east coast giving concerts all the way to New York City. As far as the audiences were concerned, they never knew how we got the pitch for each number (a closely guarded secret). We just started singing in the language in which it was written. We only missed the right pitch one time. We liked what Dr. H. Augustine Smith of Boston University said of our singing, "You had a body of tone, balance, release and attack, color values—like a symphony Orchestra."

That was valuable training. It helped me with confidence to organize, and sometimes direct, choirs in the US Air Force overseas and some bases in the USA. During the 20 years as a military chaplain, Lois accompanied me to most places in Germany, Austria and Spain. Together we did the vacation Bible schools and Sunday schools, and worship services. What a trooper she was!

My duty station in 1953 was at Parks AFB, California, near San Francisco. That year the Chief of Air Force Chaplains,

Maj. Gen. Charles I. Carpenter, wanted to try having a spiritual life conference, not just for chaplains, but for interested officers and enlisted personnel. He chose the Baptist Assembly Grounds at Ridgecrest, NC, as the site. I landed there with a plane load from California. When he saw me he said, "Phil, you're in charge of the music."

Here I am directing a congregation in song.

I was pleased and a bit shocked at first. I had brought no music, no anthems for a choir, just my little self. But I was still 6' 12" tall, and he knew I would do as good a job as possible. At dinner, I announced a choir rehearsal for volunteers for immediately after supper—before the evening session. Out of the more than seven hundred people present, twenty five showed up. Happily, among them was a skilled organist and an excellent pianist. I put both of them right to work on an anthem found at the grounds. We had an anthem that night and every night. Chaplain Carpenter had an excellent baritone voice. He chose three others for a male quartet. After it was all over, I received three unsolicited "warm fuzzies" for my efforts.

Chaplain Carpenter wrote:

> *Dear Chaplain Green: I want to express to you my appreciation for your excellent leadership of the music at our recent conference at Ridgecrest. The quality of the congregational singing as well as the choral and solo numbers was very high and was greatly appreciated by all who listened.*

The Director of The General Commission on Chaplains, Rev. Dr. Marion Creager, was a principal speaker. He wrote:

> *Dear Phil, I should like to say how greatly your leadership of the music enriched the conference. Really, I think what you accomplished in such a short time with the choir was amazing. I was personally very much moved and blessed by the whole musical phase of the conference.*

Dr. James Oliver Nelson, Professor of Christian Vocations at the Divinity School at Yale University, a primary speaker, wrote:

> *Dear Chaplain Green: Your music at Ridgecrest far overshadowed my ideas, as your enthusiasm exceeded that of any other leader.*

Lining my life's journey with enjoyable music has increased my desire to keep on keeping on. In the circumstances associated with the pure pleasure of the music have been other satisfactions. The opportunity to share my talents in a broad variety of ways brought gladness and happiness to others.

An elderly woman, who was a teenager when I was her pastor 65 years before, had read my autobiography in her church library. She wrote to tell me how much she enjoyed the duets Lois and I sang in church. She also added that I had led her to Christ and membership in the church. Maybe you think that that was peanuts to me. Wrong! It was a two-pound rib eye steak. I hardly could imagine anyone remembering with delight the music of so long ago.

When I arrived from Germany at Vance AFB, Enid, Oklahoma, I inherited a chapel worship service with no choir. Past experiences had prepared me to do something about that. I was not pleased to rely only upon temporary and occasional soloists (vocal and instrumental), as appreciated as they were. Before very long I was able to put together a small choir. It took off and grew until it was impressive. There was no one in it who would direct it, so I did that too. In the spring of 1951, we did an Easter concert. The wing chaplain, Lt. Col. Martin Scharleman, had arrived, and sang in the choir. He was so pleased with the concert—given at the base and over a local radio station—that he wrote me a letter of commendation, as follows;

> *This is to commend you for superior performance in your work of preparing and presenting Du Bois' "Seven Last Words" at Vance AFB Base Chapel and over Station KGWA. The enthusiasm and skill with which this particular project was executed has won the respect and admiration of every one associated with you in this task.*
>
> *The public response to both presentations was of a kind to enhance the effectiveness of the religious program of the Air Force Chaplain Service. The devotion to duty and the spirit of sacrifice demonstrated in this undertaking reflects great credit on Vance Air Force Base in general and on the Chaplain section in particular. The undersigned shall request that this letter be made part of your permanent file.*

At Spence Field, Moultrie, Georgia, I was the lone chaplain. It was something special! It was a civilian contract flying school. Bevo Howard, a WWII Ace, and the Hawthorne School of Aeronautics trained young Air Force officers and others, from friendly European countries, to fly airplanes. All were male students. But I was able to form a glee club. It went slowly at first. But, when I added young women from town, it caught fire.

Spence Field, Moultrie, Georgia Glee Club

Part of the time I had the direction help of the local high school music director. Extraordinary things happened. We had a concert every three months during the eighteen months I was there. That pleased the personnel of the base and people of the city and Colquitt County. You bet it fired me up to continue to make available enjoyable music for worshiping troops and their families.

Bad Kissinger, Germany, was a seven-month assignment while Hq. XIIth Tactical Air Command was closing down. There was a group of German boys who lived close by, hoping to get whatever "goodies" the Americans threw away—especially, cigarette stubs. Tobacco was the legal tender that opened doors when near-worthless German marks were little wanted. Somewhere among my photos is one of two lads along the railroad tracks of a passing train with their outstretched arms, hoping to receive something, anything. Now I was serving in a situation where everything was already in place at the chapel, with no need for a choir, or a director. They had one. Then the thought occurred to me, "Why don't I start a German boys' choir? I could get them together with chocolate bars."

Frau Boeing was musical and willing to help. The older young man, who played the organ at the German Lutheran church, said he'd help. So, believe it or not, I began training a dozen or so boys to sing together. It would have taken years before they would be anywhere nearly as good as the Vienna Choir-boys, but why wait for perfection?

My German Boy Choir

Sadly, after the headquarters folded, I was transferred, again. Often my thoughts go back to that small group of lads, wondering whatever happened to them.

When I was a young lad, at home I practiced on our piano, usually after meals. My siblings accused me of going to the piano in the parlor to escape my turn at washing the dishes. My mother often would excuse me by saying to them, "Just let him practice."

At that time, I wish someone had taught me the touch system on the piano. I used the hunt-and-peck system with my two forefingers. I still do that on the typewriter and computer. I could read musical notes and slowly pick them out on the piano. When I wanted to learn a piece of music well enough to play it, I memorized the entire piece. As a young pastor in the mountains of Western North Carolina, I often took a pump organ apart to remove dust from the reeds, because dust made some reeds stick open. Dissonance did not go well with hymns. During duty as an Air Force chaplain, sometimes I was needed to clean the reeds of a portable folding field organ.

While at the USAF Academy, Ivan Genuchi, a gifted Chief Master Sergeant, was the director of my Community Chancel Choir. In 1962 the chief of Air Force chaplains gave out several choral numbers for the contest to all Air Force choirs world wide. Those choirs in competition taped themselves and sent the tapes for comparisons.

(top) USAF Community Chancel Choir
(middle) Genuchi shaking hands on a job well done
(bottom) CMS Genuchi receiving the 2nd Place Award in the world wide competion

Music is so much a part of my existence that, most of the mornings I awaken with the music—and some of the words—of a familiar hymn or song. My soul comes awake at the same time as the day is brightened as the music and words repeat themselves in my early consciousness. My daily devotions are built around one or another of the words of a hymn. To sit on the piano bench and thumb through a hymnal, and play and think about the words, is a devotional delight. My father loved the devotional hymns of Fannie Crosby as, *"Savior, More Than Life to Me."* Lois liked hymns about Jesus, as *"Oh to Be Like*

Him," and "*Jesus, Rose of Sharon.*" I often quoted the words of a hymn when I preached, especially when the words strengthened the basic theme of the sermon.

In every place I have lived I have made myself a part of the musical scene. Where there has been no musical group, I have organized or sponsored one. Where there has been no willing director, I've done that, too. In Franklin, NC in 1940, there was nothing. What did I do? I organized the Franklin Choral Club. Can't you just see me directing Handel's "*Hallelujah Chorus*" with only seventeen singers! Then World War II came along, causing it to fold, but not before a Christmas and an Easter sacred concert.

In 1971, First United Methodist Church was coming upon its 100th year anniversary. There was going to be a celebration! Everyone was told they could contribute whatever they wanted to the celebration. Some gave money, some gave of their talents, and a few chose to write a song.

I always had hymn tunes running through my head—like "*Glorious Things of Thee Are Spoken*". In humming that tune, I was inspired to write a centennial hymn for the church. By the end of the day I had penned the first draft. After some reworking of the words, we had an official "*Centennial Hymn.*" I've shared it below.

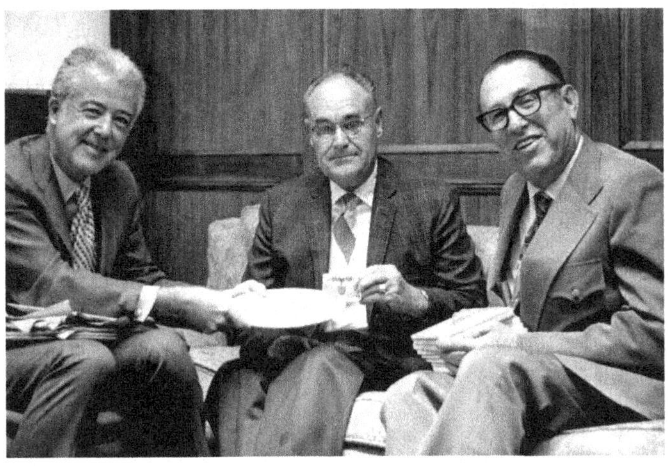

Dr. Lacour, Bill Mason and Phil Green
Planning the 100th year celebration

Centennial Hymn
1871-1971
In celebration of the first 100 years of First United
Methodist Church, Colorado Springs, CO,
I wrote these words:
Tune: Austria
Words: Philip L. Green 1971
Music: Franz Joseph Haydn 1732-1809
Hymn Tune: Glorious Things of Thee Are Spoken
(Words: John Newton, 1779)

Thanks and praise, O holy Lord of space,
For the first one hundred years,
Of thy providence and love and grace,
Through the sunshine and the tears.
We now celebrate in this hymn of praise,
Our good fortune to be known.
As thy people, who in humble ways,
Their father's God to gladly own.

Though unworthy, God of Rampart Hills,
Of a heritage so great,
We admit our very being thrills,
That in us thou didst create
With such skillfulness and such knowingness,
A desire to seek thy face.
At the altar of this church now bless,
Those who again thy name embrace.

Colorado, Colorado Springs,
First United Methodist Church.
Site of many, many christenings,
And of penitents in search,
Of the Father's house, and the way of peace,
And the place of brotherhood.
Father, in our hearts increase
Faith, hope, and love that is understood.

Spirit of God, help us to care
Through another great century.
And in servant-hood to Christ we'll dare
To be faithful through jeopardy.
Bless our church and grant its people may
From all harm and sin depart,
That the challengers to goodness say,
"Almighty God, how great thou art!"

I will keep on using music to help people want to sing joyously together, as children of a loving heavenly Father.

My beginning choir
at Enid AFB, 1949

Chancel Choir
Madrid, Spain
1954 - '57

GI Chorus celebrating
the end of WWII, 1945

Chancel Choir
Enid AFB 1952

Some of the choral groups I've directed

SECTION III

Will Rogers once said, "I never saw a man I didn't like." Neither do I know anyone who doesn't like encouragement. Well, there may be a few people who don't care about getting an encouraging word, smile, phone call or e-mail. We are all capable of giving a pat on the back. My life has been replete with oral and/or written words of encouragement. They are satisfying.

You may have had more than your share of disappointments. You could be struggling with the "if only" disease—if only I had been born in a rich family; if only my skin were different; if only I had been born in a better place. Jesus himself was probably disappointed that not everyone accepted him as the promised Savior. A look at his life in the four gospels of Matthew, Mark, Luke and John reveals that he faced every situation and person without cringing with fear, or responding in anger. He was creative in the management of his disappointments.

Everyone has struggles. Even a child struggles to stand up, walk, and obey the rules. A preacher's kid like me had struggles with the call to be a minister when I had inadequacies in public address. Then I remembered Rev. Bud Robinson. He stuttered badly. His pastor told him that he would never be able to be a preacher. He ignored that advice and became an outstanding communicator of the gospel, in spite of his stuttering.

In this chapter I have listed thirty-six fears. If you check and count more than five, it is possible that you need some help from a counselor, pastor, teacher—even a trusted level-headed friend.

The year 2004 was my "big year." At almost ninety years of age I managed the following accomplishments: (1) caught a plane to Nashville, TN to attend the National Association of United Methodist Evangelists; (2) attended the 25th anniversary of a new church I helped get started; (3) flew to Berkeley, CA to attend a five-day United Methodist Senior Adult Ministries Conference; (4) flew to St. Louis, MO, to attend the National Institute of the Military Chaplains Association; (5) attended a United Methodist District Conference in Denver; (6) helped plan and preside at "Growing Edge of Evangelism in the Pikes Peak Sub-District; (7) Attended the Colorado Christian Ashram at Saint Milo Retreat Center near Estes Park; (8) celebrated my 90th birthday and my 68th year in the ministry.

11

EVERYONE LIKES ENCOURAGEMENT

This chapter is written to lift that thought up as one that will make life more meaningful and enjoyable. Whether or not it is given or received, it is a two-edged benefit. Because it is an undisguised boon, everyone can give it or receive it. The path of my life has been decked with encouraging words from a multitude of friends and well-wishers. More than likely yours has been, also. A telephone call, a "hello there", a smile of approval can make someone's day. The cost is minimal, so give one, or two, or three a day.

At the turn of the 21st century, I gave encouragement to each of the ninety-eight members of the chancel choir of our church. How did I do that? It cost something in time and expense but it was worth it to receive the kind of response many members gave me. It was "an open letter" to the Chancel Choir Members, May 21, 2000.

Dear Choir Members,

I can delay the writing of this letter no longer. Even when I was a chaplain at the USAF Academy in early 1960, and certainly while I was a member of the professional staff from 1963 to 1980, and for many of the years until the present, I have been the recipient of the inspiration of your music. Many of you do not know me, but I see each of you week after week.

A brief history reveals that when I came on the staff, Mr. L. John Shoemaker was the director, followed by three Charleses; Margason, Hausmann, and Merritt—and our present director, Rev. Steve Harter. I have been close enough to the assistant directors, organists, and office personnel to fill them in too, but I won't. I don't remember all those who sang in the choir "back then," but I'll name a few: Charles Belshaw, Barbara Crawford, Verne Crotinger, Ann Daniel, Trudy Fennewald, Pat and Ron Fox, Helen Greenley, Fran Husser, Harriet Kidd, LeeAnn and Ron Kidd, Barbara Myers, Will Potter, Pat Puryear, Eileen Read, Wendell Robbins, Merle

Sickbert, and Suzanne Vaughan. I know a few of the newer ones like Rose Trigg.

What have you (older and newer) members meant to me? You have set a good example of faithfulness to the choir. Every Thursday and Sunday you have committed yourselves to singing in the choir. I happen to know that to some of you, this has been a real hardship, given your home and work schedules. Whether or not singing in the chancel choir is an enjoyable experience, or a personal commitment to God and the church regardless of the cost, to me, this means that it is a part of your journey of faith. When I look into your faces from the front pew Sunday by Sunday, I try to calculate the total amount of energy and purposeful effort which is amassed in the choir membership. My heart rejoices to know that, when you back your car out of the garage on Sunday mornings, you are witnessing to your neighbors your love of God by going to worship in the house of the Lord. To me, in my mid-eighties, you are an inspiration. You need not remember the couple in their 70s twenty-five years ago who came to me for marital counseling. She was accusing him of "eyeballing" the women in the choir! I'm too old and too happy with my wife, Helen, to even imagine such a thing.

I ask myself, "What is singing in the choir doing for you?" I believe it was William James who wrote, "Repetition deepens impression." If that is true, and I believe it is, then singing the basics of the Christian faith is bound to be an anchor to your soul. Whether you believe everything you sing or not, you have the option of taking to heart what you believe is true. It is impossible for you to sit at the feet of Jerry Trigg, Cal McConnell, Larry Lacour and Ben Lehmberg, and let their messages go unheeded over your heads. So you are learning, and doing, your faith.

A word about beautiful music—I am not against guitars and you need to know that I am glad they haven't made a dent in our worship music. So great is your singing of anthems that, much of the time, people are so moved at what they hear that they forget to applaud. May their tribe increase. Please know that you have my ultimate thanks and appreciation for being such a quintessential part of the worship team at first church. My wife, Helen, thinks you are great. We both enjoyed the spring concert tonight.

I sent the above choir letter at personal expense to every home address.

I had space for only one of the many responses to that letter of encouragement. It was from a long-time choir member, three months later:

Dear Rev. Green,

I appreciated very much your letter written May 21. I kept it on my desk to reread and to be sure to answer. It gives me a boost to read it every now and then; to be reminded of how important our chancel choir is to worship on Sundays. Each Thursday night is a thorough workout and I come away feeling like I've really learned more about music and our God.

I'm reminded of our early years when you started the DUO Class in the old Acacia Hotel because of lack of room in the church. That was a great time of discovery and bonding with wonderful friends. That class is still like family to me. I remember one time I visited Lois in the AF Academy hospital. You were there visiting her too. I still remember that she encouraged you to be on your way so you wouldn't have to rush. That was a wonderful lesson to me as a new husband. Instead of saying, "Please, stay longer," she said you should go so as not to hurry or be late. So many lessons I've learned from you both. I also loved hearing you two sing duets at Edison-Leader Church.

NB: In addition to my primary job as the associate pastor of a mega-church, I was asked to do an additional duty by being the Sunday night pastor of a small church, fifty-six miles out at the extreme southeast corner of El Paso County, 1964-'67. The church had thirty-five members, including resident and nonresident members. Pat's mother was the church's secretary. She and I wrote the 50-year history of Edison-Leader Church. Both Pat and her mother are now in the "great cloud of witnesses," and are hoping to see me soon.

A letter of encouragement came to me in 1978 from a woman who was a member of our mega-church. After eleven years, the senior pastor had gone to the seminary at Oral Roberts University in Tulsa, Oklahoma. That left me to fill in for four months, during which time he returned Friday nights through Sunday afternoons to preach. He had served in the US Navy so he said, "Phil, you're in charge of the ship most of the time now." So the letter sent to me surely gave me a boost I needed. I knew she considered her friendship with the Lacours at the top of her list. But here comes a personal letter of encouragement. She included these words:

> *Dear Phil,*
>
> *I am writing this letter to you as a friend, to give credit where credit is due—in fact it is long overdue. This morning after church I was thinking about the fine inspirational message you gave to us. Phil, it is really too bad you lost so much sleep over it. There was no one—I repeat no one who could not say they felt much, much better spiritually after having heard your excellent sermon.*
>
> *You know Phil, I remember so well after Dr. Ben was gone, how you guided the ship (our church) with so much strength and "know-how" during that trying ordeal. Then during these 11½ years the Lacours have been with us, you have always been right there too. Now that they have left, you are back guiding the ship with that same steady hand that keeps things running smoothly. We have always appreciated your fine work, but I'm afraid that I, among so many others, have taken you too much for granted. I didn't feel I wanted to say this to you in person, because you might not stand still and listen. Ha. So I was determined to tell you how very much you do mean to all of us via this letter.*
>
> *Whether you know it or not, both you and your lovely wife, Lois, have a "one-to-one" communication with us that makes us feel comfortable in your presence. I am so grateful*

> *for the spiritual and just ordinary help to both Cook and me, and now to me since he is no longer here. I am so grateful and proud that I can say: "Yes, I count Phil and Lois Green as personal friends."*

No one needs to guess how encouraged I felt after reading such a letter.

Rev. Dr. John A. Taylor and his wife Helen, of Sebring, Florida, came to the mountains each summer in Waynesville nearby. He and my father had been close clergy friends for many years. Dr. Taylor was not only a "Lay Methodist Evangelist," he was a successful business man, patriot, author, legislator, song writer, poet, lover of children and benefactor of young ministers, including me. Never, in all the more than nine decades of my life, have I known a more gracious and outgoing person. Although he was all of the above, he accepted my invitation to be the evangelist for a revival at two of my small country churches. During those times he stayed in our less-than-elegant parsonage.

He went with me to visit members and nonmembers with a smile of acceptance for farmer, sharecropper, or whoever. Because of the signal success of the revival at Old Brick Church—a church that had been abandoned for twenty years—it became alive again with many young families, who now had a church with a pastor, Sunday School, all the rest again. Reviving that church brought happiness to many families and put a feather in my hat. What a great encourager Dr. Taylor was! Two years later it was my joyful pleasure to direct the music at Avon Park Camp Meeting, which was a camp he and my father and Dr. Henry Clay Morrison founded. Generous Dr. Taylor gave the thirty acres in that orange-growing part of Florida for what has become a veritable spiritual center where "snow-birds" can come each year.

Four decades later, I wrote the early history of that site entitled, "*Grace Abounding in the Orange Groves*." That native of Pocahontas County, West Virginia, took off for "that great cloud of witnesses" in 1944. How many young pastors he helped with his generosity only God knows. He never sought any credit for what he did. May his tribe increase.

My job description in Madrid, Spain, 1954-'57 was that of assistant command chaplain of the Sixteenth Air Force. That was a misnomer. I was never asked by either of the two Catholic chaplains who followed one another as command chaplains. I found right away that I was expected to begin a complete chapel program and ministry for the Protestant community—and that without arousing the displeasure of the Catholic hierarchy. Spain, until shortly before the arrival of US military personnel and families, had been considered an unfriendly nation. That sentiment was ill-founded and a US Embassy had recently been established. Generalissimo Franco had come to power and stayed there after internal strife and after anti-religious Russians destroyed many Catholic churches, killed a multitude of priests and holy nuns. His only solid backing was the Catholic solidarity.

We were there building three Air Force bases and one for the Navy. He was jittery about "all those Protestant service-people" who came. In order to make the Americans less noticeable, we did not wear military uniforms the first three years we were there. Being the number one Protestant in Madrid mandated a low profile for me as well as a place of worship that didn't look like a church—i.e. in the American school auditorium. As I mentioned elsewhere in this book, every thing had to be as unobtrusive as possible. The two Catholic chaplains both left with a Legion of Merit. I was fortunate to rate a Commendation Medal.

I began alone—just a part-time secretary. A year and a half later, a sergeant was assigned. But I had a great number of volunteers who knew that, if they didn't do it, there was no one else to do it. At his own volition, Brig. Gen. Lewis L. Mundel, Commander, 7602nd Support Wing, wrote the following letter to the Chief of Air Force Chaplains, Maj. Gen. Charles I. Carpenter, that was very encouraging to me.

He said (in part),

> *In Catholic Spain, the work of a Protestant chaplain is difficult. Chaplain Green, through his energy, courage, and complete dedication, has developed in Madrid for Americans of the Protestant faith religious services and leadership that should be a source of pride to him and to the Air Force. Not only are his services always attended to capacity, but Chaplain Green himself is a rallying point for many activities*

> *of an interdenominational character. It seems appropriate to me to express to you my high opinion of Chaplain Green. He has contributed significantly to the welfare and morale of U.S. personnel in Spain. In my opinion he would be a welcome and stalwart member of any command.*

To have someone, not in my chain of command, write such a letter, encouraged me. I was alone but not lonely. It might have been easier there if I had had ministers of my faith—or clergy of any Christian faith with whom I could chat and be confidential. But, yes, there were visits by several dignitaries looking in on me.

A Letter I Needed at the Time

Two days after this letter was written on May 20, 1988, and before I even received it, Lois, my life companion of 52 years, went to her heavenly home. The last 19 ½ months she had spent in a nursing care center a mile from home in Colorado Springs. During all of this time her awareness was limited (she knew me), and her ability to respond was minimal. I had visited her most every day, three times a day for 5, 10, and up to 20 minutes. Now she was gone and the family joined me to prepare a fitting service of remembrance. While this letter was in transit, my children had picked out a beautiful spot among the pine trees of Evergreen Cemetery for her burial site.

The letter was from Chaplain Col. James E. Townsend who, for the national convention of the Military Chaplains Association of 1978, had been of inestimable help to me as host chairperson of that event. Now he was retired and serving the United Methodist Church as the Associate General Secretary of the Board of Higher Education and Ministry of the General Board of Discipleship (for United Methodist Chaplains). His predecessors in that position had often visited me when I was a chaplain on active duty in the U.S. Air Force. I was now serving as the Regional Representative for the United Methodist Foundation for Evangelism. In that work the committee that had joined me had raised $250,000 to pay for the first year of an E. Stanley Chair of Evangelism at the Iliff School of Theology in Denver. He praised our publicity brochure. Likewise, in April before Lois died on

May 22, 1988, he had sent a representative from his department to the MCA Convention in Colorado Springs. Jim did not know that Lois was near death so she was not mentioned in his letter. However, his letter did touch upon two projects for church and country that engaged my sincere attention. Here's the letter:

> *Dear Phil:*
>
> *Thank you for your letter and for bringing me up to date on the Foundation for Evangelism. Your new material is superb! It is visually exciting and can be read quickly, is inviting to read, and has about it a sense of permanence that will appeal to donors. You have done a remarkable job.*
>
> *I'm also delighted that you have the $250,000 in hand. This has been a remarkable project and one for which you are to be commended.*
>
> *I'm sorry that it was not possible for me to be at the MCA Convention. Unfortunately, I can only be in one place at a time and we have to make priority decisions. This was simpler when I was a director, not as an Associate General Secretary. Sincerely, Jim.*

12

TRANSFORMING DISAPPOINTMENTS

Most people have more than one, sometimes more than their share. What we do with them, how we respond to them, can embellish or diminish our gusto for life. Projecting the blame for them on others, or on circumstances like "if only," is an easy way but not an ideal one. Finding and doing the better, or best, way often takes strong and searching insight and will-power. Placing the blame on oneself is no better. That wipes out a needed optimism on one's self-confidence.

The more I have thought about the management of disappointments, the more I have become convinced that the best way is to transform them whenever possible. That puts a weighty load on the person who has been disappointed. Getting even won't do it. Bulldozing won't do it. Rationalizing won't do it. Facing it squarely is a good start. Treating it creatively could be the best answer. Let's turn to the master model. Jesus faced every situation, person, and challenger without cringing with fear or responding in anger.

A great disappointment in my life happened in 1947 while on occupation duty in Germany. I had entered military service as a chaplain in the US Army Air Corps. Five years later, the Air Force became autonomous—equal with the Army and Navy. My choice was to transfer from the Army to the US Air Force. One of the benefits of that decision was the possibility of moving up from reserved status to a regular commission. I made an application to be considered for that changed status because my efficiency reports by commanders had been high. Col. Woodrow Dunlop, in Wiesbaden, Germany, had encouraged me to apply. On my request to the Adjutant General in Washington, he had given a high endorsement, that said,

> *This officer is a superior officer in his field. He is conscientious, sincere and energetic in his work. He often exceeds that which is expected of him by performing extra curricular activities—all designed for the betterment of his communicants. He is amiable, extremely well-liked and unquestionably successful in his assignment as Staff Chaplain.*

> *I therefore recommend that he be considered as an applicant for a regular commission.*

The military headquarters gave an affirmative reply for this changed status. However, the Methodist Commission on Chaplains in Washington, my ecclesiastical endorsing headquarters, turned it down. Their standing rule was that only clergy with a bachelor of divinity degree from a seminary would be accepted for a regular status. WOW! Was I ever stunned and disappointed! After such high praise from my commander, to be turned down by a technicality was a blow that was difficult to take. But I had to take it, if I wanted to remain on active duty as a reservist. Benefits of regular status would have given more security, with less likelihood of being riffed before retirement age—the end of twenty years.

I hope I responded well and healthily. I didn't let it interfere with my job performance, but I went through a period of discouragement and depression. The best thing I could do was to pursue that degree and re-apply later. At my next stateside assignment at Vance Air Force base, Enid, Oklahoma, I was in the same location as Phillips University. Thankfully, Col. Tom W. Scott gave me permission to become a special student in the College of the Bible at Phillips. I earned 24 semester hours in Practical Theology during those two years. Happily, as I was leaving for another assignment, Colonel Scott thought I had done very well with my chaplain duties. In his endorsement to my monthly report, he wrote to the Commanding General of the Air Training Command, as follows;

> *It is with regret that I write the orders transferring Chaplain Green away from this base. He has done an outstanding job in all phases of his work as Assistant Base Chaplain. He has worked hard on routine projects and extended himself into development of many extra activities on the base.*

My next assignment was in South Georgia, too far from Atlanta's Emory University and the Candler School of Theology. Next I was transferred near enough to a seminary in San Francisco, but was too overloaded to take on seminary courses. For three years I was assigned as the only Protestant chaplain in Madrid, Spain. While at the Air Force Academy, I was able to complete sixteen semester hours in counseling at the University of Colorado's extension division in Colorado Springs. I was still trying to finish my BD degree.

After military retirement in 1963, I became the associate pastor of First United Methodist Church in Colorado Springs, CO. Rev. Dr. Ben F. Lehmberg gave me permission to complete my long-sought degree at the Iliff School of Theology in Denver. I got brushed off by the dean of the seminary, who said in essence;

> *Phil,*
>
> *You've completed the four-year course of study by correspondence through the Candler School of Theology in Atlanta, had a successful seven years as a pastor in the Western North Carolina Annual Conference. You've had twenty years of great work as a chaplain in the US Air Force. And now you are the associate pastor of the largest church in our Annual Conference. You don't need a seminary degree!*

That was the end of my trying to finish the degree that was needed so badly in 1948 to get a regular commission, instead of remaining in reserve status. During the remainder of those twenty years, I competed with regulars and reservists, and was never caught in a riff.

It is of some interest that the military chaplains of the Air Force, Army, Navy and Veterans Administration elected me the national president of the Military Chaplains Association in 1970-72. And, on the morning I was about to give my acceptance address, the representative of the Methodist Commission on Chaplains in Washington—who had turned me down for a regular commission—sat with me beforehand, put his arm around my shoulder, and whispered, "Phil, we're proud of you!"

As a raw beginner in the military chaplaincy, I was eager to do everything "right." I have said that I liked approval, sometime too much. My first assignment in the Army Air Corps was to the 329th Fighter Group, at the Grand Central Air Terminal in Glendale, California. I had finished the month of orientation into military service at Harvard University where I was happy to learn that my duty was to be in the Air Corps. After that graduation, I returned to North Carolina to pick up my wife and two children for the long haul across America—through Kentucky, Missouri, Colorado, Utah and on to San Francisco where I received orders for Glendale.

My trip some 400 miles down the west coast in September 1943 was perilous. World War II had begun 32 years earlier after the surprise attack on Pearl Harbor. (Many Japanese Americans had been re-located far from there, lest they could betray us "again".) To drive that coast by night required no headlights, only parking lights, so as not to let spy ships off the coast know of troop movements. The temporary building of the 329th was not impressive, as I had expected. As I entered the front door all prepared to report to my first commanding officers, I knew how to do it—Go in, cap under left arm, orders in left hand, salute and say,

"Chaplain Green reporting for duty as ordered, Sir."

But, as I opened the outer door, a major was just coming out. He was the adjutant of my outfit, and it was an awkward moment. What to do? Give a quick salute? The officer solved it by asking what he could do for me. I told him I had been assigned as a chaplain to his outfit. He replied,

"The hell you have! We've got a chaplain!

That chaplain was Aubrey Wallace, in line to be transferred to overseas duty, but the orders had not been received at our headquarters yet. So my introduction to the Army Air Corps, awkward as it was, was completed. In short order, Chaplain Wallace was gone and I was at my first duty desk. My outfit was in the business of training fighter pilots to fly P-38 fighter planes.

One of the first things I did was to devise a way to communicate with the troops about the chapel worship service and activities. Despite the shortages of a wartime situation, I found a way. I was able to purchase 8 2 inch by 14 inch colored paper, fold it once, and there was a four-page document. I had to distribute copies to barracks and work places myself. That gave some face-to-face contact so troops could know what their chaplain looked like. The next question was, "How to get the troops to open the newsletter and read the hours of worship services?"

I answered that question by the use of written humor. The GIs found routine chapel news interesting enough to flip open the newsletter to get to the humor stories. It worked well. But some person, maybe the chaplain of another faith, took exception to the humor and sent several copies of "Chaplain Green's Page" thru Channels to the Air Chaplain in Washington! Back through channels, for everyone at each intermediate headquarters to see, was the Air Chaplain's reply:

> *"The enclosed copies of 'Chaplain Green's Page' were brought to our attention as containing jokes of a questionable nature.*
>
> *It is our feeling in the matter that the best of taste is not exercised by Chaplain Green in the general tone of his regular bulletin. We well understand that the intention behind his efforts is the best, but feel that it is not advisable to compromise with propriety in an effort to be a 'jolly good fellow' and appeal to the crowd. An* occasional *good joke serves its purpose, but it does not seem good policy to have a chaplain's regular bulletin serve mainly as a joke sheet.*
>
> *The joke about the Second Lieutenant is ill-advised. The story of the Negro minister and the one about the fat bishops are hardly of an inspiring nature, and thus defeat their purpose. Popularity gained at the expense of religious dignity is hardly a worthwhile accomplishment."*

WOW! There goes my good name with the Air Chaplain in Washington! And what will my commander think of his newly assigned chaplain? I was somewhat mollified by remarks from colleagues in their endorsements along the chain of command. The chaplain at the Fourth Fighter Group wrote,

> *"It is the belief of this headquarters that Chaplain Green has made many contacts and accomplished much effective work through the paper in question. He is one of our best chaplains."*

The command chaplain of the Fourth Air Force, my immediate supervisor in San Francisco, wrote the Air Chaplain about this matter, as follows,

> *"In reply to your letter of 12 January in regards to 'Chaplain Green's Page', will say that the matter has been brought to his attention. We are assured he will be more cautious in the selection of jokes for the humorous section of his page.*
>
> *Chaplain Philip L. Green is an active and effectual chaplain. His work has been of the highest order, a fact that is substantiated by numerous complimentary remarks in various endorsements. His 'Chaplain's Page' has interested many in his unit and brought about numerous contacts, thus enlarging his sphere of service. It is quite likely that the jokes in question were an oversight or were not scrutinized carefully in the editing process."*

It was with a great deal of satisfaction that I received the following letter from an officer in our outfit who knew nothing about the criticism I had received,

> *Dear Chaplain Green,*
>
> *It is with great pride and devout seriousness that I write a humble note of commendation to you. In the few short days I have been returned to undoubtedly the finest group in the armed forces, I have heard no end of friendly remarks made by the members of our group with you as the subject. Like many others, I have enjoyed reading your weekly page.*

Happily, neither the Air Chaplain in Washington, nor my commander, took further note of my 'Chaplain Green's Page.' It turned from a criticism into a blessing.

At Vance Air Force Base 1949-'51, my duties were so approvingly looked upon that I thought I might soon be considered for a job promotion. Chaplain Glen Shaffer had written words of high praise for my work. His successor, Lieutenant Colonel Martin Scharleman, holder of a PhD degree and author of the "Dynamics of Moral Leadership Lectures" to be given by chaplains Air Force wide, was my supervisor the last six months. He was so taken with my accomplishments with the chancel choir, of which he was a member, that he wrote a letter of commendation to be added to my permanent 201-file. Colonel Scott wrote a letter of regret that I was being transferred elsewhere from his base, where I 'had done a superior job as assistant base chaplain.'

Instead of getting a promotion, I was sent to a small contingent of military troops with hardly as many as in a squadron—not a group, not a wing—where I might have been happy with a man-sized organization. The main mission of training pilots for the Air Force was done there by a contractor named Hawthorne School of Aeronautics. It was a new concept being tried out in many places by the Air Force. Why was I being singled out for a job like that? I felt a little better after receiving a letter from someone I knew who had been sent to a similar training unit. He had been at Vance AFB during my earlier days there. He thought such an assignment was right up my alley. I began to perk up with the thought that I'd be in charge of everything and would be my own boss.

With a determination to show them what I could do, in May of 1951 I reported in at my new job at Spence Field, Moultrie, Georgia. It pleased Lois because it was in South Georgia, and only a hop and a jump to the pan handle of Florida where she grew up and where most of her relatives still lived. In less than two hours she could be home. My children liked it because there was a swimming pool on the base. There was an apartment on base, so we didn't need to find and/or buy a home there. Lieutenant Colonel Steve Crosby, the commander, and his wife Flo, welcomed us warmly. Bevo Howard, President of the Hawthorne School of Aeronautics and a World War II flying ace, was pleased with our arrival.

Very soon I changed my attitude from "I'll show them a thing or two," to a desire to prove my ability to meet creatively that new one-chaplain assignment. The cantonment-sized chapel, left over from WW II, needed upgrading, altar drapes, pulpit Bible and other ecclesiastical supplies. There was no chapel annex for the trainee pilots and military families to have a Sunday school and a Vacation Bible School and no chapel choir. Colonel Crosby let me have his secretary. He needed a change. He was a survivor of the Bataan Death March in the Philippines of WW II, and was most accommodating in helping his chaplain to get everything needed for his chapel program. He even gave an unused building that could be converted into a chapel annex.

We hired a Catholic priest nearby to conduct Mass and hear Confessions. There was no rabbi in town, but I found a layman who was well versed in what to do for the Jewish service people. When the Chief of Air Force Chaplain's Representative brought the Centenary College Choir for a concert, the Methodist Church in Moultrie gave the space for it. The building was well-filled with people from Spence Field and Moultrie and the concert was enthusiastically received. Colonel Crosby was elated because, during the war, community relations between the town and the base were strained to the point of needing to have machine guns placed around city hall.

From that auspicious beginning, I began nineteen months of ministry that resulted in many creative developments in the Chaplains Six Point Program. Happily, six weeks after my departure, Jim Greenwood wrote the following summation for the Hawthorne School of Aeronautics:

> *The people of Moultrie will remember Chaplain Green for his outstanding contributions to the cultural and spiritual life of this area. He gave much of his personal time to causes for the good of the whole community, as well as for the welfare of students at Spence, his primary responsibility.*
>
> *A song leader for the Lions Club and social chairman of the local Ministerial Alliance, he was also a member of the Community Chorus and of the American Legion. In 1952 he was chairman of the membership committee for the Community Concert Association, in which he was instrumental in attracting many new members.*
>
> *Of his many fine accomplishments, Chaplain Green probably achieved widest acclaim for developing an idea that*

did much to promote international good will on a local level. Aided by local civic clubs, he established a program designed to offer a home environment and recreational outlets to Allied trainees from various foreign nations who were taking flight training at Spence under the Mutual Defense Assistance Program. He named the project, appropriately enough, "Operation Southern Hospitality."

As a result, several hundred Allied cadets here in strange surroundings and oceans away from their homeland gained a keener insight into the American way of life through their contacts with Moultrie families. And the families in Moultrie gained a better understanding of life abroad.

Chaplain Green, vitally interested in civic progress, was a driving force behind numerous projects for the benefit of the community.

13

STRUGGLES I'VE HAD

While in Guilford College (1933-1936), I did a lot of soul-searching about my "calling" into the ministry. One of the troubling factors was that a pastor had to love people. During the lunch period one fall day, I lay on my back on a bed of pine needles under some pine trees in a secluded campus area wondering how I could be a minister when I didn't love people. The only ones I loved were my sweetheart, my parents, and a few friends. The thought of loving "people" in general was foreign to me. Wanting to be in the ministry, I prayed hard for God to put the love of people in my heart.

He didn't do it right away. Over the decades I wound up being the Minster of Pastoral Care in a church of more than 6,000 members. As demanding as my job was—caring for the hospitalized, the shut-ins in homes and care facilities, for seventy to ninety bereaved families annually, and counseling multitudes in need of a listening ear—I never complained once over the long hours, the interruptions, the middle-of-the-night emergency calls. It was God's ultimate answer to that earnest prayer under the pine trees at Guilford College. Tired I was, badly overworked to be sure, but God always renewed my strength. One ten-day period I was sorely tried—with seven overlapping funerals including a suicide and a crib death. During that time I drove home different ways to vary the routine and spent Friday night at a motel in a nearby town with my wife before returning for a wedding and a funeral. I was so confused once that I drove my car to a crowded funeral-home parking passage and, knowing that an attendant would move it out of the way, I left the motor going, but locked the car doors! I accepted the load I carried in the belief that God would mete out strength adequate for the duty. And He did.

Inadequacy in oral communication: A most painful experience in college is the day I had to give an annual presentation. My whole body rebelled at the prospect. My face flushed red and my voice was unsteady. It wasn't that I was not acquainted with the material at hand. I was overly aware of other class members and the professor and what they would think of me. A year later I was given an opportunity to speak to the young adult group of a church. Some of the same dynamics of inadequacy attacked my efforts, although—since the group was sympathetic—not to the same extent as in the college classroom.

If every public speaking appearance were to plague me with such painfulness, did I really want to continue toward the ministry? In 1934, I had already been granted a local License to Preach in the Greensboro District of my denomination. Singing and leading musical groups was not a problem, unless I had a solo to do. I hated for all eyes to be focused upon me, and me alone.

I knew that there would have to be a solution to this dilemma. It became a major object of earnest prayer. God helped me to understand that the "message of truth"—"The Good News of the Gospel"—I would be giving was not my message, but God's message passed on through me. This thought encouraged me and I soon learned to give His message with confidence, leaving the results of each sermon to God.

Oral Speech Impediment: At times I was aware of an uneven flow of oral presentation resulting from occasional interruptions in my chain of thought. Most of my life as a minister I struggled with trying "to be more eloquent." Finally, I came to the realization that I didn't have to preach like some of the expert "pulpiteers" of that day, that God and the people expected, only that I do the best I could, in my own way. My own feeble way caused me to consider myself to be a great shame to the God who had called me into the ministry and who deserved my better.

Walking the Talk: It came to me early that, to preach the gospel truth, meant that the preacher would need to be a willing and living example of what came from the pulpit. It would be patently unethical for me to expect the laity to live by one standard and the minister by another. One of the temptations of that early day—and still of today—was that of becoming involved with a woman in the congregation, or in the community. The example of Rev. Elmer Gantry was to be avoided at all costs. But the temptation was always there, waiting deliciously with a bite of the forbidden fruit. I was glad that the promise of Scripture was fulfilled. There was always a way of escape.

14

SCALE DOWN YOUR FEARS

(Some could be fulfilling)

Especially the fear of dying. Dr. ElisabethKubler-Ross wrote a book entitled *On Death and Dying*. I attended a workshop she gave at Penrose Hospital in 1971. I was asked to bring a woman who was about to die for an interview. To get her from the hospital to the site of the workshop across the street, she needed to be wrapped warmly because a blizzard was on outside. Very calmly Dr. Kubler-Ross asked her about her situation and, to the surprise of everyone, she spoke quite openly about the fact that she was dying. She answered every question asked. She said she was not afraid of dying because God had given her a long life. Not many days afterward I conducted her celebration of life. Her son was in charge of the custodial staff of our church's super-large building. He had given me permission to ask his mother if she'd be willing to come for that interview.

During twelve of the seventeen years I was the associate pastor, I prepared eight sessions on the topic of death and dying. One of the sessions was led by a funeral director, another by an attorney (who helped prepare wills), and one by a hospice nurse (who provided care for those who were not expected to live longer than six months.) One of the topics covered was about a less expensive way to have a funeral and bury those of lesser income.

It was of interest that there were people, especially the younger adults, who didn't want to think about the end of their lives, much less talk about it in the presence of other people. But they needed to address many issues related to the end of their lives and the lives of other loved ones.

Scale Down Your Fears

(√) Check and count the number of fears you have. If you have more than five, you're in trouble enough to see a trained counselor or doctor for help to scale down your fears. Your pastor might suffice, or your school counselor. Even a level-headed and trusted friend might help you.

List of some fears

Fears of:

() Accepted, not being
() Accidents
() Animals, some
() Antiquated, being
() Blood
() Contamination (germs)
() Close places
() Crowds of people
() Darkness
() Dying
() Desires, unacceptable
() Delinquent, being
() Detection
() Disease
() Disease, sexual
() Failure
() Falling
() Fire
() Flying
() High places
() Illness
() Impotence
() Inadequate, being
() Insane, going
() Job loss
() Left behind, being
() Lightning
() Mistreatment
() Open places
() Pain
() Pregnancy
() Solitariness (being alone)
() Storms, thunder, tornados, floods
() Suicide, committing
() War
() Weapons, bombs, guns
() ______________
() ______________

15

WHEE! HOW GOD USED ME!

The year 2004 was the big year, the year of my 90th birthday and 68th year as a minister. Not only would I be a nonagenarian, I would be the paternal head of five generations, a great-great grandfather. God honored me by using me extensively. He had known for many years of my prayer of dominant desire, *"Lord, use me whenever, wherever, and however you may wish."*

I began that year by flying alone to Nashville, Tennessee, to attend the National Association of United Methodist Evangelists (NAUME) of which I have been a member since 1981, followed by my denomination's Congress on Evangelism, January 4-7. This repetitive event occurred in January each year and I attended most of them in other cities. Many of my colleagues in NAUME were also friends, as were some who attended the Congress. Each year for me it was a time of spiritual renewal and feasting.

On Sunday, January 11, I was invited to attend the 25th Anniversary of Mountain View United Methodist Church, up the mountain to Woodland Park a few miles from Colorado Springs. I had been instrumental in helping that church get started. My son, Phil Jr., was one of the first pastors for four years. Rev. Betty J. France was the very successful pastor under whose leadership the church had grown to some four hundred and fifty members.

On February 7, I flew to Berkeley, California, to attend a partial class reunion of a few members of high school classes who had been in the American School in Madrid, Spain, 1954-'57. Phil Jr. and Marcia had both graduated while I was the Protestant Air Force Chaplain there.

While in the San Francisco area, I attended a five-day United Methodist Adult Ministries Conference. I was one of the oldest ones present. My daughter Mickey and her husband Bruce Salimi lived close by, so we enjoyed visiting and staying with them.

April 20-23, I flew to St. Louis, MO, to attend the National Institute of the Military Chaplains Association. I was president 1970-'72. With the passing of the years, there were fewer chaplains I remembered, and who remembered me.

I drove to Denver May 15 to attend the Mile High/Pikes Peak District Conference of the Rocky Mountain Annual Conference.

For my 41st time, I attended the Rocky Mountain Annual Conference, in Denver, June 16-19. The Colorado Christian Ashram met at Saint Malo Retreat Center in Allens Park, CO, June 25-28. Since 1971, I have been a leader, director, and evangelist.

Aug. 21, was the day we celebrated my 90th birthday—we moved it from September 15 to this date so my great-grandchildren from Minnesota would not miss a school day. It was 1-4 p.m. at First United Methodist Church in Colorado Springs.

Aug. 28, 9:00 a.m. to 4:30 p.m., I was chairman of the "Celebration of the Growing Edge of United Methodism in the Pikes Peak Sub-District" at First Church, Colorado Springs.

Sept. 10-16, flew to Greensboro, NC to attend the Family Reunion. Gave the sermon in the family church, after which I spent three day with Rachel, my niece, in the mountains.

Sept. 21, drove to U. Methodist Hq. in Denver for an International Pot Luck.

Oct. 27-30, flew to Lake Junaluska, NC to attend the annual trustees meeting of the Foundation for Evangelism. I was a Past Regional Director and a member of "The Seventy" for eighteen years.

A Memorable Day! On Sunday, October 31, 2004, I left Lake Junaluska and drove the 45 miles to Western Chapel, Leicester, NC, and gave a brief sermon where I had preached my first sermon in 1936. Jo (Lunsford) Herron was there with her husband Lew. She was 12 when she began her journey of faith, when I was there. They took us to lunch in Asheville and to visit Bishop and Mrs. Hunt in the infirmary of Givens Estates.

Afterwards, I drove the 75 miles to Franklin where I had served the Franklin Circuit (1940-43) and was met by NC Senator Bob Carpenter and his wife, Helen. They spent four precious hours driving me around to all the churches and to dinner when his reelection two days later was still pending. Helen was a star student in Lois' French class at Franklin High while I was there, and Bob was one of her students, too. Imagine how I felt visiting a church on my first circuit where I began my ministry (1936-40), and the same day spending time with longtime friends at Franklin. If I live to be 100, I will never forget Oct. 31, 2004.

As this was my 90th year of life and 68th year as a minister, and as paternal head of five generations, I put together in January the above rather extensive itinerary.

I need to swing back a few years because that's when Jo (Lunsford) Herron read a copy of my autobiography in her church library. She wrote a two-page typewritten letter after reading it. Among other things she wrote,

> *Greetings from South Turkey Creek;*
>
> *I just finished reading "The Mountains Are Happy" and enjoyed every page (of 385). You have done a wonderful job of sharing a beautiful life with us all. I am Jo Lunsford Herron and I joined Western Chapel Methodist Church of the Sandy Circuit in 1937, when you were our pastor. Congratulations on a wonderful life of service. Your beautiful singing with Lois is remembered with my best memories of my early years as a Methodist.*

I want to explain "The Celebration of the Growing Edge of United Methodist in the Pikes Peak Sub-District," on August 28, 2004. In January there were three retired ministers who regularly met Monday mornings for refreshments and fellowship—Rev. Dr. John M. Vayhinger, Rev. Bill Cooper and myself. Weighing upon my conscience was how the membership in our denomination had dropped more than 3,000,000 over the past two decades. I took it upon myself to put together the facts about gains and losses in our sub-district over the past thirty years. The three of us studied those facts and decided we ought to take the lead in helping the active pastors to do a better job of reaching out and bringing in un-churched people to help replenish those people our churches lost. It was not a small undertaking. After all, we were retirees wanting to nudge our colleagues on the firing line.

July 9, 2004

TO: All ministers of the Pikes Peak Sub-District
RE: The Celebration of the Growing Edge of United Methodist Methodism in our area (the Pikes Peak Region), at which event we hope to discover new ways to help our churches grow.

Dear Colleagues in Ministry,

The thrilling story of church growth in our area is being told by the new congregations founded during the past three decades. Included is Sunrise, Wilson, Mountain View in Woodland Park, Korean, Korean-American, and Tri-Lakes in Monument. In part, the new churches came into being at the expense of losses in the other churches. The willingness of existing churches to reach out with a helping hand and share resources and people to the new congregations has been an exciting part of the story.

We will gather on Saturday, August 28, 2004 at First UMC, to listen to the first-hand sharing of the stories from Marvin Vose, Betty France, Keith Watson, Robert Leeds, and others. Rev. W. James Cowell, founding pastor of Sunrise, has been invited to MC this celebration event. A statistical survey of church membership from 1968 motivated this event. Overall, like our denomination, we have suffered a continuing decline in church membership. We want to turn this trend around, for the sake of Jesus, "who for the joy that was set before him, endured the cross."

A special treat will be the video account given by Adam Hamilton, senior pastor of one of the three most dynamic United Methodist congregations in America. His United Methodist Church-of-the-Resurrection in Kansas City, Kansas, grew from less than 100 members to more than 11,500 members in 12 years.

Those Invited: 39 Pikes Peak Sub-District appointed pastors and staff ministers, 32 resident retired ministers and a key lay person from each of the 21 congregations. The hours are 9:00 a.m. to 4:30 p.m. Reservations for the event, which includes a free lunch, must be made by August 16.

I covet your valued presence at this event.

Philip L. Green, Chair, Celebration Event

SECTION IV

Whatever ails you is helped by a good laugh, even a smile. In today's modern world, humor is being used by doctors and other therapists to attack health wreckers as serious as cancer—yes, advanced stages of the same. This chapter includes as much humor as I can remember from all my years. But you are not limited to mine. There are books and movies galore that address themselves to humor therapy.

A serious crisis can kill you, if you let it. It has been authenticated that a trauma of serious proportions, if not handled healthily, can cause the beginning stages of cancer, and the growing cancer can kill you. I have outlived the dying months of two beloved wives partly because I didn't let it get me down, and partly because I was undergirded by many caring and loving family members and friends.

A guilty conscience is a drag. Something a simple as a theft of a twenty-cent can of apricots can nag, and nag, and nag until rectified. I know because every time I knelt to pray a stolen can of apricots appeared to remind me. Once I was tempted to rob God—yes, rob God of the tithe that I hesitated to give to the church. A seventy-five dollar sick Jersey cow taught me that I, even a pastor, needed to practice what I preached.

Keeping on keeping on doing the right thing is a never-ending challenge. Sometimes it means getting out of the easy chair and doing something still waiting to be done. I have been a pastor who couldn't quit, that didn't want to quit. I enjoyed obeying God's call to do "something more." When I retired from the being an Air Force chaplain for twenty years, I was only fifty. Who would want to quit at that age? Following the next seventeen years as the associate pastor in a 6,000-member congregation, I was prompted to say, "I ain't done yet!" So I became a founder of a new congregation. At age seventy-four, nine years after retirement age, my bishop wanted me to pastor a church of a hundred members sixty miles from home. I did that until I was eighty. At that age the pastor of a Korean congregation needed someone to conduct an English-language worship service at 9:30 a.m. because his English language ability was not good enough to do that himself. So, until age eighty-five, I did that. At that turning point in my life I became an author. This book is but the last of four books I have authored.

16

SPRINKLE HUMOR ON IT

Laughter is good for many things, even cancer. The Associated Press released an article to the news media through the Colorado Springs Gazette newspaper on Friday, November 28, 2008, entitled, "*When Cancer Is Laughable.*" That article told of cancer patients, some with advanced stages of the disease, gathered and exchanging laughable stories at the Montefiore Einstein Cancer Center at the Montefiore Hospital during one of their monthly "*Strength Thru Laughter*" therapy sessions. It was just one of several types of laughter, or humor events, being offered by medical facilities for patients diagnosed with cancer or other chronic diseases. Included at these humor sessions are clown appearances and funny movies.

After military retirement in 1963, for many Monday mornings I met with a number of clergy colleagues for an hour or so for coffee, refreshments, fellowship and an exchange of mutual concerns. Over more than thirty years, from that sub-district group, motivation came for the origination of several new congregations. The annual roster I published was a piece that promoted mutual collegiality. We also exchanged humorous happenings, events and stories, many of which are included in this chapter.

It is impossible for me to give accurate credit to persons and sources for what I will include for the readers' grins, smiles, and healthful belly-laughs. I intend no infringement upon copyrighted material that appears here. I apologize for stories that are common knowledge among my clergy colleagues and which might have originated with them. Some stories may be a bit delicate for some readers but there has been no intent to embarrass anyone.

Famous Dallas Cowboys Coach

In 1961, I accompanied the Falcons from the USAF Academy to a game in Dallas, Texas. After the game I spent a few days visiting friends in that area. I was invited and thrilled to attend a banquet where the famous Coach Tom Landry was the guest speaker. I will never in this life forget the story he told, as follows,

> *The game was tied. By injuries, the team had lost both of its quarterbacks and the coach was desperate. He called to a player on the bench and said, "I know you've never played quarterback, but we must have someone to finish the last two minutes of this game. Do you think you could remember the four calls I give you?" The player thought he could. The coach said, "Now listen and listen well. Call the first play to go over left guard, the second to go over the right guard, the third is to be a pass to one of our ends, then kick it. Do you have it?" He had it.*
>
> *To the surprise of the coach and fans, the non-quarterback made a first down on the first play, another first down on the second, and the right end carried the ball to the two-yard line. To the dismay of everyone except the opposing team, the non-quarterback obeyed to the letter the prior instructions of the coach and punted on the two-yard line! After the game the coach asked the non-quarterback, "What on earth were you thinking when you punted on the two-yard line?"*
>
> *"I was thinking what a dumb coach we have,"* was the reply.

The Devil in His Britches

The pastor had only one Sunday suit. Each Sunday night before bedtime he removed it and hung it in the unheated closet on the back porch. Each Sunday morning he brushed the dust from it and wore it to give the weekly sermon. On freezing cold Sundays he donned the suit as usual. What he didn't know was that during a warm week at the beginning of the fall season, some wasps had made a nest in one leg of his pants. In the sudden change to freezing weather the wasps became dormant. In the warmth of the church they began to thaw out and sting the pastor's leg. He grabbed his leg after each sting. Feeling he owed the congregation for his erratic action, he explained,

"Friends, I know I have the Lord in my heart, but I surely must have the devil in my britches."

My Dog Fala

President F.D.R. was campaigning for a 3rd term. Some had said harsh things about him. He said to curious other people, who asked if those words hurt him,

"I don't mind the criticism very much, and Eleanor doesn't either. But Fala doesn't like it at all."

A Texan Tells One

The Rev. Dr. Benjamin F. Lehmberg, pastor of the largest congregation of my denomination in the Western Jurisdiction, brought me aboard as his Associate in 1963. He was a marvelous teller of stories and was happy for every new one he heard. Attending every Sunday night service was Mr. Tex Bundy, an elderly cowboy whose name was inscribed in the Cowboy Hall of Fame. In addition to admiring Dr. Ben's messages, he enjoyed Dr. Ben's humor. When the cowboy recognized the beginning of a story, he'd move to the front edge of his front pew and leaned far forward. I will never forget the happiness on his face when Dr. Ben told the following bit of Texas humor:

> *"During the depression years of the 1930s, a Texas sheep-rancher was having great difficulty selling his lambs. In fact, he had so many lambs in his large flock one year that he was able to sell only a third of them. One sunny day one of his lambs fell into a vat of pink dye. It turned into a lovely pink lamb. A passing motorist slammed on his brakes, backed up, and wanted to know the price on "that" pink lamb. The rancher realized that he had a serious buyer in his yard and raised the price accordingly. The buyer drove off without batting an eye about the price of the lamb. From that day onward the rancher dyed all his lambs and sold every one*

at a good price. That rancher became known as the biggest lamb-dyer in Texas."

One from My Sister

When I was age eighty-two, my only living sister, Ruth, phoned to tell the following bit of humor: An elderly gentleman was taking an elderly woman out several nights a week. One night he said to himself, "*I think I'll ask her to marry me.*" He did and she said, "*Yes!*" On the way home afterwards, he said to himself:

"*I distinctly remember asking her to marry me, but did she say 'yes' or did she say 'no'? I'd better call and ask her.*" He did and she replied, "*Oh, I told some fellow I'd marry him, but I've already forgotten who he was.*"

Why France Tried to Buy the Rock of Gibraltar

While serving with the 16th Air Force Command in Madrid, Spain, I learned that the Spanish people were unhappy that the British had taken and fortified the Rock of Gibraltar, and kept it for centuries. At one time, France tried to purchase it from the British. They wanted to rename it "*DeGaulle Stone!*"

On Raising Children the Military Way

Al Davies was a gifted magician, as well as a volunteer at one of the chapel dinners in my congregation in Madrid, Spain, in the late 1950s. After showing some of his magical wonders, he delighted us all with the following:

During the Korean conflict, the North Korean armed forces—augmented by Chinese Communist troops—were successful in overrunning the U.S. forces in trenches. Each time they did so, our troops fell back to secondary trenches. When our troops had to fall back again, they fell back until they could hold against the enemy.

Rearing children is somewhat like having to "fall back" when necessary, absolutely so.

Example 1: At Meals: Rule one—"Children must clean their plates." If that doesn't hold, rule two becomes necessary—"No desserts for those who don't." If rule three becomes necessary, it is "Absolutely no second dessert!"

Example 2: On Going To Bed at Night: Rule one was "Eight o'clock sharp." Rule two—"Not one minute past 8:30." Rule three—"Children who stay up late will not be carried to bed." Rule four—"Unless they won't wake up."

Example 3: On Watching Scary TV Programs: Rule one—"Children may not watch scary TV programs." Rule two—"Children who watch scary TV programs may not come and sleep with mom and dad afterwards." Rule three—"Children who must come and sleep with mom and dad after watching a scary TV program, may not bring the dog to bed with them." Rule four—"Oh well."

The Difference Between "Politeness" and "Tact"

The new hotel bellboy needed all the instructions there were in order to be successful on the job. His instructor told him he needed to know the difference between politeness and tact. *"For example,"* he said, *"if you enter a hotel room and see a woman in the shower, you should say, 'Oh, pardon me sir'. That 'Oh pardon me' is politeness. The 'sir' is tact."*

Old Senator Barclay

Some years ago, one of the oldest senators, but still very popular on Capitol Hill, was Allen Barclay. He tried to attend every party to which he was invited. On some weekends, this meant three or more parties. He attended most of them, even if only for a short time. In the midst of one party, the hostess found him in the hallway looking at his list of parties for that night and asked politely, "*Senator, are you looking for the address of your next party?*" "*No,*" he replied, "*I'm looking to see where I am right now!*"

Before A Cross-Eyed Judge

The judge addressed the first of three defendants standing before him and asked, "*Why did you steal the car?*" The second defendant answered, "*I didn't steal the car.*" The third defendant replied, "*I didn't say anything.*"

Punishing the Blameworthy

At recess, two students had a Jewish lad down and were beating him unmercifully. A teacher pulled them off and asked, "*What are you two boys doing?*" They responded, "*The Jews killed Christ!*" The teacher exploded. "*But that was more than two thousand years ago.*" "*We just heard about it!*" replied the boys.

Whistle the Doxology

When I was pastor of six country churches for four years in Western North Carolina, we observed Communion on the first Sunday of each quarter—January, April, July and October. Most Methodist churches in the mountains did the same. In one of the churches of a colleague, the woman in charge of preparing the elements of bread and grape juice awoke on the first Sunday in October. She had forgotten that this was one of her Sundays and rushed about the house but could find no grape juice, only a bit of apple juice—but not enough. To get enough juice, she went and gathered persimmons from under a tree in her yard. Frost had yet to fall on the fruit. The persimmons were not quite ripe enough to keep them from being puckery in one's mouth. Consequently, after everyone at church had communed, the pastor said:

"*Now let us all rise and whistle the doxology!*"

Billy Graham in a Limousine

He and I were born in Western North Carolina near Asheville. I was five when he was born and we lived only thirty miles apart. He became an evangelist of gigantic proportions as well as a confidant of presidents. I met him near his home in 1953 and was a member of his team to help provide buses to transport people in Colorado Springs to his stadium services in Denver in 1967. Recently, I heard the following made-up story about him:

Billy Graham landed at the international airport in Charlotte where a limousine had come to pick him up and take him the seventy-five miles west to his home. He said to the driver, *"I'm in my eighties but I've never driven a limousine. Would you let me drive a bit?"* The driver gave consent and they turned west towards his home.

A rookie cop pulled the limo over while it was going seventy-five miles per hour in a sixty-mile zone. When he saw Billy Graham as the driver, he excused himself and returned to his vehicle, and called his supervisor.

He said, "*I have a problem. Please help me to decide what kind of ticket to give to a very important driver.*"

"*Well, who is it, the governor*?" asked the supervisor.

"*No*" replied the cop.

"*He's more important than the governor.*"

Next he asked, *"Is he the President of the United States?"*

"*No. He's even more important than that,*" said the cop.

"Well, quit stalling, who is it?" stormed the supervisor.

"It surely must be Jesus Christ," said the cop, "*because Billy Graham is his chauffeur!*"

Top-Level Animosity

The hostility began when two British lads were in the primary grades in school. Why they disliked each other no one knew. Later years of education found them still hostile to one another when they were in the same college. They lost track of one another after graduation. Twenty-five years later one of them had become an Admiral in the British Navy, the other an Anglican bishop. On a train platform some distance from London, the bishop came up the steps and there stood the admiral in all his braids. They both recognized each other. To cut the admiral down, the bishop in his ecclesiastical gown hustled up to the admiral and asked,

"*Station-master, when does the next train leave for London*?" The unflustered reply was, "*At ten o'clock, madam, but should you be traveling in your condition*?"

For My Longevity

I doff my hat to a life of good humor. I was ever alert to remember good stories. In the Methodist Church of my first seven years in the ministry, the women's organization was called The Woman's Society of Christian Service. Each year at the Annual Conference of all the clergy and an equal number of lay delegates, that organization had one night for dinner and programming. A prominent minister within the conference gave the main address. He wanted to praise the president of the woman's Society and did so with the following made-up story:

"*Many months ago I visited in the home of Mrs. Abercrombie, your President. While waiting for her to finish preparing a delicious meal, I wandered about the house from room to room. In one room her little daughter was playing with two other neighborhood girls. I didn't want to intrude but stayed outside a short time listening to their interesting conversation about which one could remember events earliest in their lives. The first said, "I can remember when I was four years old." The second one said, "I can remember when I was able to reach up and touch the bottom of a chair." Our President's daughter said, "That's nothing. I can remember the day I was born. Yes*" she said to unbelieving friends, "*No one was home but my grandmother and me, my mother had gone to the Woman's Society of Christian Service.*" It brought the house down. And I still remember it.

Question to a Woman

This was at a time when very few women were employed outside the home. "*Do you work outside the home*?" Answer—"*No. My husband makes the living and I make the living worthwhile.*"

Prayers Were Forbidden in Public Schools

Except in Colorado . . . during final exams . . . in trigonometry.

The Bob Hope Show

Bob Hope during one of his shows in Berlin

1948 Bob Hope Christmas Caravan, Berlin Airlift

Every Christmas season, for many years, comedian Bob Hope visited military troops in troubled parts of the world to bring a touch of humor to grim situations. This time it was West Germany and was called "Operation Vittles." Among those who came with the Caravan were Irving Berlin, Tex McCreary, Jinx Faulkenberg, Irene Ryan, Tony Romano, ten Rockette dancers from New York City, and others. I was one of several escort officers for the shows. My role was to train, in advance, a number of GIs to sing the refrain of Operation Vittles, a song composed for the show by Irving Berlin who sang the stanzas. I was both pleased and excited to be one of the escorts of the caravan but regretted having to be absent from my little family on Christmas Eve and Christmas Day. They seemed to understand.

It was a liberal education to be behind the scenes of the Bob Hope Show. He was in charge and was the main attraction, but he was more than that. He managed every performance from back stage and on stage. He critiqued every show afterward. He instructed the performers "If you're going over great, stay out there. If not, get off fast." There were no dead spots. The response to each actor made each performance somewhat different. The Rockettes were always a success, as was Bob Hope himself.

During each of his seven shows, Bob Hope had a GI prompted to jump up during the show and shout, "Where's [Bing] Crosby?" Then Bob could give such an answer as, "He's in the hospital. He fell off his wallet." Or "One of his [race] horses was dying and he stayed to see one of them 'finish.'"

A Few Other Jokes by Bob Hope

Bob: We have some wonderful newscasters back home these days. We have some that can tell us the news behind the news. Others tell us the news before the news. Wouldn't it be great if some of them could tell us what is going on right now?

Bob: I visited the GIs in Europe during World War II. On the plane over here I read a book. On the way back I read the second page. It was a bomber that brought me. I wish I knew who wrote "Gentleman" on the bomb bay doors! That first step was a dilly. O well, I wouldn't have made it anyway.

Bob: We've just come through a presidential election. At 10:00 p.m. on election night, a prominent commentator exulted, "I predict Dewey!" At midnight he was less sure and said, "I predict!" At 2:00 a.m. he wailed, "Eye-yie-yie!"

Years later when I was on duty at the USAF Academy, Bob Hope gave a show. The tri-faith cadet chapel was nearly completed. There were criticisms about the design, especially by some that had wanted another design. One said that the 17 spires looked like sharks teeth. Another said twelve of the spires were for the twelve Apostles and the remaining five were for the congressional committee. Bob knew about the controversy before he came. When he arrived he said, "The cadets are confused about the chapel. They don't know whether to pray TO it, FOR it, or IN it."

Irving Berlin

Irving Berlin (who wrote 'Alexander's Ragtime Band' in 1911, three years before Philip was born, as well as 'Easter Parade', 'White Christmas' and many hundreds more) told us about a song he wrote for the special benefit of the women on duty in the Pacific Theater during WW II—Red Cross hostesses, nurses, WACS, and WAFS. The war department had mandated the wearing of slacks, not dresses. That was before slacks became popular. So the lips of the women were on their shoelaces. He sang that song. I remember only the refrain. Here it is:

> *O for a dress again, to caress again, in a dress again. There's no romance when you dance cheek-to-cheek and pants-to-pants. Oh, for an old fashioned dress!*

Phil, Would You Marry Me?

After I fell and broke my right hip in early 2005, after hospitalization and rehabilitation, I needed some home care. An agency called "Right At Home" was in business locally but I hadn't learned of it. So I found a young woman who was willing to spend a few hours three days a week to help this old retired preacher for so much an hour. A few months later, she had some bad news and some good news for me. The good news first, she wanted me to marry her. Now the bad news, She wanted me to marry her to someone else.

One Thanksgiving Morning

At 10:00 a.m., the people of seven downtown churches came together for worship at one of them. All seven pastors had a part. The main speaker was Rev. Dr. Paul Peel, the Senior Pastor of First Lutheran Church. He grabbed our attention as follows:

Early one morning at daybreak, a woman said to her startled husband, "Dear, don't forget what day this is." He jumped out of bed thinking, my goodness, I've forgotten her birthday!

To make up for lost time, he hurried to a store for an appropriate card to place on her dresser, bought a dozen red roses (her favorite), a box of chocolates, and took her to a matinee. For dinner, he took her to the best restaurant in town. At bedtime his wife said to him, "Sweetheart, this was the nicest Ground Hog Day I've ever had!"

Which god?

Off the coast of Savannah, Georgia, a mother and two young daughters found their boat stuck on a sandbar and in need of being rescued. The Coast Guard men soon came along, saw their dilemma, and rescued them. The woman was so grateful for their kindness that she wrote a note to their commander and thanked him for what his seamen had so skillfully done. She added a word about what occurred between her two daughters at the time they went aground. The five-year-old began to cry. The three-year-old tried to comfort her by saying, "*Don't worry. God will take care of us,*" to which the five-year-old said, "*Where was God when we went aground?*" The younger sister replied, "*Oh, I'm not talking about that God. I was talking about the Coast god.*"

Ayatollah Khomeini's New Robe

He swept into power from exile in Paris to Teheran on a wave of religious fervor, and was accepted nowhere except in his own country. There were Fundamentalists who went wild about him. He bought a large bolt of white satin, took it to the royal tailor for a new robe. The tailor took his measurements and told the Ayatollah that there wasn't enough cloth for the job.

Later Khomeini took the bolt to his tailor in Paris. After measurements, he was informed that there was too much cloth on the bolt. Much puzzled, the Ayatollah asked why his tailor in Teheran might have thought there wasn't enough cloth. The Paris tailor said, *"Sir, you are a larger man in Iran than you are in France!"*

He Knew "Perfectly" English

It was unusual for a Brazilian to want to excel in the English language. But this professor wanted to master all the idiomatic expressions and pronunciations before accepting an invitation for a lectureship in the United States on the topic of "Family Life." On the tour, a student asked how it was that he was such an authority on family life when he had no children of his own. He replied, *"That's an easy one, you see, my wife is unbearable."* Seeing the humor on the faces of his audience, he realized he had not chosen the right word. He clarified by saying, *"That is, my wife is inconceivable."* When the humor in the audience became vocal, he hurried on to say, *"What I mean is, my wife is impregnable."*

What To Do Last

In 1963, I visited the troops stationed where missiles on the North American Dew-line poised in their underground launching pads. At this particular site, military personnel were well aware that, should Russia point and fire an intercontinental missile, there could be no escape; death would occur within a few minutes. They were on alert much of the time. I was interested to know how morale stood up under these conditions. It was the chaplain's duty to find out. Humor under these conditions must be the kind I saw on the bulletin board in the common area. In large letters was this heading, "What to do if an Enemy Missile Heads This Way." Below were these instructions,

"Go immediately to your room. Lower all your blinds. Remove all your clothes. Pull the chair well out from your desk. Sit on the edge of your chair and lean all the way forward and downward. Kiss your [behind] one last goodbye."

The Preacher's Horse

He sold it to a layman in his congregation. In doing so he needed to explain the language to which the horse would respond.

To ask the horse to go, you say *"Praise God."*

To get him to stop, you say *"Amen."*

After a few weeks the layman decided to ride the preacher's horse but couldn't remember the right words. As hard as he tried, he failed to make the horse go. Finally he was lucky to say the right combination. The horse immediately took off at great speed but in the direction of a thousand-foot cliff. In great anguish, the right word would not come to him. Facing eminent death, he hurried through "The Lord's Prayer," at the end of which he said the right word. The horse stopped at the very edge of the cliff. The layman was so glad that his life was spared that he shouted, *"Praise God!"*

A Navy's Brief Orientation

In 1962, I was among a group of Air Force Academy officers who were invited by the US Navy for a brief orientation at North Island in San Diego, CA. While there, we were given an aircraft ride over the Pacific Ocean where we landed on Aircraft Carrier Oriscany. Seen from a distance, it was scary to think we'd have to land "on that postage stamp." We both landed on, and took off from, the carrier. Later we went aboard a submarine for a trip beneath the waves. On board I heard about what happened on board a nuclear sub somewhere. The seaman said that the commander of the sub piped for all crew members to come together where he said, *"I have some good news and bad news. The bad news first—we'll be under for three more weeks. Now the good news—you will all get a change of underwear. Joe, you change with George. Allen, you change with Smitty. Ralph, you change . . ."*

Epitaph On A Tombstone

"Ma loved Pa. Pa loved women. Ma caught Pa with one in swimmin'. Here lies Pa."

Three Mischievous Youths

Between 1936 and 1943, I was pastor of country churches in Western North Carolina. One of the stories I remember was about a farmer's three sons who spiked the preacher's milk. When preparing to leave after the meal the pastor wanted to buy the cow.

Blue Ridge Breezes

That was the title of a book given to me on Sandy Circuit by a retired math professor at a state college nearby. It had been written by one of his colleagues and contained humorous stories gained while teaching there. One story I remember could have been a true one, though I doubt it.

The pastor of the local Baptist Church, faithful to his calling, tried to persuade as many un-churched people he knew to confess their faith, be baptized in the French Broad River, and join his church. Many people responded to his invitation. One woman had received several invitations across the years but never gave any interest in responding. The reason was that she was large; very large, and afraid. Therefore, the minister would be unable to "put her all the way under," a necessity for the baptism to be acceptable in the Baptist tradition.

To his surprise, one summer, he looked up from the river and saw her coming. He remembered that she was large, but not "THAT" large. The reason—she had put an inner-tube under her dress to be sure the minister would not let her drown. During her baptism, the pastor lost his footing while trying to get her "all the way under." The last the people saw of them was as they rounded the bend in the river singing, "I am bound for the Promised Land."

Forbidden Humor

In some quarters it is gauche to tell stories about ethnic persons, such as the Irish, Jews, persons of color, etc. I have had to stop telling a number of stories that I thought were priceless, and now when I tell some of them, I omit the ethnic element—only the "human" situation remains. To the rescue came the eminent Rev. Dr. Oswald "Ozzie" Hoffmann, preacher of the National Lutheran Hour. When he was a principal speaker for the convention of the Military Chaplains Association's a couple of decades ago, he said he could (and did) tell an ethnic story about a Hittite. He said that all the Hittites had died centuries ago and now there were none to take umbrage.

There was once a Hittite named Eric who went to his bank to cash a check. The teller asked him to endorse the check on the backside. He protested that such was not necessary as his name was on the front of the check. The teller insisted and finally Eric stormed out of the bank and went into another across the street. There he was told that they would cash his check if he would sign his name on the reverse side. "That's what they told me at the bank across the street," he protested loudly. "But that's what you must do if we cash your check," the woman said. As he was about to storm out of that bank, the teller took him by the lapels of his coat, banged his head on the counter and said, "Sign it!" He did, and as he was crossing the street to his car, the teller from his bank came out and saw him counting his money. He asked, "Did they cash your check over there?" "Yes!" proudly declared Eric. "Did you endorse it on the back?" "Yes," he replied. "Why in tarnation didn't you endorse it at our bank?" He clarified by saying, "Over dhere dhey explain dings!"

Late Coming Home

His wife wanted to know why he was so late golfing that day. He said, *"Dear, today it was just swing-and-drag, swing-and-drag."* She said *"I've never heard that excuse before. What do you mean 'swing-and-drag?"* He replied, *"Bill, my golfing partner, had a heart attack on the second hole and it was just 'swing-and-drag' for all the other holes."*

How's That Again?

The beauty salon was ultra, with a clear sign out front that said, *"No pets allowed."* But Fi-Fi went with her mistress everywhere. Who was to tell her she could not take well-groomed Fi-Fi to the beauty salon. The manager confronted her with, *"get that bitch out of here!"* The manager noticed how offended she was and thought she might never have heard the "b" word before, and said, *"Haven't you ever heard that word before?"* She replied with honest incredulity, *"Well, yes, I've heard it. I've heard it many times. But this is the first time I have heard it applied to a dog!"*

Prime Minister's Response

At a London party a woman confronted Sir Winston Churchill with these words, *"Mr. Churchill, you're drunk."* He replied, *"Yes, I'm drunk, and you are ugly, but tomorrow I'll be sober."*

Heavenly Punishment

Moses and God were looking down to earth over the parapets of heaven one Sunday morning and saw a preacher playing golf. *"Shouldn't you punish him?"* asked Moses. God said, *"Well, yes, but I don't like to. His congregation finally gave him a Sunday off after three years, and he deserves some recreation. But yes, I'll punish him."* The next hole was a 255-yard three-par one. The preacher teed the ball, swung mightily, and the ball landed on the green and rolled right into the cup for a hole-in-one. Moses said to God, *"That's no way to punish a preacher for playing golf on Sunday. You've rewarded him."* To which God said, *"I did punish him. Who's he going to tell?"*

An Old New York Businessman

One of his accounts was far off in the Midwest. He and his daughter caught a train to meet and settle that account—which was for a horse and buggy and five hundred silver dollars. The two of them climbed into the buggy and began the long journey back to New York. Bandits stopped and robbed them along the way. The old merchant lamented, *"I'm ruined, I'm ruined. I've loosened my horse, I loosened my buggy and I've loosened my horse and buggy."* His daughter said, *"Don't cry, Papa. I have the 500 silver dollars." "O, you have? That's good. But where did you hide it?"* She replied, *"I hid it in my mouth." "Vhat a pitty your Mamma wasn't here. We might have saven'd the horse an' buggy!"*

A Big Difference

The six-year-old Catholic boy finally had a playmate. Moving next door was a Protestant family with a six-year-old girl. They enjoyed playing in a lake behind their unfenced homes. The problem was—they were punished for getting their clothes wet. They solved that one by removing their clothing. When they did that the Catholic boy exclaimed, *"So, that's the difference between Catholics and Protestants."*

Big in Texas

The man had heard many stories about how big everything was in Texas. At last, he had driven from Kansas to Fort Worth. Because he had failed to pause at the last "rest stop," he entered the hotel lobby, rushed to the desk and asked for the location of the nearest rest room. The clerk pointed down a hallway and told him it was the third door on the left.

The third door on the left turned out to be the wrong door. It opened on a large indoor swimming pool. The clerk realized he had indicated the wrong door, rushed down to alert the man and found him struggling in the pool with his clothes on. When he saw the clerk he cried out, *"Don't flush it!"*

Historically Speaking

In 1845, the Methodist Episcopal Church in America divided over slavery and ended as ME Church and ME Church South. Not until 1938 did the two branches get back together. At that time I was in my second year of my first pastoral appointment. It was wonderful to wind up with simply The Methodist Church. I heard one speaker humorously explain the process of that union. He explained that;

Two inebriates entered a hotel lobby and asked for *"one bed with two rooms in it."* The patient clerk could not make such an arrangement. So the drunks changed their request to *"two beds with one room in it,"* which the clerk was unable to supply. Finally, the clerk persuaded them to take a single room with a double bed and sleep together. Off they went to do that. During the night, number one awoke and shook the other man and said,

"Say, there's someone in bed with me."

The other replied, *"That's funny. There's someone in bed with me."*

Said the first man, *"Let's kick 'em out."*

Number one kicked number two out. Number one said, *"I kicked the guy in my bed out."*

The one on the floor said, *"That's funny, the guy in my bed kicked me out."*

Number one threw back the covers and said magnanimously, *"That's all right. You just come and sleep with me."*

Did I Say . . . .

Seventy years ago I was a young pastor who was just beginning as a pastor. The retirement age at that time was not more than sixty-five, or less. In those years many retirees died within two years. I heard about a man who, when he reached age sixty-five, was asked by a reporter from the local newspaper about his plans after retirement. The conversation continued as follows: (key: N=reporter, R=retiree)

> *N: I wish I had known your father. It would have been great to interview him.*
>
> *R: Did I say my father was dead? He's eighty-one.*
>
> *N: Oh, that's great. Could I interview him?*
>
> *R: Well, no. Not now. He's on a visit down south for a month.*
>
> *N: Then, maybe you could tell me a bout him and his deceased father.*
>
> *R: Did I say my grandfather was dead? He's a hundred and two.*
>
> *N: That's just wonderful. Do you think I could interview him?*
>
> *R: He's not here just now. He's gone to town.*
>
> *N: Gone to town? Who took him, and why'd he go there anyway?*
>
> *R: Oh, he still drives, and he went there to get a marriage license.*
>
> *N: Who would want to marry at age one hundred and two?*
>
> *R: Did I say he wanted to get married?*

17

YOU CAN OUTLIVE CRISES

A famous hospital in Houston, Texas, proved an interesting and frightful fact. Not only can an accident take your life, or a poison, or yet a gun, but a major crisis in your life can initiate a fatal disease—cancer. The death of a spouse, a sudden major loss of employment, or a serious physical health problem can trigger the onset of cancer IF one cannot, or does not, come to grips with it in a successful and healthy way. It may take a couple of years for it to become known. As a minister of pastoral care in a six thousand-member church for twelve of seventeen years, I saw how often the elderly showed up with that dread disease.

It is often difficult to identify which crisis weighs most heavily upon one's emotional stability. What would give one person very little concern could throw another person into a deep depression. A divorce in one's marriage could solve a simmering problem or bring an end to great happiness. The depth of the wound is to be measured by what it does to one or both spouses.

I know of a colleague whose ministry was outstanding for decades. For some reason known only to God, he took his own life—leaving many loved ones and friends to wonder why he did it. Was he afraid that he would be unable to "keep up the pace" as in former years? Did his wife decide to leave him?

During the Great Depression following the stock market crash of 1929, many managers of the funds of their friends and associates were faced with disaster—with banks closed and no way to make good on promises of profit. First, the managers ruined. As a result their clients were ruined. Many could not face the hard reality and took their lives.

My oldest grandson was killed in an eighteen-wheel truck accident, caused by a drunken sports car driver who crossed the yellow line. He left two teen-aged daughters. My daughter was devastated! However, in time she handled the tragedy well. Later the man who had caused the accident was scheduled to show up in court to meet the results of his crime of driving while intoxicated, and insurance charges that included the care of my grandson's two minor children. On the day of court he did not show up. He was found dead by his own gun.

If you find yourself in a serious crisis and are tentatively trying to decide how to handle things, it would be a good idea to talk about it with a trusted friend, pastor or counselor. Do not hurry for a quick fix. It pays to wait awhile.

18

MAKE FRIENDS WITH YOUR CONSCIENCE

While I was a senior in Valdese High School, two other boys and I took off from classes for "Skip Day." Wasn't that what skip day was for? We had decided beforehand to go fishing in the river three miles north. On the way to the river we passed through a small village and stopped to purchase "supplies" for the day. The country store had a lone old man inside who had to move slowly and couldn't see or hear very well. While my two classmates engaged his attention on the other side of the store, I took an opportunity to take (steal) a can of apricots. I knew better than to do that. My early training was to live a Christian life.

So, on that fishing trip, we had apricots and whatever the other boys bought at the country store. But I had apricots every time I said my prayers. My conscience proved to be very much alive. Each time I prayed, I told the Lord that I was sorry for what I had done and promised to "make it right." Procrastinating didn't make things better, though my promise lowered the pressure. Then the family moved a hundred twenty miles from there. But when I tried to pray, there was that can of apricots to deal with. I had worn out my promise to God and my conscience. So I did what every person needs to do. I did something about it. I wrote a letter to the old merchant and confessed to what I had done and included in cash much more that the can was worth. I told him that I was trying to live right and would he forgive me? He answered my letter and forgave me. He was glad that I was trying to live right. After that, the can of apricots never showed up again. I learned my lesson that "you can't be right with your conscience, and God, and wrong with your fellow-man."

In 1936-'40, I served my first appointment on the Sandy Circuit, Buncombe County, North Carolina. I was twenty-six at the end. There were six small mountain country churches to serve—three on the first and third Sundays, and the others on the second and fourth. The four fifth Sundays were free Sundays off. My salary was $1,000 a year—$600 from the churches, $300 from the Board of Missions, and $100 from a fund an unknown benefactor gave. A scantily-furnished parsonage was also included. I had married Lois D. Ritter on January

5. And I had borrowed money to purchase a 1932 A-model Ford car. Living on a tight squeeze was nothing new to me. Marcia Helen was born on Easter Sunday, March 28, 1937, and Phil, Jr., on September 15, 1938 (also my birthday). It became necessary for the little ones to have more milk than Lois had to give. We needed a cow. So I bit the bullet and paid $75 for a Jersey cow. I had no lawn mower, so I staked the cow here and there for her food and for her to "mow" the grass.

One day I staked old Jersey in the back yard. Outside the back door we had a garbage container that she overturned. In it were many salt crystals that had been left over from making homemade ice cream. After she ate them, she became very ill. I phoned the local veterinarian who said she'd probably die. He said there might be one chance to try out. He told me to go into Asheville, the County seat, and to the Revenue Office, where whisky from stills had been raided, and ask for a half gallon of whisky. Can you imagine a twenty-four-year-old preacher doing that? I did it and was pleased that they knew the vet and gave me some.

The vet told me to find a bottle with a long neck, put some whisky in it, lift the cow's head and allow the liquid to gurgle down her throat. If she swallows it there might be a chance of saving her. I tried it, and it worked. The vet told me to make some oat meal and make it very thin. I tried that, and she could, thank God. So I saved my investment of seventy-five dollars. That cow taught me a lesson about paying a tithe of my income to the church. I had been wrestling with whether or not a minister, on such a meager salary, ought to pay a tithe like everyone else. During the cow's struggle to live I promised God that, if he'd help me save the cow, I would ante-up with my delinquent tithe for that year. I tallied up what I owed and, to my surprise, it came to exactly $75—the exact amount I'd paid for the cow. So, happily, the cow was saved and my conscience smiled. I've paid my tithe ever since.

Last week, after some seventy years, I read in the newspaper the results of a survey of the honesty or lack of it in high school students. Most of them admitted cheating, stealing and sexual misconduct. At the same time they claimed to be good young people. When was there such a decline in moral integrity? How long have young people and adults allowed their consciences to become so callous? We browbeat our conscience, we flatter it, we do anything to get what we want—like getting to be chosen to enter the college of our choice, or like parents who, to please their own ego, press their children into molds of mamma's choosing, no matter what.

As people hoping to age with integrity, it is difficult for us to do that when selfishness is allowed to lower the floor of ethical and moral behavior in our homes, businesses, and daily living. We hold tightly to our ideals but compromise on our practice. If it's good for business, let's do it. If liquor will bring more trade, let's sell it. A commercial states that this kind of beer helps one have a "brighter tomorrow." Is the only choice that youths have between brands of tobacco? What about not smoking at all? It seems that a huge circumference of dishonesty and deceit has enveloped us. In short, in our time it is difficult to stay friends with our consciences.

So we have on our hands the herculean task of stemming this great tide of corruption, this decomposition of truth and right. The way to live longer, happier lives might well be to join in the battle against the stranglehold of advertising that suggests to the young that smoking is a manly and desirable habit. At this point, some hostility toward the media is in order. It will displease the media, but your conscience will smile.

19

KEEP ON KEEPING ON

Following is a list of my involvements that kept me 'keeping on.'

- After seven years as a pastor in Western North Carolina, during World War II, I was a volunteer chaplain, first in the Army Air Corps, then after those five years, in the US Air Force. Retiring after twenty years, I kept on going.
- "*The Mountains Are Happy*," my autobiography of 387 pages kept me occupied because I only used the hunt-and-peck system of typing. The next book, "*Prayers Jesus Might Have Prayed*," though less than one hundred pages, took a long time because I only wrote as I was inspired. I had a difficult time putting words in the mouth of Jesus, and did so only after limiting myself to ten restrictions. So here I am at nearly ninety-five and trying to put together this book entitled, "*Much Alive at Ninety-five*."
- What to do to keep on going? Mickey, my daughter, said she wanted me to buy her computer so that she could buy a newer model. I had been struggling with an electric typewriter but needed to re-type too much of my work. She told me that with a computer I could easily make corrections without retyping. That appealed to me.
- I was invited to become an associate pastor in a six thousand-member congregation. I retired from that staff after seventeen years in 1980. Three years later I retired from mandatory appointment by the bishop of my denomination in 1983. What to do next? How to keep on keeping on?

Public Institutions Committee,
Pikes Peak Council of Churches
19 January 1967

1. Services have been provided the year round at 3:00 p.m. Sundays at Pikes Peak Manor and Colonial Columns Nursing Homes.

2. Services were provided during the winter months at the Union Printers' Home at 3:00 p.m. on Sundays.
3. Devotional services have been led by various ministers at the Good Will Industries Plant on West Colorado Avenue on Monday mornings during the winter months.
4. Some pastors have provided sermons for the Men's Service Center of the Salvation Army as called upon.
5. Pastors of the Broadmoor Episcopalian Church and the Broadmoor Congregational Church have provided programming and counseling for the Zebulon Pike Youth Center.
6. Contact has been made with the management of the Memorial Hospital relative to a request to establish a volunteer chaplaincy program of weekly services and other pastoral ministries. An attractive chapel and organ plus altar appointments are on hand. This will be a primary objective for the New Year.
7. The chairman served on the Military Personnel Services Task Force of the Community Planning and Research Board and made a comprehensive study of the services being provided for the religious enrichment of servicemen and their families in local churches. This study showed that greater liaison between clergy and chaplains at the three military installations would result in more efficient ministries for these people. Last spring the committee sent rosters of the three of the thirty-three military chaplains to all the local ministers, priests and rabbis. Likewise, each chaplain sent a copy of the Council roster of local pastors and churches. A letter of each group encouraged personal contacts on a denominational basis and greater utilization of mutual resources.
8. The chairman has attended two meetings of the Public Institutions Committee of the Colorado Council of churches in Denver.
9. As a result of a study made earlier this spring, it was discovered that there are many nursing homes where

services are being conducted by churches and ministers who are not members of the Pikes Peak Council. No information as to the adequacy of these programs is available.

10. I cooperated with the Family Counseling Service, Mental Health Association, and Mental Health Center, in planning a series of six seminars for the training of local clergy to be better counselors. These were held at First Methodist Church on six Mondays, 8:30-12:30 beginning 19 April 1966.
11. The appreciation of the committee is expressed for the many, many members of the clergy, and members of the Council Staff, who assisted in the above work so willingly and so well.

Philip L. Green, Chair.

Martin Luther King Memorial Education Fund
Founded by the Pikes Peak Council of Churches in 1968

At its Fourth Annual Dinner Meeting held at St. George's recently, the Martin Luther King Memorial Education Fund, an organization established in memory of Dr. Martin Luther King, Jr., elected the following officers:

Dr. Julian P. Tatum, President
Mr. John Holley, Vice President
Rev. Philip Green, Treasurer
Mrs. Beatrice Jackson, Secretary

Since its inception in 1968 the Martin Luther King Fund has received many applications from economically disadvantaged youth and adults who have wished to continue their education and gain marketable skills. Despite its limited financial resources the King Fund has helped a considerable number of blacks, whites, Chicanos and other deserving applicants.

Members of the King Fund board were among the first to urge Colorado colleges and universities to set up special programs to provide greater opportunity for economically disadvantaged youth and adults.

Applicants have received amounts varying from $15.00 to $200.00. Many applicants have been helped a number of times. Much of the assistance has been used for tuition and books. The King Fund has received most of its contributions from Colorado Springs churches. Other contributions have been given by individuals, board members, and various business firms.

Some of the educational institutions attended by those who received assistance include:

Academy of Hair Design
Adams State College
Blair Business College
The Colorado College
Colorado State University
El Paso Community College
Loretto Heights College
University of Colorado Boulder
University of CO Colo. Springs
University of Denver
University of Northern CO
Morristown College
Southern Colorado State College
Trinidad State Junior College
Western State College

- Thirty-six pastors from the USA and I went for preaching missions in Mexico in 1970. During those two weeks we were assigned to various churches to conduct evangelistic services. I was assigned to Templo Bethel in Tepititla where, in only four of the nine services, an interpreter was assigned. I had served as a chaplain in Madrid, Spain, 1954-'57, so the planners must have thought I didn't need one all the time. I struggled with my limited vocabulary but the people were very kind and leaned forward to supply words that escaped me. The Holy Spirit helped me.
- The late Dr. E. Stanley Jones founded The Christian Ashram. Beginning in 1971, I was very active in the Colorado Christian Ashram and have been ever since.

- In 1974, I was responsible for a conference on Ministerial Excellency, to which the clergy of large churches were invited. It was interdenominational and interfaith. A hundred and forty-one came from all across America. Dr. Seward Hiltner of Princeton University was the Dean, and Bishop Wheatley was one of the principal lecturers. He later paid me a "warm fuzzy". He wrote;

  "I am indebted to you for elevating the position of associate pastor to the level of distinguished and distinctive service where it properly belongs."

- The Bicentennial of our nation and the Centennial of the State of Colorado were celebrated in events and ceremonies in 1976. There were no plans for the religious communities to celebrate the freedom to worship God according to one's choice. I protested and was given permission to promote something, provided no single group like the Association of Churches did it, and that there were no funds available to do it. With the wholehearted cooperation of all the religious groups, I was chairperson of "The Grand Festival of Faith Celebration" that was held in Wasson High School Stadium. We had a 600-voice union of choirs for three great numbers, the symphony, and a nationally reputed speaker for this two-hour event. The complete 'program' is re-printed in the back of this book.

Church-Sponsored Sunday Dinners
for Senior Citizens—1976
(12:00 noon-2:00 p.m. beginning soon
at the Acacia Apartment Hotel), Colorado Springs, CO
RE—Information Report to the Pikes Peak Association
of Churches

The Ad Hoc Committee, which has been in the process of involving nine downtown churches in a Sunday extension of inexpensive meals for senior citizens and sponsored jointly by interested church people, (with the help of federal funds under Title 7 money, and the Acacia Meals program, in cooperation with the Colorado Springs Housing Authority), has been successful in getting the following churches to sponsor a meal every two months:

St Mary's Catholic, Grace Episcopal, First Christian, First United Methodist, First Lutheran, Immanuel Lutheran, First Presbyterian, First Congregational (UCC).

Although, at this moment, the meals have not begun to be served, it is hoped that all co-ordinations will be completed so that meals under this wonderful arrangement can begin in February.

Dr. George Fagan, Co-Chairman
Rev. Philip L. Green, Co-Chairman
(Note: As of 2010—nearby churches are still serving meals)

- I was one of nineteen pastors from the USA who went for a month to Liberia, West Africa, in 1977, to attend their Annual Conference, visit their churches and a workshop to teach pastors and key lay persons how to conduct New Life Missions. Some of us visited Ganta, an outpost mission station for lepers. A few years after our visit, there was an insurrection. The head of the president, a Baptist pastor, was cut off. The vice president was our bishop who "happened" to be in the USA at the time. Did someone tip him off?
- Being chairperson of the Temple Hills Conference Camp near Woodland Park, I took advantage of being there to found the "Aspen Glow Camp for Seniors" of the Annual Conference. It was during a week late in September 1981-'84.

Ecumenical Social Ministries, Pikes Peak Association of Churches September 13, 1982

SUBJ: Letter of Affirmation
RE: Ecumenical Social Ministries (ESM)
TO:
Rev. Dr. Robert A. Frykholm, Senior pastor, First Baptist Church
Rev. Father Dennis Grabrian, Senior Pastor, St Mary's Catholic Church
Rev. Dr. Warren M. Hile, Senior Pastor, First Christian Church
Rev. Robert G. Hewitt, Rector, Grace Episcopal Church
Rev. Dr. Jerry M. Jordan, Senior Pastor, First Congregational Church
Rev. Dr. Paul R. Peel, Senior pastor, First Lutheran Church
Rev. John H. Stevens, Senior Pastor, First Presbyterian Church
Rev. Dr. O. Gerald Trigg, Senior Pastor, First United Methodist Church

FROM: Rev. Philip L. Green, President, Pikes Peak Association of Churches

1. The bold step you have taken in bringing into reality ECUMENICAL SOCIAL (WELFARE) MINISTRIES prompts me to express great affirmation and appreciation for your action. By doing this cooperatively and ecumenically you have affirmed that there are things churches can do better together than in an uncoordinated way.
2. I was present for the official opening of ESM Center at 514 North Nevada Avenue and was both pleased and excited that this united ministry was becoming a reality.
3. Of course, many of the ministries of ESM were already being rendered, but by piecemeal, individualistic kind of way. CARE and SHARE ministries, and FISH of the Pikes Peak Association of Churches were already

cooperating in ministries to persons in need. Only some of you were "in" on this now. Now you have all made a major commitment to do a better job by being responsible together.

4. You and your churches have also been carrying the responsibility of providing funds and personnel for SUNDAY DINNERS FOR SENIOR CITIZENS at the Acacia Hotel. On behalf of the Association of Churches (that handles the funds for this needed ministry), I express appreciation that you continue to see in this outreach an answer to "whatever you did for one of the least of these brothers of mine, you did for me."
5. Thanks are extended through you to all those in your congregations who share the vision of ESM, CARE and SHARE, and FISH. Most Sincerely Yours, Philip L. Green, President

- In 1984 I continued in a ministry I incorporated as "Pastoral Care Evangelism." Under that ministry, on the fourth Sunday of October, another retired minister and I founded a fellowship called the Flying-W-Ranch-Church-in-the-Making. It became a church of more than three hundred members and is thriving under follow-on pastors who took over when my wife collapsed into a state of near-unconsciousness. During her nineteen months in a nursing home—unable to speak or move her arms and legs, I made three brief visits a day to let her know she was the most precious person in my more than fifty years of life. However, I kept on doing the work I had chosen.
- In 1986, the Rev. Dr. Charles Kinder came to visit me in September. He was the President of The Foundation for Evangelism of our denomination. He wanted me to consider becoming the Rocky Mountain Regional Director of that organization. I was, at that time, divesting myself of a number of responsibilities and told him I would only be interested in something really important to me. But I knew and admired the founder of that organization, Dr. Harry Denman. Also, the word "evangelism" struck a sympathetic note in my consciousness and in my soul. Agreement occurred. One of

the objectives of the organization was to raise funds to put an E. Stanley Chair of Evangelism in all our seminaries. The committee I put together helped to get a chair at the Iliff School of Theology in Denver.

- At age seventy-four, I was asked by my denomination to pastor Avondale United Methodist Church sixty miles from home. Some of my retired colleagues told me I was under no obligation to do that. They said I was nine years beyond retirement age. I was reluctant to take that challenge at my age and so far from home. However, when I was interviewed by leaders of that church, they surprised me by saying they wanted me to come in spite of my being seventy-four. So I took it and spent six and a half of the happiest years of my life. When I was eighty, I asked to "retire again."
- When I was back in Colorado Springs full time again, the pastor of the Korean United Christian Church (non-denominational) had a few people who wanted to have a worship service in English. He was unable to do that because his English was inadequate. He asked my help in finding a minister to do an English-language service at 9:30 a.m. Finally, being unable to find anyone for that spot, he asked if I would do it. So I became the English-language pastor of that church until I was eighty-five, at which time I was able to find a replacement.

My New Life/Key Event Ministries 1965-'96
(An affiliate of the General Board of Discipleship of the United Methodist Church)

- ➢ Sept 1965—Director, Pikes Peak Sub-District New Life Mission, with Rev. Bill Peckham of Nashville, for Methodist and United Brethren Churches at First Methodist Church in Colorado Springs, CO.
- ➢ May 1967—Arranged a New Life Mission at First UMC with Rev. Dr. Larry L. Lacour as the evangelist in Colorado Springs.

- Feb 1971—Directed a New World Mission at First UMC in Colorado Springs with Bishop Alejandro Ruiz of Mexico City as the evangelist.
- Jan 1977—Assisted Rev. Dr. Eddie Fox of the Board of Evangelism in Nashville, to train a group of native clergy and laity in New Life Mission techniques, in Liberia, West Africa.
- Sept 11-13, 1979—Attended a New Life Mission orientation by
- Dr. Eddie Fox at St. Andrews United Methodist Church in Littleton/Denver, CO.
- Sept 1986—The evangelist for a New Life Mission in Huntsville, AL.
- Oct 1987—The evangelist for a New Life Mission in Cincinnati, OH.
- Mar 3-5, 1989—Attended a New Life Upgrade Conference in Nashville, TN.
- Oct 1989—Conducted a New Life Mission at Wesley UMC, Pueblo, CO.
- Oct 21-24, 1996—Attended a Retooling Conference on New Life Missions in Nashville, TN.

- The Pikes Peak Association of Churches had been the "Council" of Churches. Because there was disagreement locally with the policies of the National Council of Churches, the name was changed and ties to the national Council were cut. Three times I was elected president. As a member, I served as Treasurer of the Martin Luther King Memorial Education Committee; Garden of the Gods Easter Sunrise Committee, and the Hospital and Institutions Task Force. That body was responsible for funds and goods for the needy who came to the churches for help.

20

NEVER A DISCOURAGING WORD

At Whiteman Air Force Base at Knob Noster, Missouri, 1957-'60, I happily received "never a discouraging word." The efficiency ratings were numerically near the top and the word pictures were enviable. At the end of my stay there, I received the best of news.

"Chaplain Carpenter wants you at the Air Force Academy."

Carp, as he was affectionately known, was the former Chief of Air Force Chaplains and had chosen to remain on duty as the Staff Chaplain at the recently established Air Force Academy. "*Wants me*" were magic words with me any time, but especially so from one who, for many years, had been at the top.

At the end of each rating period, my commanders boosted my career and my ego (too much), with the following words:

(NOTE: Most of these evaluations were not shown to me but sent through military channels to files that were copied later at my request, years later, and sent to me privately).

Sept. 1, 1957-Aug.12, 1958: Colonel William C. Lewis wrote:

> *"Chaplain Green is held in high esteem by everyone. His contribution to the morale and welfare of the base has been outstanding. His pleasing personality, military bearing and polite mannerisms are the best. He has furthered the religious education program by meeting people socially and joining the various social activities of the base. He is a very sincere and genuine person who mixes well and yet maintains the dignity of a religious leader. I consider him to be one of three outstanding chaplains I have known in the service."*

Reviewing Officers Report: Colonel Harold E. Humfeld, Commander:

> *I frequently discuss morale, welfare and religious status of personnel under my command with this officer and therefore am well acquainted with his performance of duty, which I must state is superb. He is a dedicated "sky pilot" who has the respect and admiration of all officers and airmen assigned this station.*
>
> Aug. 13, 1958-May 31, 1959
> David A. Freeman, Colonel, Base Commander
>
> *Chaplain Green is an outstanding chaplain in every respect. He is tolerant of those who do not practice strict religious discipline but maintains a fine example as a religious leader under all circumstances. His pleasant personality readily makes him friends against the confidence of military personnel and civilians. He enjoys the confidence and respect of his co-workers and subordinates alike.*
>
> June 1, 1959-June 30, 1960
> Colonel Walter F. Todd, Base Commander, 340th Bomb Wing
>
> *Chaplain Green is friendly, helpful, kind, well-humored and pleasant. He has a very even disposition. He and his family are wonderful citizens of our community. He keeps the grounds surrounding his quarters immaculate and has beautified them from his own personal funds to the extent that in two different years he won first place in the annual base beautification contest.*
>
> *With a minimum of command guidance, he planned and directed the dedication and acceptance ceremonies of the new chapel. They were extremely well received, not only by the attending personnel from the base, but by Major General Finnegan, Chief of Chaplains of USAF, and Colonel*

> *Slivinski, both of whom complimented me on the chapel and the professional and competent manner in which the total program was handled. Chaplain Green's greatest strength is that he practices the principles of Christianity every day of the week and not just on Sunday. He is a good man and this basic goodness shines through and favorably colors everything he does.*

Soon after leaving the Air Force Academy and retiring from military service, the Rev. Dr. Ben F. Lehmberg invited me to become his associate pastor. He had built up First United Methodist Church in Colorado Springs from 3,000 to over 6,000 members. I was flattered, of course, as it was a much greater responsibility than I ever expected. As his associate, he wanted me to share his very heavy load. First, he asked that I begin as Minister of Outreach (Evangelism), which duty I performed for five years.

In the midst of that period, he was hospitalized with a heart attack. His doctor advised him to off-load as many of his less necessary duties as possible and give them to me and the other members of his staff. He began getting better after a few weeks and was sent home to convalesce further. In October, while he was "out of the harness," he wrote me a note, as follows:

> *Dear Phil,*
>
> *I don't have the words in my vocabulary to express my true appreciation for the way that you have managed things so beautifully and loyally during these past weeks while I've been engaged in the job of getting well. I guess there isn't a better word than the word "Thanks." So, even though I am sure it is an overused word and often used carelessly, I'll use it again and I hope with special meaning. Thanks, thanks a million! With sincere good wishes, Ben.*

Bishop R. Marvin Stuart was in the Denver Area of the Rocky Mountain Annual Conference during the time Dr. Ben had this attack. I contacted him immediately with that disturbing news. He came to the church's assistance by sending outstanding preachers to fill our pulpit for a few weeks.

Dear Phil,

How I wish I could adequately express my appreciation to you for the great way you have been moving in to fill the gap at First Church! Again you have been most thoughtful in keeping me informed all along. I am deeply grateful to you for this. I thank God many times that you were there and I am sure the Church feels the same way. I feel you are a tower of strength to the Staff and to the Church and I know God will strengthen you to face this heavy responsibility.
Most Sincerely, R. Marvin Stuart

Thank you, Phil, for your part in helping us have what I believe was an outstanding Conference. Signed, R. Marvin Stuart

While Dr. Lehmberg was trying in vain to recover from his first heart attack, on September 23, 1966, Bishop Stuart wrote:

Dear Phil,

You and your cohorts there have done a tremendous job. I was thrilled at the spirit back of your letter and with the communication you sent out to all the Staff of the Church. I know that you have been a tower of strength through these critical days, and I thank God that you have been there. Most Sincerely, R. Marvin Stuart

Rev. Dr. Benjamin Franklin Lehmberg, Senior Pastor, First United Methodist Church, Colorado Springs, CO (1950-'66). During those years he built the membership up from around 3,000 to more than 6,000, built a wonderful new sanctuary and added a much needed massive north wing. I came to know him while I was a chaplain at the USAF Academy nearby. We worked together on a welcome brochure sent to cadets and permanent party people at the Academy. "Dr. Ben," as he was affectionately known, surprised me by asking me to become the Associate Pastor of his huge congregation. I was most pleased to learn that he thought so well of me but saddened to realize I could not accept at that time.

On February 7, 1963, he wrote me a letter in which he said:

> *Dear Phil,*
>
> *I am still interested in talking with you about First Methodist Church, Colorado Springs.*

On February 13, I answered:

> *Dear Ben,*
>
> *Thank you for your letter of Feb. 7, which was received with both pleasure and surprise—pleasure, because it revived a lost hope, surprise, because I thought you had long ago filled the vacancy in your staff. I am definitely interested in joining your wonderful staff.*

After future exchanges of letters and telephone calls, I asked my bishop in the Western North Carolina Conference to transfer my membership to the Rocky Mountain Conference. In June of 1963, six weeks before my Air Force retirement in the grade of colonel, I attended my new Annual Conference and was appointed as Associate Pastor.

Ashamed, Unworthy

In view of all the things listed below, I consider myself not worthy of the opportunities that have been mine, and of the many expressions of affirmation and praise that have been lavishly given to me.

I was barely able to finish high school after having changed schools four times, and having to take six solid subjects the senior year. I wound up having to complete and deliver a paper after the graduation ceremony.

My piecemeal completion of college courses showed that I wound up near the bottom of my class—39th of 41. This was not because I was unable to do the studies, but for other poor reasons. My thesis for graduation was not completed until after graduation and I was graduated during the summer of 1936. Some of my courses were done at a non-accredited school.

My father believed I had potential as an evangelistic preacher and gave my name to the officials at a church called City Temple in Baltimore. He had preached there a week and they liked him. I had been a successful "country" pastor in the mountains of North Carolina for nearly four years at the time I was invited to preach at that evangelistic center. The people there were seasoned Christians and used to being challenged to a better life in Christ. For me it was a poor fit. I did not know how to preach to people like that". They seemed pleased with my efforts and gave me an honorarium and a new suit of clothes. But I felt I had been a failure there.

Once again my father had misjudged my talents. I had directed some of the music at Camp Free, NC, a 10-day meeting under a tabernacle that he had founded in 1921. I failed to meet the expectation of the evangelist to whom I had been recommended by my father. So that closed one avenue to that kind of ministry. But I was a success as a singer in duets, trios, and quartets for the Bible College my father had founded in 1932.

Years later, my father was aging to the point of putting his mantle as president of John Wesley College on someone else. In his generous spirit he offered me the opportunity to do that. My poor showing in Guilford College convinced me that again my father had misjudged the extent of my capabilities. At the time I was on the way to success as a military chaplain. So I turned my father down. Ten years down a career as an Air Force Chaplain, I was offered the position of Vice President of Pfeiffer College by a PhD I had known years before in Franklin, NC. What a pity I had too poor an educational background to accept that offer. But I was pleased that Rev. Dr. J. Lem Stokes thought that highly of me.

When I began to enjoy a few successes, I absolutely couldn't let them make me into someone I wasn't. I remembered what the Apostle Paul said about my model, Jesus:

> *"who being in the form of God, thought it not robbery to be equal with God, but made himself of no reputation, and took upon him the form of a servant, and was made in the likeness of men: and being formed in fashion as a man, he humbled himself, and became obedient unto death, even the death on the cross."* (Phil 2:6-8) KJV

Humility—*"Humble yourself under the mighty hand of God, and he will exalt you."* James 4:10 KJV

When I began to think about the truly great men and women who blessed the generations of their day, my few accomplishments dwindled to nearly nothing. As a result I became ashamed that I had not accomplished more for my Lord.

In 1986 I became a member of "The Twelve" at the headquarters of the United Methodist Foundation for Evangelism at Lake Junaluska, NC. Like the other eleven, I gave a thousand dollars a year to keep the organization up and running. That amount added up to a tidy sum ($21,000) and I toyed with the thought of being proud of myself. That is, until I learned about a layman and his wife who, out of their wealth, gave the Foundation several million dollars.

That invidious comparison burst my balloon of pride into a thousand pieces. The words of *Isaiah 5:21* put me back on the track toward a humble spirit, i.e. *"Woe unto them that are wise in their own eyes and prudent in their own sight"*. Then I remembered a warning about comparisons by the Apostle Paul who said, *"And you, comparing your selves among your selves, are not wise"*. My mother's wise quote hit me squarely on the nose, *"Self brag is half scandal"*.

SECTION V

Being a survivor during the desperate times in your life is a necessity. There are those who give up and suffer the results. I survived a burst appendix in 1934; pneumonia and dehydration in the sub-tropic of Liberia in 1977; diabetes 1978-2010; two prostate operations 1990, 2003; two blood clots 1997, 2009; shingles 1996; hiatus hernia 1987-2005; two hip replacements 2005; three falls on icy pavement. In 1918-'19 the world-wide Spanish flu pandemic killed millions. I was age four and my six siblings and parents and I all survived.

I was the Minister of Pastoral Care in a mega-church for twelve years as I began to age. That was a good time for me to help many people who were aging. It was a learning situation. When a former senior minister of the church died, he and I realized he and I had been born the same year. That brought me up abruptly with my own mortality. My first wife of fifty-two years collapsed into unconsciousness four months after our 50th anniversary. She regained consciousness five weeks later and lived for nineteen months, unable to speak or move her arms and legs, in a nearby care facility. This also was a learning experience.

During some years of my life I have "played second fiddle." Some think I did that quite well. But several of those years were at the top. I was in charge. In Madrid, Spain, I was the only Protestant chaplain for three years. I had to take charge and initiate a full chapel worship program including space, equipment, all volunteer personnel, Sunday school teachers, chancel and youth choirs and everything else. I was in charge. In most churches I served I was in charge. In 1970 I was elected the national president of the Military Chaplains Association. Twice I was the interim (acting) senior pastor of a 6,000-member congregation.

I sincerely believe that God is to be thanked and given the glory for all he has done through me.

Faith, hope and love cannot be seen. Hebrews 11 clearly states that what we see and consider real and touchable, was made by the Creator whose powerful word did it all. I have made the words of that chapter the inspirational guide of my life.

21

SURVIVING THE ODDS

I was once caught in a Colorado blizzard! The storm had begun during a sermon I had persisted in preaching 56 miles out in the extreme southeast corner of El Paso County in February 1965. Edison-Leader Methodist Church, two miles from the nearest house on the plains, was an additional duty for the second, third, and fourth year on the staff of First Methodist Church. District Superintendent Hugh Pritchett had persuaded the Rev. Dr. Ben F. Lehmberg that he could spare me for Sunday afternoon and night duty and sermon as pastor of that 35-member church. The people had accepted me well—well enough to look at the gathering clouds that winter, even before the service, and recommend that we not have a service.

I had driven an hour to be there, so it was easy for me to say that it would be all right for me to give the sermon I had prepared. I have long forgotten what it was about, but I will never forget what I learned from not listening to what the "dry-landers" of the plains thought best. Storms were no threat to me. After all, hadn't I already driven in a snowstorm across Wolf Creek Pass—the most treacherous pass in the Colorado Rockies—and in a VW Bug at that? And hadn't I spent a winter in Upper Michigan where snow storms hid the car in my driveway so I had to dig out and tie a red banner to my radio aerial so that passing cars could see me coming out of the driveway? That's enough now for my poor knowledge of a blizzard on the plains.

During that brief service (my sermon was not long), snow had begun to fall, and two inches covered the cars and the road. Large fluffy flakes were flying in the wind, "a northern." I led the way past Mrs. Arlie Hamilton's turn-off. Clarence and Rella Correll drove in my tracks the nine miles to their turn-off. I gave a parting honk on the horn as I drove on alone to the crossroad where I turned west. The VW Bug seemed to do well in the storm until that turn. Now the snow was even more blinding. It was difficult to see where I was in the road. With high beams on it was worse. Parking lights were insufficient. Soon I found myself off the road and high-centered on the left-hand side. I was stranded and partly in the ditch. I had a shovel but it did no good. Every shovel-full of snow was swirled by the wind right back into my face. What to do?

The VW had nearly a tank of gas so I decided to leave the motor running and the heater on. I would spend the night right there, I decided. Then, it occurred to me that the under part of the car had dragged the ground. What if I became asphyxiated and never woke up? I couldn't ask a neighbor to let me call my wife for two reasons. There was no neighbor and my wife was visiting Marcia, our daughter, in Minneapolis, MN. No one would be alerted to come looking for me.

I didn't know how far I had traveled west from the crossroad. I knew there was a store there. Maybe I should head out for there. I had on a suit coat and a light topcoat. They could possibly keep me from freezing if I were not too far from the store. When I turned off all car lights, I made a happy discovery. The moon above the clouds gave enough light to see when I was in the road. It also made it possible for me to see a short distance on either side of the road. I soon came to a house. It was unmistakably a house where someone lived. Making my way into the yard and up to the front porch I noticed there were no lights. What if everyone had gone visiting? Or were already sleeping out the storm? There was no response to my urgent knock and no light came on. I cried out that I was freezing. There was still no response.

I decided that no one was home and finally found a wagon wheel spoke in the yard to use to break the glass in the upper half of the door. The screen door was already open. With bated breath, expecting (but not hoping) that my head might be blown off by fearful people believing their home was being robbed. I scraped the jagged edges of glass from the door and climbed in. The house was vacant. There was no electricity as the switches proved. There was a stove, but no wood. I had no match even if I could free some planks from a wall. The sweat from my efforts began to turn cold from the frigid house.

There was no other alternative but to try to make it to the store at the crossroad. As I struggled through the storm, I remembered hearing about a man who had tried so hard to save himself that he had a heart attack and died. So I slowed in my struggles against the wind and snow. The light of the moon above the storm clouds made me reasonably sure that I would be able to know where the road was. I didn't want to be like the man who started to the barn in a blizzard, got lost, and froze to death. What if I made it to the store and no one was there? I quickened my pace, then thought better of it, and slowed down again. No heart attack for me.

The store was locked and the house next door was locked also. I learned later that the man who ran the store was stranded somewhere else in the same storm. What to do now? I was becoming frantic until I remembered that becoming frantic could kill me. Then I thought, "It couldn't be more than a mile south to Clarence Correll's house. Could I make it? I must try—but not too hard. I was thankful that the north wind at my back helped push me along. When I finally arrived at the Corrells' home, Clarence was out on the porch sizing up the storm. He was very surprised to see me. I was overjoyed to be safe from the blizzard. He took me in and put me to bed. The electric bed covers felt delicious. I was soon thoroughly thawed out. The only physical damage I sustained was that the top of one of my ears was frozen—a matter of little consequence, thank God!

Later, I paid to have the damaged house repaired. Everyone seemed happy that "the preacher" had made it safely to shelter in time. From that time on, I listened to the wisdom of those who knew how dangerous an on-the-plains blizzard could be. They were wise in other ways, too. Mrs. Virgil Gieck, and others, helped me write the 50-year history of Edison-Leader Methodist Church for its 50th Anniversary celebration.

In 2005, with two hip replacements three months apart, and the death of my wife, Helen, I came face-to-face with two questions: (1) "Could a nonagenarian with a broken hip recover?", because past experience indicated that in most such cases, it was the first of steps down to life's end. (2) The next question was, "Do I want to get well?" It was a question I needed to face and answer honestly. I had held onto the top of five generations for several years and wanted to remain there. Eleven great grandchildren and nine great great-grandchildren beckoned me to hang on a while longer. Not reluctantly, I decided to try to get well and survive that challenge.

So here I am at nearly ninety-five (in 2009) and eagerly awaiting a twelfth great-great grandchild on the family tree. I'm already beginning to think about what I want to do in my second century. Until then, I will finish this book and continue my prayer of dominant desire, "Lord, use me!"

Helen, my second wife of fifteen years, had her own health challenges. As a child in Chicago, she had a disease that prevented her from the physical activities of her age group. She also needed to sleep in a tent out of doors where her parents were seeking to escape tuberculosis. In mid-life she was brought low with paralysis, at which time she bravely fought and won her war against that crippling disease. When her husband died, she had the challenge of caring for her mother until she was almost one hundred years of age. When she was past seventy, she felt called to use her great talent in communications to enter the ministry in the Presbyterian Church. Before she completed her formal training for that challenge, we became friends in her widowhood and mine, and married. Eleven years into that relationship, during which time at age seventy-four, I was pastor of Avondale United Methodist Church near Pueblo, CO, that most talented woman started down the four-year road of dementia.

She never knew at which point along that continuance she began passing downward. She even forgot that I was her husband, and called me the name of her first husband who had died twenty years earlier, or her father. She knew always that I was a person of interest to her. At one time she confidentially suggested that it would be very nice if we'd plan a simple ceremony and get married. For three of those years she needed the additional care given in Assisted Living, and later even more care in a nursing facility for those with extreme dementia and Alzheimer's disease. I was accompanying my son at a workshop at the Crystal Cathedral in CA when a call came from a nurse saying that she was about to end her earthly pilgrimage and would I say a word on the phone to Helen. I said, "Hello, Helen, I love you!" Though she was unconscious, experts say that the last part of one to go is hearing. I hope she heard me. Thirty minutes later she crossed over into God's great tomorrow where she entered that "great cloud of witnesses" of the heroes of faith.

In 1977, I was included by the General Board of Discipleship, to go with some thirty other clergy, to Liberia in West Africa at the invitation of the Methodist bishop there. He had attended some sessions of the New Life Mission in America and wanted his pastors and key lay leaders to know about how to plan and use it.

During that month I became very ill and spent two days in a hospital in Monrovia, the Capitol. My wife was with me and was very solicitous. She'd honor my request to walk a little down to the beach where there was a strong breeze blowing. At the beach I was disappointed with that breeze. It was not a fresh breeze as I had hoped. Rather, it was from off the Sahara Desert. The weather was so hot in that tropical country that I found it difficult to get enough water, even warm water. Food would not stay down. I "just knew" I was coming down with some such disease that came from the tsetse fly or some other foreign malady.

Mercifully, the President allowed Lois and me to leave Liberia a couple of days earlier because of my illness. Entering and leaving that country was only permitted by the President. I was one of those who had been invited by the Bishop, who was the Vice President of Liberia. We flew out on an airline called British Caledonia. When we reached the altitude of fresh cool air we went peacefully to sleep on the way to London. What a relief!

I was still very weak the ten days we were in England, so weak that just getting up out of a chair was a major undertaking We got rooms in the hotel where most Americans stayed while in London and contacted the physician at the American Embassy. He kept close tabs on me the whole time. I was very relieved when he finally told me why I was so ill and had lost fifteen pounds. He said I had pneumonia and dehydration. I was so relieved on the flights back to the USA and Colorado Springs, CO. I survived that ordeal, thankfully.

The next year I learned from a USAF doctor that I had diabetes. I had driven up there to a military hospital during a New Life Mission in Cincinnati to which I had flown from Colorado, because the pastor schedules to fill that spot had a death in the family. I was needed there for I had been trained and was the only one available at that time. The type of diabetes was not the worst variety, but was capable of becoming worse.

The danger points of a person with diabetes are: (1) Feet and legs. Watch for sores. Get a technician to trim your toenails. If a sore gets ahead of you as it has of me, doctor it fast. I failed to care immediately on my right heel that had blistered and peeled to the quick. For several months the nurse, my daughter and two hours-a-day helpers from "Right At Home" have worked together to turn the sore around to healing status, saving me from the disaster of losing that foot. (2) Kidneys and urinary system. An examination of my kidneys showed that they were badly damaged. Who would want a kidney machine each week!? The last word of the doctor was that they would last until my death which, at my age as a late octogenarian, would not be long. (3) Eyes. I am glad that I have survived transplants in both eyes and can see to read as usual, watch television, and enjoy the beauties of nature.

For the past twenty years, through diet, exercise and regular medication, the disease has been kept under control. So, at age ninety-five, I am surviving this challenge. In 1985, I had painful shingles, but with medication, I survived.

Beginning in 1987, I had the first bout with hiatus hernia. That affliction became untenable to the extent of my having to wait a long period of time before even water would go down my esophagus. But by skillful medical procedures, I am able to eat normally, hoping it will stay "fixed." Survived, again!

In the following year, 1988, I had vertigo. I had flown many times in the US Air Force but never had experienced the debilitating effects of vertigo. At its worst, I could not stand up or walk because of the dizziness and nausea. The verdict is still out on this survival but I haven't had it since 2001. It first hit me in 1988.

When I returned from a visit with some 220 other United Methodist leaders, to the Bible Lands including Istanbul, Athens and the Greek islands in 1990, I went to my doctor and said that the pain in my right hip had become excruciating. The trip abroad had been wonderful but very painful. He took x-rays of that part of my body and said, "Yes, the pain is in your hip but the cause of the pain is in your spine. A nerve in your lower back is pinched." He called it spinal stenosis. His son also was a doctor who agreed to do the necessary operation. Afterward, I had no pain in my hip until 2005 when I fell and broke that hip.

In the fall of 1990, a USAF Academy doctor found that my prostate sac was greatly enlarged and needed special attention. He operated through my lower abdomen and called it a super-pubic prostatectomy. He said he cut away part of that sac and gladdened my heart by telling me that the area was not malignant. In 2003, another doctor found it necessary to do a routine prostatectomy. There I was still not infected with cancer. Hallelujah!

In 1992, a blood clot was discovered on my left shin. I had been walking the dog with Helen in a nearby park when I felt pain in my left leg. After examining it, Helen said I should show it to a doctor. So, off I went to the Academy hospital. The doctor that examined me put me right to bed and started a blood-thinning medicine. He said, *"That clot could break loose, pass through your heart to your lungs and kill you!"*

After treatment in the hospital a week or so, I was asked to leave military care and find a civilian doctor in Colorado Springs. I found Dr. Scott Sickbert who took me on and continued the blood-thinner until it was safe to discontinue it. He told me that it was not necessary to remove the clot, that the human body would make another channel to my foot. And it has. Am I glad to survive that threat!

In 2002, in a minor auto accident, the seatbelt dislocated my left shoulder. A month after Helen died in January 2005, I tripped on the edge of a carpet at a US Post Office near Peterson Air Force Base, requiring a right hip replacement and three weeks in a rehabilitation facility at Healthsouth. Ten weeks later at home, I fell again, breaking the same hip further down. That necessitated another hip replacement, time in rehabilitation, and follow-up help at home for several weeks. (See first paragraph).

In 2009, I was hospitalized for anemia and urinary tract infections needing two blood transfusions. Earlier there was an examination of my sleeping needs. I was found to have sleep apnea with a recommendation that, at night, I needed to have oxygen.

In 2007, the physician took x-rays of my aching neck and said that I needed an operation on three vertebrae. He recommended against that operation because I was past ninety years of age, but would operate if I asked him to. I elected not to have it, but I do suffer with it. It's a constant low level of hurting (1 to 3) except when prone. In an auto or bus on the way to church Sundays, it moved up to 4 and 5. I don't like it, but I have chosen to live with it. I want to keep on surviving.

But my bladder began giving me a challenge. Enuresis is not a pleasant thing. The medic measured the remainder of the urine remaining in my bladder after emptying and found much too much. He put me on a catheter for three weeks. He tried changing it to three times a day, then twice a day. I was sent home to personally change it at that level. In time, I reached the level of once a day. For a year now, it has been my happy privilege of no catheter at all. But I am still pestered with occasional urinary tract infections. But I am surviving, thank the good Lord!

I have survived three falls on icy pavements, bumping my head each time, and two falls from step-ladders one of which rendered me unconscious. In 1958, I attended a month of training for twenty-five USAF chaplains at the Hogg Foundation for Mental Health at the University of Texas in Austin. Near the end of training, we were entertained and royally fed at a Texas ranch. The trampoline in the recreation area was huge and a temptation to bounce up and down and try other stunts. I tried one and came down on one of my shoulders and neck, dislocating a middle-of-the-back vertebra. A doctor at a nearby military hospital replaced it during the overnight stay. I've not had any trouble there since that time.

The bumps and scrapes of childhood and youth were many, in my case. Walking with bare feet was hazardous. Stumped toes and injuries from stepping on a variety of things such as rusty nails and broken glass were the order of the day. Then going blackberry picking with bare feet and legs was an open invitation for snakes, especially rattle snakes, to strike you if you failed to heed the sound of its rattles. Somehow, God knows how, I survived all of these.

In the fourth grade at school, during the midmorning recess, I stepped in front of a classmate who went high in a swing. The seat assembly caught me just west of my left eye and cut a deep gash. My father was called. He took me to a doctor who sewed it up. Happily, it missed my eye.

During the years when cars had running boards on each side, I broke the rules and rode on the running board of another youth's car. We were in a wooded area and missing trees to save bent fenders. On the side of the car there was a broken stub protruding. The door handle was broken off. Regrettably, my hip was positioned over that stub when the car squeezed between two trees, pushing that stub into my hip. I never stood on a running board again.

Being on the basketball team in my junior high school year in 1930 in Wilmore, KY, we went for a game beyond Lexington. On the way home, the car, filled with six teens, was in a wreck at high speed. I was in the middle of the rear seat. The player on my left was badly injured and later died. Luckily, during the wreck, I lifted my playing gear from the floor and covered my face. A piece of flying glass hit my right hand that was on the other side of my gear and cut a deep gash on the knuckle at the juncture with my hand. It was sewed up and, in time, healed. I was glad I survived but was sorry that a teammate didn't.

Valdese High School had no football team. At noon, some of us played touch football. During one such session, I ran to catch a pass. That's when it happened. As I went high to catch the football, the head of one of the players from the opposite side hit me in the mouth, breaking one of the two front teeth in half. Later the tooth died. Some years later a third tooth began to grow there under the replacement, but at a severe angle. Being in service at that time, I went to a military dentist who found a cyst growing at that place. He had to chip the supernumerary away. He warned me that the cyst might cause trouble, and for me to keep an eye on it and report if didn't go away. It went away without becoming malignant. I was happy to survive.

While swimming the edge of the Catawba River near my home in Burke County, NC, I dived under the boat around which several of us were playing. I knew how to get out from under a boat, but every effort to locate the edge of the boat eluded me. I stopped struggling and began to give up, but another teenager pulled me out before I drowned.

I was a chaplain (sky pilot) in the USAF for twenty years. During that period, I flew in several kinds of aircraft. When in Germany, 1946-'49, the command chaplain of the European Air Force asked me to take the place of a chaplain who was on emergency leave for his Sunday worship service. A fighter pilot promised to fly me to that base. On that weekend, the weather was threatening. The pilot asked me whether or not I wanted to go to that base. I told him that I needed to conduct that service, so we took off. The plane was the kind that took off very fast and landed very fast. When we arrived near the airfield on which we would land, the pilot told me that the runway was made of a metal grill and was frozen over. He said his brakes would do no good. I asked him if there was any way he could safely land. He said he might try coming in and landing at the very beginning of the runway and reverse his propellers to slow the plane down, and "did I want to try that?." I said, "Let's try it." We overshot the runway but not enough to damage the plane. I fulfilled my duty, and, Gracias a Dios, I survived.

During a flight in a B-25 bomber from the east coast to home base in Enid, OK, we had a discussion about whether or not to stop and refuel in Memphis, TN. The pilot said we had enough gas without stopping but that it would be okay to refuel. We wheeled around and prepared to land. But when the light saying the landing gear was down would not come on, we didn't want the plane to wreck with all of us in it. So we headed for Vance AFB and home. As we neared our field, the pilot asked everyone except himself and the co-pilot to move to the utmost rear of the plane so that the extra weight there would keep the nose-wheel high until the speed of the craft was as slow as possible. We all hoped that the weight of the landing would make the wheel go down. And, whee! It did go down! Survived again! As I look back over nine and a half decades of my life, I can remember the desperate times of my life and the places and ages at which they happened.

Desperate Times

My Age

4 Older siblings threw me in the swimming hole. I couldn't swim. I was rescued.

5 When our touring car overturned and spilled us all out. I said to Papa, "Get a man! Get a hundred mans!"

10 When I heard adults say, "When you eat fish and drink milk at the same meal, you will die!" I had just done that.

11 When a school bully wouldn't let me pass, on the way home.

12 While hanging arms' length from the tabernacle rafters over a fresh sawdust pile, unable to climb back up and too afraid to turn loose.

19 When I learned that the car I was supposed to drive 120 miles through several towns had no brakes, I drove it anyway, but very carefully.

20 Stopped at night with a flat tire, a drunk driver sped by on the ditch side of the car, seriously injuring one of my passengers. I saw what might happen and jumped across the ditch to safety.

22 When waiting for the Bishop to read my name for my first pastorate.

23 My first funeral. I happened upon a funeral in progress at a schoolhouse. A member of my church saw me and rushed up to tell me that the minister of another denomination was 30 minute slate, and would I hold the service for a man whose name I didn't even know?

42 In Germany, lost at midnight near the infamous Dachau Extermination Camp.

43 When I awoke to discover that I had slept through the sermon time I had promised my chaplain supervisor to take for him so he could take a trip.

55 When I let the time for a retirement-home sermon pass by.

69 When I was called on to make a few remarks and pass the torch from the retiring ministers to those being ordained—with very short notice.

72 When I heard the voice of my wife of fifty years cry out from her bed one afternoon, "My heart is killing me!"

75 When I learned, on a long trip, that my top-drawer committee to raise funds for an E. Stanley Chair of Evangelism at the Iliff School of Theology had fallen apart because the faculty had jumped the gun and chosen someone not approved by the Foundation's Trustees.

84 When my second wife, Helen, couldn't breathe for a couple of minutes.

85 When a sudden serious attack of vertigo put me in bed, I realized that neither Helen nor I were neither able to drive for medicine—she because of temporary blindness, and I because of a sudden attack of vertigo. Shades of the future! What if I were to be struck down with something permanent?

90 With two hip replacements, could I recover and did I want to recover?

91 When my doctor advised me not to drive any more. That was a low blow but it relieved my three children.

94 When my kidney doctor put me on a catheter permanently, requiring a daily cleansing of my pubic areas by a nurse's aide.

22

LEARNING TO AGE WELL

While I was growing older, I was too busy to think about how to do that. What I was doing was helping others to grow old in workshops on death and dying. I began writing the 385 pages of my autobiography entitled, *The Mountains Are Happy*, in which was included a chapter entitled, *Sunset Years*, which was my age from eighty to eighty-six. It was high time for me to begin practicing some of the things I had been teaching others to do.

When I was seventy, I put together a twenty-year plan, hoping I would not dry up and blow away before ninety. I lost precious Lois after fifty-two years. Later I found and married Helen. She had a twenty-five-year plan. We both drank to her plan until her passing in 2005. I'll drink alone to the remaining years of her plan. Then I'll need to devise another plan—five-year? Ten-year? A ten-year-plan would put me well into my second century. A familiar quote is,

Age is a matter of mind—if you don't mind, it doesn't matter.

Learning to Grow Old with Lois

The love of my life for 52 years.
Lois Dawson Ritter-Green, 1907-1988

The aging phase of one's life is the time to look toward how to stay physically and mentally well. Now that I was in my early seventies, it was certainly time to begin taking serious thought about that reality. Lois and I drew up a list of all our possessions in preparation for a

Last Will and Testament for each of us. We were amazed at the total accumulation of things in each room, in the garage, in the storage area beneath part of the house. Then we settled down to enjoy the multitude of flowers in our front and back yards at 2215 Condor Street where we had lived for twenty-three years. Imagine getting to live in the same house that long instead of the many moves during twenty years as a chaplain in military service.

Four months later tragedy struck suddenly and with little warning. I had cancelled a New Life Mission engagement back east for the Board of Evangelism because, for the first time ever, Lois had said she wished I would not go. She wasn't feeling well enough to be alone for four days. How glad I was that I was at home the afternoon of her collapse. She had been in bed all day and had eaten little of the food I had brought to her bedside.

At about 4:15 p.m. on Thursday, October 26, I heard her cry for help and rushed up the half-stairs to our east bedroom. She was holding her chest and crying,

"My heart is killing me!"

I thought she'd be able to ride in our car to the hospital, so I began picking her up on her feet to help her to the car. But she collapsed into unconsciousness in my arms. And I laid her gently on the carpet. I reached for the phone and dialed 911. The attendant on the phone sounded the alarm for help and asked me to stay on the phone while she asked some questions. In five minutes the neighborhood fire station personnel showed up to do whatever they could as directed from 911. An ambulance arrived very soon and transported her to the emergency room at Memorial Hospital.

The emergency room doctor (Dr. Wong) called for extra help, because of her unconscious state indicated that everything possible needed to be done quickly. The doctors were perplexed because Lois did not have the symptoms of a heart attack. I had told them what she had said a few minutes earlier at home, "My heart is killing me." Dr. James Edgerton became her physician of record. He asked Dr. Graul to perform the necessary operations. They opened her chest and found that blood had filled the sac around her heart from a leaking aneurysm. Lois had taken an aspirin tablet that caused her face to become bloated and later allow the thinned blood to seep through the tissues. The doctors advised that Lois' chance of survival was about

20%, and did we want them to try to save her? We said, "*Yes, please try.*" So twice more within the first twenty-four hours they opened her chest to try to control the bleeding. In the first three days eighty-three units of blood, platelets and blood derivatives were used. Thank God for the many friends who were generous with their blood.

My daughter, Mickey Salimi, and son, Phil, Jr., and families came immediately and Marcia Thompson, our oldest daughter, flew in from Minnesota. Vern Swim, hospital chaplain, stayed close by during our times of decision.

A CAT scan and arteriogram were performed on the fourth day that revealed a partial blockage of the blood flow to her right arm and the right side of her head. A "simple" crossover bypass surgery was performed to get more blood to her right side. When she remained unconscious, Dr. Peters did an EEG on her head. It revealed a blood clot on the left side of her brain—that the upper brain was essentially dead—that she would never regain consciousness—and that, if she were to live, she would be in a vegetative state.

The big decision that needed to be made right away was whether or not to keep her all hooked up in intensive care to maintain life until she might come out of it, or to disconnect emergency life support systems and allow her to die naturally. Knowing that Lois would not like to live "like that," the family made a difficult decision. Whether or not she was able to hear us, we all verbally gave her permission to leave us, as we moved her into a private room. I'm not sure I was very convincing with my permission. A single tube to a vein in one of her hands remained to give her nourishment and liquids.

Amazingly, her lower brain did not deteriorate. Her blood pressure adjusted itself, her breathing and coughing ability stabilized, her kidneys continued to function (they had never failed). A week later on November 7, I conferred with Dr. Edgerton and told him that she didn't seem to be dying—that she was no worse than she was the week before. He agreed and told me that Lois was no longer in eminent danger of dying. He said that she might live in that condition for an indefinite period of time. The matter of allowing her to starve to death was out of the question.

In preparation for a move to a care facility, the doctor made a hole through her abdomen and inserted a feeding tube into her stomach. With that done, on November 11 an ambulance took her to Pikes

Peak Manor Health Care Center, one mile from our home. We asked a longtime friend and member of our church, Dr. Lewis A. Crawford, M.D., to become her physician of record and to care for her precious body until her death. We asked that she be kept comfortable, that life be maintained, but that no extraordinary measures be taken to prolong her life in that condition.

Seven months after her collapse, I made the following memo for the record;

1. Smiled at me, the nurses, friends on several occasions.
2. Closed her eyes during my bedside prayers without being asked.
3. Wept silently a few minutes after I told her how much it hurt me that she was unable to say back that she loved me, too.
4. Kept her eyes open hour-after-hour at a time . . . and upon hearing the voice of a visitor.
5. Opened eyes wide when shown family pictures.
6. Made vocal sounds with the movement of her lips as "MaMaMaMaMa" in a sort of mumble, and looked pleased at her accomplishment.
7. Smiled when I told her to hurry and get well and come home and show me how to roll my socks.
8. Turned her head on her pillow a significantly larger turn than heretofore.
9. Wiggled her toe at my request once.
10. Focused her eyes upon visitors and refocused then on another person farther away or in a different position.
11. Appeared to pay attention to the devotional reading and Bible verses.
12. Exercised her jaws and tongue more freely.
13. Blinked her eyes (only once) when shown a large sign which read,
14. "If You Can Read This, Blink Your Eyes"

At Christmas time, two months after Lois' collapse, I tell all of you now how such a trauma did not end with cancer or some other dread illness. I wrote the usual Christmas letter to more than one hundred and fifty people to whom we sent one each year, and added many more of the helpful people in the church where I served for seventeen years. The letter is shared:

> *Dear Loved Ones and Friends,*
>
> *Because of Lois' condition, this will be a very different Christmas from any heretofore. And yet I know that neither I at home on Condor Street, or Lois at Pikes Peak Manor Health Care Center, will be alone. Ever since her collapse into (five weeks of) unconsciousness, we both have been bathed in prayers, in loving concern, in tokens of affection constantly. Such an outpouring has both humbled and encouraged me, Philip, as Lois has yet to regain awareness. When and if she does so, you may be sure that she would reiterate my eternal gratitude for every prayer, visit, letter, card, telephone call; as well as every donation of blood, food, time devoted to answering the home telephone; and every meal "out", and other expressions of solicitude for the two of us and for the members of our family. In all my years of ministry I can not remember any family that has been the object of so much loving, caring, and undergirding as that given so freely to us. How can it ever be repaid? It cannot, but this Christmas letter hopes to begin doing so.*

At the same time, in view of Lois' present condition, I remembered how we had both agreed as an engaged couple fifty years beforehand that we would be happy with thirty or forty years together—if we could just have each other. Now I was faced with a "put up or shut up" situation. Beyond the thirty years we had twenty more, with children, grandchildren, and great-grandchildren. Besides all this, I continued to see her two and three times a day and she had regained consciousness enough to squeeze in a smile of recognition.

As a matter of fact, the remainder of the nineteen months of her life were marked with many smiles and a couple of chuckles. She was never able to speak or move her body. Responses to questions never were given. However, responses to one's presence when coming into her room were often shining by a brief smile. After the first year, she would lower her lip when she saw the bottle of salve in my hand, would close her eyes at the beginning and end of my prayer, watch the ceiling above her bed when I projected pictures of the flowers in our yard, listen to gospel music, stay alert during short visits by family members and close friends. One day I said to her, *"Darling, it nearly kills me to tell you how much I love you, and you can't tell me back."*

It took a few minutes, but not long afterwards I saw tears on her beloved cheeks. How more eloquent can a response be?

Fifteen months into her incapacitation, her body was still rather stiff and fixed in one position. She never again took anything by mouth and was completely helpless as to bodily functions. Her autonomic system worked very well as to breathing, coughing, yawning, hiccupping and the like. During my visits I would read the Upper Room daily devotionals, and a promise out of the daily Promise Box. I wiped the "cobwebs" from her dear eyes, washed her glasses, brushed her hair and rubbed her shoulders. At times she would lower her lip for Vaseline. She cooperated with the process and seemed to want it. She had some bleeding ulcers and pneumonia earlier in the year. But she was as well as she was a year before. Her face remained full.

Her peaceful end came in the late morning of May 22, 1988, at the end of more than nineteen months of incapacitation. Fred and Kit Ross, visiting from California, were with me when we returned from lunch. We found that she had just taken her last breath. I had known that the end was near, but not how near.

Lois' service of remembrance and the celebration of her wonderful Christian life was conducted in the large full sanctuary of First United Methodist Church, Colorado Springs (her church and mine since 1963). The entire mini-concert of the music she loved and/or sang, as well as the principal service, was graciously videotaped in sound and color by loving friends at the church. Marcia, Phil, Jr., and Mickey picked out a beautiful spot under some tall pine trees in Section 30 of Evergreen Municipal Cemetery. On her headstone are the words (from Psalm 121) she loved so well,

"I will lift up mine eyes unto the hills . . ."

There her body rests, waiting for the day of resurrection. Beside her is a spot for me, when the time comes.

The Kind of Woman Lois Was

A highly organized person
A quiet builder of persons and organizations
A provocative conversationalist
An excellent listener
A professional, always up-grading
Always gracious and hospitable
A choice story-teller
An avid reader
The family cheer-leader
One whose primary interest, consideration was home
A person who modeled her beliefs
Fiercely loyal & protective of loved ones

Growing Old with Helen

Helen Thompson McMillan-Green.
We were happily married 1989-2005.

Helen was ninety in the year 2000. Even though her general health was good, the years had taken their toll of her reliable memory. She recalled many things with considerable clarity, but remembering accurately had mostly departed. On-time and follow-through projects could not be relied upon. To expedite the process of preparing meals, I took the responsibility of taking us out for one meal a day so that dietary sufficiency was maintained. She washed my underclothes and put them in my drawer regularly and made the bed—changing sheets mostly every Monday. We walked her dog together in a nearby park. I took her with me everywhere, except to the meeting of the ministers on Mondays and to Rotary Club luncheons of Fridays. If I "went under", both of us would have needed institutional care. Frightening!

Now and then she asked me if I had ever been to Roswell, New Mexico. Her parents had left her a five-acre homestead on a six-mile hill just west of the city. During the first ten years of our marriage I had taken her there at least a half-dozen times, and helped her get a well dug and the property surveyed. She didn't remember the 40-acre farm we jointly bought while I was the pastor of Avondale UMC 1988-'95. She couldn't remember where her parents were buried, despite the fact that I had driven her to the cemetery in Updike, Illinois and had taken her picture standing behind the headstones. She couldn't remember when her husband died (1980), or where we were married (in Colorado Springs). With her mind in such a condition, I knew that everything depended upon my physical and mental ability. Helen's condition reminded me of the words of Ecclesiastes 12:1-6.

> *Don't let the excitement of being young cause you to forget about your Creator. Honor him in your youth before the evil years come—when you'll no longer enjoy living. It will be too late then to try to remember him, when the sun and light and moon and stars are dim to your old eyes, and there is no silver lining among your clouds. For there will come a time when your limbs will tremble with age, and your young legs will become weak, and your teeth will be too few to do their work, and there will be blindness, too. Yes, remember your Creator now while you are young, before the silver cord*

of life snaps, and the golden bowl be broken, and the pitcher is broken at the fountain, and the wheel is broken at the cistern.

-*The Living Bible* (paraphrased),
Tyndale House Publishers

In February 2000, Helen had a cataract removed from her remaining good eye. On Sunday afternoon of November 26, we celebrated her 90th birthday at an open house in our home on Chestnut Street. Helen was on cloud nine. Her dementia became more pronounced after that. By 2002 her dementia had encroached to the point of an inability to give a Power of Attorney in time to prevent the Court from making her daughter and me Co-Conservators/Guardians. To avoid the same thing happening to me, I have given Phil and Marcia power of attorney. A word to the wise is sufficient.

I recommended to Sara and to my children any one of six options for our changed life situation. They chose the most expensive one—that of placing Helen in a good assisted living unit and me in a one-bedroom apartment across the street from her at $2,000 a month. My apartment at the Inn at Garden Plaza allowed two meals a day. I needed to get to the dining room from the third floor. In the apartment also were a small kitchenette and microwave oven for snacks.

I regularly drove her to church with me each Sunday, then out to dinner, followed by a little drive. On September 1, 2002, I ran a red stop light, hit another car and wound up with an A/C left shoulder separation. Helen suffered some broken left ribs. The woman in the other car was shaken but uninjured. We both recovered rather quickly. I got an $85.00 fine and four points on my driver's license. In addition, I was required to take a written and road driving test, which I passed. Our children cautioned us about continuing to drive. I still drove.

In her cute small apartment, Helen accepted the change from home living, only after I was required not to visit her for a short time. That gave her enough time to get into a routine of her own in her new home. One day she said she thought it might be a good idea for us to plan a simple, inexpensive wedding and get married. She had forgotten that we had been married for thirteen years. Well, anyway, I was still the kind of guy she'd wish to marry. Aides walked her to her meals (she didn't remember when), gave her medications, helped her with personal hygiene and saw that she got dressed enough to go out of her room. Her dog, Joy, died of cancer that March at age fourteen. She took the loss with difficulty.

We sold her home on Chestnut Street and put the money in court-approved investment accounts. Fortunately, she had enough money to meet her requirements—even later at a cost of $4,500 a month at Cypress Court, a facility for Alzheimer residents, including dementia. She didn't remember who I was except that I was always the one she expected for a visit. Sometimes she called me her father, sometimes the name of her first husband who had died two decades before.

Three times in 2004 she failed to wake up in the morning. One time she was so tardy the hospice doctor warned me that she might be dying. But she gradually came back without heroic efforts. I saw her three times a week on average and she always smiled a welcome when she saw me. I tried to decide whether my effort to bring bright spots into her life was more important to her or to me.

In January 2005, Phil Jr. and I flew to California to attend a workshop at Schumer's Crystal Cathedral. Before I left to go, I went by to see Helen. At first she seemed indifferent to my presence. So I went to the desk of the aide and explained that I'd be out of state for a few days and asked her to call me on my cell phone in case anything happened to Helen. On the second day away I received a call from the hospice nurse who said that Helen was dying and would I talk to her on the phone. At my signal she put the phone to Helen's ear, hoping that she might hear me in her unconscious state. I said to Helen,

"Hello, Helen, I love you!"

Helen drew her last breath thirty minutes later. Those who know say that the last sense to go is hearing. I do hope Helen heard me. I caught a plane back and set up a service of remembrance at First United Methodist Church, where—as long as she could—Helen had attended with me. As I started to leave the sanctuary at the close of her service, I impulsively turned and waved farewell to the urn that held her precious ashes.

The Kind of Woman Helen Was

I came to know her late in life—in 1965, shortly after she and her husband Stiles arrived from Roswell, N.M. She was educated in Chicago, IL where she earned college and graduate degrees, and had taught in schools there. Despite health disabilities, she became a specialist in the field of communications—radio, television and news media. In Roswell she hosted three television shows and was the principal newsperson for the state Presbyterian Denomination.

In Colorado Springs, she was soon to be employed as the Executive Director of the Pikes Peak Council of Churches—later the name was changed to "Association" of Churches. In my chapter called, "I Could 'Cry for Happy'" are more details about her and her outstanding work in that association. In Colorado Springs she excelled in getting the churches to be members of, and active in, the association. She had, for fifteen years, been in charge of a television weekly show over KKTV entitled, "The Church Game." In time, she was for many years in charge of the famous Garden of the Gods Easter Sunrise Service.

After our marriage in 1989, she left membership in the First Presbyterian Church to become the wife of the 74-year-old pastor of Avondale United Methodist Church, near Pueblo, sixty miles from home in Colorado Springs. During my six and a half years as pastor there, she used her expertise to help that church expand its small Easter Breakfast to an ecumenical event that was called The Arkansas Valley Easter Sunrise Service at Inspiration Point.

23

WHEN IN CHARGE, TAKE CHARGE

Taking seriously Paul's admonition about those called upon to lead, when that is needed, and with more than an ordinary amount of trepidation, I wrote the following letter to the Officers, Executive Committee Members, and Trustees of the Military Chaplains Association in the form of a memo from Philip L. Green, Incoming National President:

Dear Colleagues in MCA,

Post convention greetings to all of you! Another interesting and profitable convention has come and gone. Some deep insights were surfaced and dealt with—in part at least. To me, Dr. Moon's address and tribute to chaplains, and the presence of our Secretary of Defense to speak and to receive the National Citizenship Award, were the high points of our time together. The convention members referred some issues to the Executive Committee. We will address ourselves to them at our first meeting. I'll ask Karl (Justus) to extract them from the Convention notes and get them to all of us in time for mature consideration when we are together.

I am honored beyond merit to serve as president and as chairman of the executive committee. One great joy in this connection is the privilege of being associated with you, the leaders of MCA. I promise to be as open to your suggestions and guidance as I can be.

The Nominating Committee is to be commended for giving painstaking care, and nearly three hours of precious convention time, before coming out with such an excellent slate of officers, executive committee members, trustees and area vice presidents. I congratulate each one of you on being chosen for your specific office. Those of us who are carry-overs will wish to welcome more fully the new members at our

Executive Committee Meeting, which will be scheduled in late June or in July (Karl Justus will pass the word on this soon).

I hope we will all recognize the unique position held by our staff executive, Karl B. Justus. While he is employed by and therefore amenable to the executive committee, he is also the most knowledgeable link of continuity in our organization. He has been through the decision-making process with three administrations and eight conventions. Indeed, we must admit that his capable, vigorous and enthusiastic leadership has helped to bring MCA to its enviable state and size. He would be the first to admit that he is not perfect and that he has not in every case made perfect decisions. I know him well enough to say that he would not want us to buy without questioning all his ideas. On the other hand, I believe he has earned the right to push ahead and to make suggestions in his role as Executive Director. Also, his views—against the background of years of experience with us—need to be heard and considered on issues vital to the organization. Of course, we will expect him to perform his duties in keeping with established policies and written guidelines.

In this first letter, I have an item of interest and importance to share with you. On his final two-week trip to Europe starting 7 May, Chaplain Major General Edwin R. Chess, Chief of Air Force Chaplains, has invited Karl to be a member of his party. This means that at all official stops, Karl will be given an opportunity to talk about MCA to the chaplains there. He will also attend the latter part of the NATO Chaplains Conference.

I note that the date is midway between the Convention in Chicago and the completion date of the June post-convention issue of The Military Chaplain*. This will be a good time for him to be away from the office.*

Karl has raised in excess of $1,100 in designated gifts, mainly from longtime West Coast friends, to cover the cost of the trip. Thus, the cost against the budget of MCA is negligible. Were he not to go, most of the gifts would have to be returned to the donors.

I have heartily approved of this trip for our Executive Director, and wanted to share this good news with all of you.

One reason we should all be glad for this trip is that, as a result of Karl's trip with Chaplain Chess to the Pacific Area last year, MCA now has five chapters there. We have none in Europe. It is possible that this trip could result in some chapters there.

Let us be thinking about how to make MCA grow in membership, in the number of chapters, and in conventions that involve, enrich and motivate.

Most Sincerely Yours,
Philip L. Green, President

Letter of Response from a Monsignor

On April 22, 1970, I had written the above letter to colleagues in my newly-elected position as national president of the Military Chaplains Association. Twelve days later the following letter was in reply to my letter. It was from the former Chief of Army Chaplains, Major General Patrick Ryan. He and Dr. Karl Justus had breathed new life into the MCA and started it afresh as a meaningful and helpful organization that it was intended to be. During World War II, and a few years following, it was largely something chaplains were invited to join if they so desired. Now dues were mandatory and national conventions were annual events. For six years at an earlier time, Patrick Ryan had been national president of MCA and was responsible for hiring Dr. Justus as a full-time Executive Director. Together they had brought MCA to responsible "adulthood." The letter from him brought great encouragement to me. Here it is:

Dear Phil:

Your 22 April letter was in my mail when I returned from a trip. Your letter was very good and I am sure it will be accepted by the membership of the Military Chaplains

Association and will be appreciated by them. There might be two or three exceptions and I think you know who they are.

I am glad you have taken over the presidency so completely and quickly and I look forward to a fine tour of duty for you. I will be available for any assistance when you need me.

All good wishes,
Msgr. Patrick J. Ryan,
Major General, U.S.A., Ret.

On August 22, 1978, I wrote a letter to the congregation at First United Methodist Church, Colorado Springs, CO, to let them know that there would be a firm hand in control of things, with Dr. Lacour present only on weekends. I sent a copy to Bishop Melvin Wheatley, the Staff Parish Relations Committee and to Dr. Lacour.

Dear Fellow Members:

Greetings! By this time we have all heard of Dr. Lacour's decision to become the Professor of Preaching at Oral Roberts University. Although we are reluctant to give him up, we are glad for three things: (1) for more than eleven years of pastoral leadership and great preaching; (2) for ORU which will be getting one of the very best preachers in America—one eminently equipped to train young men and women to communicate well when they preach; and (3) for the ministers-in-the-making who will have the privilege to be in his classes.

Although Dr. and Mrs. Lacour have already gone to begin their work at ORU, Dr. Lacour will be here Friday nights through Sunday afternoons to preach until October 8, the date of his farewell sermon. Mrs. Lacour has been named the Coordinator of Graduate Student Life at ORU.

Our Staff-Parish Relations Committee of nine elected members, chaired by Mr. Harlan L. Ochs, is busily engaged with Bishop Melvin E. Wheatley and his Cabinet in finding a worthy successor to Dr. Lacour. (See attached explanation of the selection process).

You will be interested to know that the congregation is taking the change of pastoral leadership with equanimity and with a maximum of hope for the future. Attendance remains up, the finances better than last year, and a spirit of optimism and providential thinking grips us.

I need not tell you, therefore, that the church needs your continuing interest. It is important that we see to it that the work of our church does not suffer a setback or a diminution of its God-ordained tasks. I appeal to each one of you in this time of transition to make your church an object of earnest prayer and diligent effort during the next few months. It would be very helpful for you to be regular in attendance, faithful in the stewardship of time and talent, as well as generous with the funds necessary to keep the church on an upward trend. God bless you, every one.

Most sincerely and hopefully, Philip L. Green, Minister of Pastoral Care, Part-time Acting Senior Minister.

On August 27, 1978, I received the following note from Dr. Lacour:

Dear Phil,

When you asked me about the letter you wrote, I had only glanced at it. Since then, I've read and reread it and pronounce it a masterpiece. Several lay persons have commented on it. Also, I understand you gave great strength to the meeting of the Administrative Board. Bless you on your great leadership.

Sincerely,
Larry

NB: Dr. Lacour flew back Friday afternoon till Sunday afternoons until Oct. 8, 1978. From then on until June 1979, I served as interim senior minister.

On 17 September 1957, I finished a three-year tour at Headquarters, 16th Air Force, Madrid, Spain. I was honored with a Good Conduct Medal. The background for it is included herewith:

> *Chaplain Green successfully accomplished the precarious task of initiating and maintaining a most effective Protestant Chapel Program from 3 October 1954 to September 1957 in a country overwhelmingly Catholic without arousing resentment prejudicial to the United States Military Mission.*
>
> *Realizing that no religious facilities were available in the local Spanish community and, fearing that widespread attendance at local Protestant Spanish-speaking churches on the part of U.S. Forces personnel might create a serious public relations threat, Chaplain Green greatly augmented the Chaplain Six-Point Program, thereby attracting a maximum number of U.S. Air Force and Department of Defense personnel on duty in Madrid.*
>
> *At a time when Protestant leaders in the United States were gravely fearful over that possible abridgement of the religious privileges of their members on duty in Spain, their misgivings were allayed by learning of such a vigorous and comprehensive Chapel Program as envisioned by this officer.*
>
> *In order not to compromise the delicate position of the Chapel Program for U.S. Forces personnel, Chaplain Green cut himself off from social and fraternal contacts with local Protestant church leaders—contacts which he would normally enjoy in other localities.*
>
> *This chaplain assisted the commander and staff chaplain by organizing and supervising the development of Protestant Chapel Programs at Zaragoza and Sevilla, Spain—making monthly trips to those areas to give religious coverage for sixteen months prior to the arrival of resident chaplains.*
>
> *Chaplain Green achieved the above praiseworthy accomplishments with minimum personnel, equipment and facilities. Beginning with no ecclesiastical supplies, he equipped a provisional auditorium in the Dependent*

> *School. He monitored the enlargement of this facility to meet minimal needs and shared it with the leaders of the school; military organizations for group meetings and courts-martial; community youth activities such as Scouts, Campfire Girls, rod and gun club; and square dance club.*
>
> *The shortage of military personnel assigned to the Chapel Program was overcome by a staff of more than one hundred and eighty (180) volunteer workers who were recruited, organized, trained, assigned and supervised by Chaplain Green. During this tour the problem of personnel turnover required the replacement of these people from one to three times. Protestant personnel arriving in Madrid were most agreeably surprised to find a chapel group enthusiastically welcoming them to a wide variety of religious activities.*

Many unsolicited expressions of approval of the Chapel Program were made, among which are those from responsible senior and flag officers of JUSMG, Spain, including: Major General August W. Kistner, Chief JUSMG, Spain, in a letter to a prominent leader in the National Lutheran Council, said:

> *"Percentage wise, we have one of the most active and growing Protestant religious programs anywhere in the Air Force."*

Rear Admiral Wallace B. Short, previously Deputy Chief of JUSMG for Construction, and first President of Chapel-men, stated publicly that: the Chapel Program in Madrid was the most active he had known in 32 years of military service.

So I was in charge and a bit lonely. There were no other chaplains or local pastors in that Catholic country with whom to chat or learn from. When I was on vacation, a chaplain from Germany was sent to cover my multitude of duties.

Three years earlier, I was sent as the only chaplain to Spence Air Base, Moultrie, Georgia. In like manner, my task was to begin and implement a chapel program. But there I had the pleasure of pastors in local churches nearby for fellowship.

Duties of a United States Air Force Chaplain
(Some are mandatory, others are recommended)
Chaplain Philip L. Green, 1943-1963

WORSHIP

General Protestant Worship Services. Other kinds of services: weekday services, annual preaching mission, sacramental (communions, etc.), junior church, patriotic, hospital, confinement facility, seasonal, facility, denominational, group devotions, spiritual retreats, in the field.

PASTORAL FUNCTIONS

Pastoral visitations in barracks, homes, GI dining halls, recreation areas, confinement facility, hospitals, troop tactical units, service clubs, choir rehearsals, crash sites; letters, phone calls.

MORAL & RELIGIOUS EDUCATION

Dynamic and moral leadership lectures, rehabilitation efforts, character projects, sex education and social hygiene, Sunday school, vacation Bible schools, youth fellowships, Boy Scouts, audio visuals, leadership training.

PERSONAL COUNSELING

At the mandatory visit with the chaplain, advise each of the availability of the chaplain's ministry, worship services, religious education, etc. Deal with problems of adjustments, mal-assignments, promotion, family and marriage, discipline, finance, religious matters of conversion, practices, doubts, bereavements.

PUBLIC RELATIONS

Parish news paper, free nursery service, PA system, bell, welcome brochure, Sunday bulletin, pastoral letters, USO, bulletin board, posters, movie spots, letters to civilian pastors.

HUMANITARIAN PROJECTS

Overseas relief for orphans, those made homeless by war, disasters, relief for churches destroyed by war, humanitarian annual project by the Chief of Air Force Chaplains, Church World Service Relief Fund, "One Great Hour of Sharing."

CULTURAL ACTIVITIES

Base choirs and glee clubs, concerts by visiting musical groups, dramatic presentations, music appreciation groups, special lectures, book review, film and fellowship hours, tours to museums, art galleries, etc.

OFFICE ADMINISTRATION

Maintain office hours and an updated policy file, supervise the preparation and flow of all military and professional correspondence, maintain representation on all pertinent base councils, direct, supervise, coordinate and evaluate all chapel personnel and activities, recommend budgetary requirements for appropriated and non-appropriated funds for chapel facilities, prepare a quarterly summary of all chapel activities on base, attend wing and base staff meetings weekly and discuss unusual trends in behavior.

24

TO GOD BE THANKS AND GLORY

"It is a good thing to give thanks to God in the morning, and to offer praise to him every night". (Translated from Psalms 92:2)

"In everything give thanks, for this is the will of God concerning you." (Ephesians 5:20)

It may appear to some readers that I intend to hit people over the head with Bible quotations. I do not. Here it is just to give a beginning place to the subject of thankfulness. The spirit of being grateful is enormous in setting the stage for a longer life. Not everyone needs to do what I have done. Many years ago, I typed up a seven-page list of the names of people who had added a special dimension to my life. If I subtracted relatives, I'd still have five pages of people to whom I owe a debt of gratitude.

While writing this book, I asked a medical doctor what he thought would help a person to live longer. His immediate reply was,

"Attitude!"

Bingo! What an answer! How insightful! How comprehensive! The quotation above is only part of the answer. Why? Because there are many things in our daily lives for which a good attitude is necessary—one's existential situation, race, sex, limitations, unseen realities, body, job situation, and on and on. The attitude one has toward daily blessings opens or closes one's mind to satisfactions. Thanking God that everything is as well with us as it is puts the picture in a good perspective.

Being thankful *for everything* gives me pause for consideration. Everything? "Yes!" For ear and eye, voice and tongue, beauty, delights, family and friends, employment, human love, life, certainties. But being thankful for *everything* makes us question what God means by that. I struggled at first with 'pain.' No one likes pain. Why be thankful for it? As I thought about it, pain is a two-headed coin. Pain comes to tell you something is not right, that you need medicine, a visit with your doctor, a stay in the hospital. One of the dangers of diabetes is the loss of feeling in your feet. That requires a podiatrist to examine the feet regularly to assure you there are no cuts or bruises. Sores become unnoticed because there is no pain. What about bad teeth that go unnoticed because there is no pain?

Rev. Dr. James Stokes, a friend, was pastor of a church in Reidsville, NC. He became quite ill and his doctor tried everything to cure him. He was about to give up his church. His brother, Lem, knew of a doctor in Charlotte who was a specialist in what was wrong with Jim. That doctor would not take Jim as a patient unless he was first examined thoroughly by an expert dentist. When Jim asked him why a dentist, the doctor told him that he had the same symptoms as Jim—that his doctor told him to have all bad teeth removed. He did and he recovered right away. So Jim followed the doctor's request, was seen afterwards, and his health was restored. So, thank God for pain.

There is suffering that comes from a variety of sources—from living in a society that gets involved in wars; from natural causes such as earthquakes, fires, floods, and storms; from poisons that creep into our air and food from the touch of other humans; from economic distress; from oppression by civil and religious authorities; from strife within the home; and from being a Christian in a hostile society. One must never forget the death of loved ones and cherished friends who leave lonely spouses, or fatherless children. In the midst of it all, is it not possible to find a spot for which to be thankful? Yes, Jesus my role model shows us the way.

Our way is not always God's way. His is not the way of self-pity, of hiding our heads in the sand, of cutting off our heads to rid ourselves of the headache; or escape by calling it the will of God; or deny its existence. His way is to use it. He did not bear his cross—he transformed it into a throne of love and grace. The end of his life became an open door to a new beginning.

I have an abundance of reasons to be thankful to God for what he has done through me. In my study I have an album chuck full of the ways he has used me. My prayer of dominant desire is to be used by my Lord and to be a blessing. Because both he and I were on the same track, there were doors of opportunity opened to which others turned a cold shoulder. After a successful career as a military chaplain, and the associate pastor for seventeen years in a mega-church, I laid myself on the line to pastor a small congregation sixty miles from home at age seventy-four. At age eighty, God found for me a small Korean church whose pastor needed an English-language worship service. At eighty-five, I helped him find someone to take my place.

These duties constituted only the tip of the iceberg of ways God has used me across seventy-two years as his servant. Along the way, he helped me to write a book in which there were more than seventy prayers, entitled, *Prayers Jesus Might Have Prayed.* Without the nudges of the Holy Spirit at the feet of Jesus, I would never have had the audacity of putting words in the mouth of my Savior. Happily, 55 percent of those who received a test-marketing copy read or looked at it and responded in writing of its excellence. With two fingers on my computer, I wrote, *The Mountains Are Happy,* a three hundred and eighty-five page autobiography to give to my family members and to the library of every church I have served, as well as to many colleagues.

25

UNSEEN REALITIES

"We fix our eyes not on what is seen, but on what is unseen, for what is seen is temporary, but what is unseen is eternal." 2 Cor. 4:18

Hebrews 11:1-12:2
(The great "Faith Chapter")

Now faith is being sure of what we hope for and certain of what we do not see. This is what the ancients were commended for.

By faith we understand that the universe was formed at God's command, so that what is seen was not made out of what was visible. By faith Abel offered God a better sacrifice than Cain did. By faith he was commended as a righteous man, when God spoke well of his offerings. And by faith he still speaks, even though he is dead.

By faith Enoch was taken from this life, so that he did not experience death; he could not be found, because God had taken him away. For, before he was taken, he was commended as one who pleased God. And without faith it is impossible to please God, because anyone who comes to him must believe that he exists and that he rewards those who earnestly seek him.

By faith Noah, when warned about things not yet seen, in holy fear built an ark to save his family. By his faith he condemned the world and became heir of the righteousness that comes by faith.

By faith Abraham, when called to go to a place he would later receive as his inheritance, obeyed and went, even though he did not know where he was going. By faith he made his home in the promised land like a stranger in a foreign country; he lived in tents, as did Isaac and Jacob, who were heirs with him of the same promise. For he was looking forward to the city with foundations, whose architect and builder is God.

By faith Abraham, even though he was past ageCand Sarah herself was barren—was enabled to become a father because he considered him faithful who had made the promise. And so from this one man, and he as good as dead, came descendants as numerous as the stars in the sky and as countless as the sand on the seashore.

All these people were still living by faith when they died. They did not receive the things promised; they only saw them and welcomed them from a distance, and they admitted that they were aliens and strangers on earth. People who say such things show that they are looking for a country of their own. If they had been thinking of the country they had left, they would have had opportunity to return. Instead, they were longing for a better countryCa heavenly one. Therefore God is not ashamed to be called their God, for he has prepared a city for them.

By faith Abraham, when God tested him, offered Isaac as a sacrifice. He who had received the promises was about to sacrifice his one and only son, even though God had said to him, It is through Isaac that your offspring will be reckoned. Abraham reasoned that God could raise the dead, and figuratively speaking, he did receive Isaac back from death.

By faith Isaac blessed Jacob and Esau in regard to their future.

By faith Jacob, when he was dying, blessed each of Joseph's sons, and worshiped as he leaned on the top of his staff.

By faith Joseph, when his end was near, spoke about the exodus of the Israelites from Egypt and gave instructions about his bones.

By faith Moses' parents hid him for three months after he was born, because they saw he was no ordinary child, and they were not afraid of the king's edict.

By faith Moses, when he had grown up, refused to be known as the son of Pharaoh's daughter. He chose to be mistreated along with the people of God rather than to enjoy the pleasures of sin for a short time. He regarded disgrace for the sake of Christ as of greater value than the treasures of Egypt, because he was looking ahead to his reward. By faith he left Egypt, not fearing the king's anger; he persevered because he saw him who is invisible. By faith he kept the Passover and the sprinkling of blood, so that the destroyer of the firstborn would not touch the firstborn of Israel.

By faith the people passed through the Red Sea as on dry land; but when the Egyptians tried to do so, they were drowned.

By faith the walls of Jericho fell, after the people had marched around them for seven days.

By faith the prostitute Rahab, because she welcomed the spies, was not killed with those who were disobedient.

And what more shall I say? I do not have time to tell about Gideon, Barak, Samson, Jephthah, David, Samuel and the prophets, who through faith conquered kingdoms, administered justice, and gained what was promised; who shut the mouths of lions, quenched the fury of the flames, and escaped the edge of the sword; whose weakness was turned to strength; and who became powerful in battle and routed foreign armies. Women received back their dead, raised to life again. Others were tortured and refused to be released, so that they might gain a better resurrection. Some faced jeers and flogging, while still others were chained and put in prison. They were stoned; they were sawed in two; they were put to death by the sword. They went about in sheepskins and goatskins, destitute, persecuted and mistreated; the world was not worthy of them. They wandered in deserts and mountains, and in caves and holes in the ground.

These were all commended for their faith, yet none of them received what had been promised. God had planned something better for us so that only together with us would they be made perfect.

Therefore, since we are surrounded by such a great cloud of witnesses, let us throw off everything that hinders and the sin that so easily entangles, and let us run with perseverance

> *the race marked out for us. Let us fix our eyes on Jesus, the author and perfecter of our faith, who for the joy set before him endured the cross, scorning its shame and sat down at the right hand of the throne of God.*

If we join faith with love and hope, we have the big three of unseen realities. All are of primary importance to the spiritual well-being of people. They transport us in the direction of happiness and contentment. All three contribute to a longer and more satisfying life.

Love cannot be seen but, oh! How its presence can be seen all around us! We have the joy of its warmth and transforming energy. God's love, at the fingertips of his generous hands, assures us that we are not only loved but abundantly cared for. We read that.

". . . . *not a sparrow falls without the Father's notice.*" And a poet wrote it thus,

"Said the robin to the sparrow, *'I would really like to know, why these anxious human beings rush about and worry so.'*"

"Said the sparrow to the robin, *'Do you think that it could be, that they have no heavenly Father, such as cares for you and me?'*"

Because of God's love for us and our love for him and his other children, things have happened during the past two thousand years. In just the nearly one hundred years of my own life, in our country alone blessings hardly dreamed of, and hopes yearned for, have appeared to benefit us—polio vaccine, insulin, sulfa drugs, vitamins, heart transplants, internal pacemakers, radio, television, video discs, worldwide web, nuclear power, jet propulsion, microwave ovens, and many others—even frozen foods.

The immense expansion of humanitarian institutions during the past three centuries has come from the efforts and love of many dreamers and doers—hospitals, public schools, colleges, universities, orphanages, and homes for the care of the infirm, aged and indigent have blossomed, because deep within us has come a desire to help people live longer, healthier, happier and more vigorous lives. We cannot see God. He is a Spirit. But "*he that would come to God must believe that he is, and that he rewards those that diligently seek him.*" *Heb* 11:6. The mysteries of life on earth, as we view it, become known to us a little at a time—not fast enough—only in God's time and then without our merit.

Thirty years ago, I knew about the wife of the professor at the Iliff School of Theology in Denver. She knew God in a personal way. He revealed to her the words and music of a *Hymn of Promise* while she was ill and dying in 1984. It was published in the United Methodist Hymnal of 1988 and has quickly become a favorite with me and many others. I share it here because it highlights things that only God can see. Here it is:

"Hymn of Promise"

In the bulb there is a flower; in the seed, an apple tree; in
cocoons, a hidden promise: butterflies will soon be free.
In the cold and snow of winter there's a spring that waits to be,
unrevealed until its season, something God alone can see.

There's a song in every silence, seeking word and melody; there's
a dawn in every darkness, bringing hope to you and me.
From the past will come the future; what it holds, a mystery,
unrevealed until its season, something God alone can see.

In the end is our beginning; in our time, infinity; in our doubt
there is believing; in our life, eternity.
In our death, a resurrection; at the last, a victory, unrevealed
until its season, something God alone can see.

Written by Natalie Sleeth

Although God may not be seen with the human eye, people know he is there. A man who stands on the Golden Gate Bridge in San Francisco, when fog shrouds both ends of the bridge, may not see either end, but he "knows" he is safe—that the bridge will not collapse because he cannot see the ends. In like manner believers rest assured that the God who created the universe will continue to uphold it. Hallelujah!

It took more than patriotism to preserve the life and sanity of prisoners of war during World War II. Chaplain Robert Preston Taylor suffered through the torturous Bataan Death March. Those who couldn't keep up were shot or bayoneted. He was imprisoned by the Japanese in prison camps for more than three years—camps in the Philippines, Japan and Manchuria. He credited his survival through mistreatment and starvation to his Christian faith. His stance was an inspiration to fellow prisoners.

My commander at Spence Field, Moultrie, Georgia, was a survivor of the same death march. He never spoke to me about that terrible experience. But I saw in his frail body the evidence of suffering.

Senator John McCain, Republican candidate for President of the United States in 2008, was a prisoner in the Viet Nam war. He suffered torture for five years rather than betray his country's trust. His faith kept him and others with him. My small challenges are nothing beside these giants of faith.

Religious faith is one of those things that is unseen, yet very real. It cannot be weighed, measured or purchased. Faith has an answer to a troubled conscience, a double-mindedness, and a misguided direction. With a peace that nothing else can give, one can not only rest, but rest in the knowledge that nothing can separate us from the peace-giver. As I look back over most of a century, I am glad to affirm the belief that "the heart of the Eternal is most wonderfully kind." Throughout life, from above, I have heard "echoes of mercy" and "whispers of love." How good it is to go to sleep knowing there is He whose promises are true and unfailing. Long ago my choice was fixed on him who is abundantly able to do more through me than I could do alone. Although I cannot accept the Bible as the exact word of God, I do believe it gives me more guidance than can anything else in this world. My preacher father said he always "posted his books" every night, so to speak, so that if the end came unexpectedly, he'd be ready.

I believe I was put here on earth for a purpose—not of my own making or choosing—but to be a part of the solutions to earth's problems, rather than of their causes. The world needs a reconciler. Though I am only one, my entry into the ministry in 1936 was a response to a divine call to do what Jesus began doing when he was here on earth.

Without a doubt, I can look back and see how things have fit together, and built upon each other, to get me through troubled waters to the finish line. I firmly believe God has helped me to reach my present age of ninety-five to do needed ministries—even extra months to write this book, which I hope will help others find the path to faith, hope and love, and longer years of service.

SECTION VI

Where are you going? Are you headed in the right direction? If your answer to both questions is "I don't know," you may wind up like "Wrong-Way Corrigan" who thought he was flying toward England and landed in Oregon. The decisions you make can start or fail to head you in the right direction. Your decisions are indicators of what you really intend and want to do with your life. I thought about becoming a minister like my father and two of his brothers. As a result all my planning took me in that direction. After twenty years as a military chaplain I had to decide whether or not to accept an invitation to become the associate pastor of a large church or to return to the Western North Carolina Conference and take my place at the bottom of the ladder. That one was easy.

Your heritage is somewhat responsible for how long you live. To live in an earthquake part of the world, or in a hurricane-prone area, or any other threatening situation on earth will make the length of life "iffy." Some parts of the world are healthier than others. Poverty-stricken homes where there is a limited amount of good water and other health needs make for a shorter life. Educational excellence, or lack of it, is another consideration.

Self messages can make or break us. Some are positive, others are negative. But a lot of them are mixed messages and they are the ones that may be difficult to unscramble. Take, for example, what we tell ourselves about obeying the law, as in Phil Jr.'s chapter 28.

I ended my military career at age fifty. A second career was seventeen years on the staff of a very large church. At its end I was sixty-seven. I was still not ready to take my oar out of the water and put my clerical robe in the closet. So I had to decide "what next and next and next."

When I was seventy-four God and the bishop gave me another church sixty miles from home. But I had to decide whether or not to accept that opportunity to pastor a small congregation. I had six and a half wonderful years there.

26

DECISIONS MAKE DESTINATIONS

Life's major and minor decisions add or subtract from the length of life. Good decisions add to our satisfactions and thus to our life's span. Faulty decisions cause worry and make for turnarounds in the direction one needs or wants to go. Couples who make joint decisions make more good decisions. They talk things over and compare what is good and best. Some choices are difficult and require adjustments in one spouse or the other, or both. For one spouse to do all the deciding, management of finances, choosing new friends, and the like, the adequacy and fairness of the choices often bring up the disastrous question of "who is right and who is wrong?" Divorce Courts are crowded with couples who can't agree on who "wears the britches" of decision-making. Break-ups make for much unhappiness in the home and that unhappiness tends to diminish long life expectations. Good partnerships do not allow this to happen.

In 1943, I wanted to join most of the young people in military service from my six congregations. I volunteered to become a chaplain in the armed forces of World War II. My wife hesitated but joined me in that wish. We needed to get concurrence from our District Superintendent and the approval of our bishop, before we drove from Western North Carolina to Washington, D.C., to be interviewed by the Methodist Commission on Chaplains.

After five years of successful and enjoyable service in the US Army Air Corps, I decided to stay in as a reservist. At that time I was stationed at MacDill Field, Tampa, Florida and, before making that decision, I took leave and flew to Greensboro, North Carolina, to talk it over with Lois, my dear wife. She had some doubts about that direction for our lives. But, seeing how important it seemed to me, she was a good trooper and gave approval.

In 1947 the US Air Force became autonomous—separate from the Army Air Corps. Another decision needed to be made, stay in the Army Air Corps. or transfer into the US Air Force. Lois was with me at the time in Wiesbaden, Germany, and approved once again. When the Russians threatened to drive their armies all the way to the Atlantic

Ocean, American dependents in Germany were given the choice of staying on or going home. Happily, Lois decided to stay with me to complete my three years of duty there. As I look back over these decisions, I marvel at Lois' equanimity and wonder whether or not there was trauma enough to have shortened her life. She died at age eighty.

Over the past retirement years, I have majored in making good decisions. I retired from mandatory appointments by the bishop in 1983. I had been Conference Evangelist for three years and wanted to continue that appointment in retirement. I learned, too late, the rules that prevailed at the time said that one could not be given the same appointment after retirement that one had just before retirement. So I incorporated under the name, "Special Care Ministries" and took the position of Special Care Minister. My duties were much the same as the Conference Evangelist. It was a good decision, as it allowed me to continue what I loved to do. I didn't want to quit. I wanted to retool and keep on keeping on.

A Word about First United Methodist Church

The church was founded in 1871, three years before the City of Colorado Springs came into existence. An earlier church (Trinity) had already been established in Old Colorado City in what is now a part of west Colorado Springs. The new congregation had steady growth in three different church buildings under the leadership of the early pastors. During World War II, the Rev. Cyrus "Cy" Albertson became a beloved pastor who filled the Akron-type sanctuary on the northwest corner of Nevada Avenue and Boulder Street. His successor was the Rev. Dr. Walter M. Briggs who stayed only two years (health factors). The next senior pastor was the last, Rev. Dr. Benjamin F. "Ben" Lehmberg who was transferred from Texas. His powerful preaching and winsome personality caused the church's membership to grow from around 3,000 to over 6,000. To make room for this expanding congregation to worship, a new 1,500 seat sanctuary was completed in 1956.

The time of my joining the staff was soon after F. Byron B. Cory became the business manager. Ninety-one-year-old Clem Morris was still teaching the largest Sunday school class (the Odds and Ends). Fritz Funk played special solos in worship on his Stradivarius. The men who sang at worship in white jackets Sunday nights were directed by Barnard Vessel and assisted by paid gifted soloists, George Garrigues and Arlene McKinney.

Dr. Lehmberg preached at night in addition to major morning services at 8:25 and 10:55 a.m. He was concerned that attendance sometimes dropped below the 150 mark Sunday evenings.

With membership above 6,000 and usable space at a premium, I was interested in how the senior minister would lead the church in another major building program—so soon after the completion in 1956 of the magnificent new church building. I found him wise enough to gather support from key leaders of the congregation who were besieged by functional groups unable to operate efficiently, much less expect to grow. Although "Dr. Ben," as he was affectionately called, was obviously behind every plan for a new office complex, he tried (without convincing many people) to stay in the background of the planning. Three years after my arrival, consecration services for the new expanded facilities were held September 18, 1966. Now there was space for Sunday school classes, a choir robing-room, offices for the staff, a little theater, and even more space for other activities. An added parking lot was already too small. Later, across the street northward, additional space was purchased for parking. At that time, First Methodist was the largest congregation in Colorado Springs of any denomination. Because so many of the members came from Kansas, Nebraska and Oklahoma, Dr. Lehmberg liked what someone said, "First Methodist in Colorado Springs is the largest 'country' church in America."

On the fourth Sunday of October 1984, the Rev. Dr. Lloyd C. Nichols, another retired colleague, and I decided to found a new congregation at the Flying W Ranch in northwest Colorado Springs. It was a good choice because it allowed me to continue what I loved to do. That fellowship became Wilson UMC and now has over three hundred members.

My wife was 100 percent with me on this endeavor. In October of 1986, her journey with me everywhere came suddenly to an end just four months after we had celebrated our golden wedding anniversary. She collapsed into unconsciousness for five weeks from a leaking aorta and a blood clot on her brain. For the remainder of nineteen months in a nursing home, she was unable to move her arms and legs or to speak. Sadly, joint decision-making came to an end. I had the privilege of visiting her two or three times a day mostly for those months, but continued in ministry as Special Care Minister and as a New Life Missioner. Another retired Air Force chaplain, Col. Charles "Jack" Richards, carried on to the chartering of Wilson UMC in 1987.

A Church Is Born

"God moves in mysterious ways, his wonders to perform." A little better than four decades ago a rancher named Don Wilson and his wife owned a large ranch in northwest Colorado Springs. His wife gave birth to two daughters, Marian and Marietta. Marian married Russell D. Wolfe on land she inherited from her parents. Marian and Russ developed a western-style dinner operation called the Flying W Ranch.

This project was a success. As it grew, an evening of entertainment was added to the early American cowboy meal. The summer nightly guest list expanded to well over 1,000 per night, seven days a week. A group of musically talented men were employed to provide vocal-instrumental western music. They were billed as the "Flying W Wranglers." They also helped to run the place. Their musicianship ran a close second to "The Sons of the Pioneers," the original "out west" musical group.

At the expense of the Flying W Ranch, Russ and Marian added to the eating areas and gift shops, a 100-seat country-style church building in 1980. They wanted a place where some of their Sunday afternoon supper guests could worship. At 2:00 p.m. on May 18, 1980, the Little Church at the (Flying W) Ranch was opened and dedicated:

"To the glory of God the Father, to the honor of his Son, and to the praise of the Holy Spirit."

The Rev. Calvin D. McConnell, their pastor and Senior Minister of First United Methodist Church, gave the sermon. I assisted Russ and Marian in arranging the services and conducted Sunday afternoon services for ranch guests and others for a while.

But the above is only the prelude to the later birth of Wilson United Methodist Church in that building. The genesis of the church came as a culmination of several dreams. First, Russ and Marian dreamed of a United Methodist Church in northwest Colorado Springs near their home—an area about to burst into new home developments. So important to them was their dream that they promised to donate the land for a new church when the need for it came. But who would step up to the challenge of getting the nucleus of a Fellowship formed? Who would commit to a new church project for which there was no money, no constituency, and only a need? Everyone was so busy, and the requirements of first getting together 100 charter members, and $100,000 for the building fund were formidable.

When the need for a new church there became a goal of the Sub-District Council on Ministries during the United Methodism's bicentennial year, the idea met with instant and enthusiastic support, and was immediately referred to the Pikes Peak United Methodist Church Extension Society, where it was approved. It was approved even though that Society had no funds to undergird the project. However, the Wolfes had the Little Church at the Ranch, where the utilities were paid, as a place in which to worship. In addition, they had promised a building site for later on. What an inducement!

The District Superintendent was heartily in favor of starting a new Fellowship, and the New Church Development/Redevelopment leaders of the Rocky Mountain Conference acquiesced. No one, however, had any start-up money. As a nest egg, the two initiating ministers gave personal donations.

When Russ and Marian Wolfe learned that definite plans were afoot to begin forming a nucleus of a Fellowship in their Little Church at the Ranch, they were delighted, and affiliated as pre-charter members.

The Pikes Peak Church Extension Society approved two retired ministers to take on the responsibility of getting things going, backed up by the promised cooperation and help of sister churches in the Sub-District. The United Methodist Sub-District Ministers' Fellowship, which met Monday mornings, pledged its support. The ministers chosen as co-leaders were: The Rev. Dr. Lloyd C. Nichols (81), former Dist. Superintendent in the Evangelical United Brethren Church, and now retired as preaching minister; and the Rev. Philip L. Green, Sr., (69), equal associate.

After a survey of adjacent housing developments north of the Garden of the Gods Road and west of I-25 (but including Holland Park), the first worship service was conducted at 9:30 a.m. Sunday, October 28, 1984, in the Little Church at the Ranch.

Feeling the pressure of age, and his involvement with the local Hospice, Dr. Nichols gave over his duties after four months. In July of 1985, George Spencer, son of a United Methodist minister, and a ministerial student at the local Nazarene Bible College, was employed at $150.00 a week to assist Rev. Green with Christian Education and Outreach.

After 19 months of pastoral leadership at the Wilson Fellowship, Phil Green asked the Church Extension Society to find someone to succeed him. He served this initial and crucial period without salary or other remuneration, and gave generously as well.

Appointed to take pastoral leadership in June 1986, was the Rev. John F. "Jack" Richards, Chaplain, Col., recently retired from the USAF. As later developments attest, this was a fortuitous choice, for the fellowship grew rapidly to chartering on December 6, 1987. Coming also to the staff of this fledgling fellowship at the same time were Mr. and Mrs. King and Eppie Hastings, who volunteered to help expedite the growth of the new Fellowship for only an apartment and travel expenses for their work.

There is no way the Fellowship could have been initiated and come to chartering without the sacrifices given by Dr. Nichols, Rev. Green, George Spencer, Rev. Richards and the Hastings.

That is only a part of the story of the first three years until chartering in December 1987. Trying to be known is how the pre-charter members dedicated themselves to the task of making the dream come true. Russ Wolfe opened the gates during the first winter months, and lighted the fires in the big pot-bellied stove that "baked the preachers" but warmed the church. He grew weary of doing that and installed a heating system. He sat on the hard, cold pews during the sermons until he found it would please the people, as well as himself, to sit on cushions.

I still remember the some 50-75 wild turkeys that spend winter nights in the tall pine trees and breakfasted on Russ's generosity. Led by George and Donna Spencer, the small congregation started a Sunday school and staffed the first two Vacation Bible Schools. We found a pianist to make it possible to have a choir. We had a printed Sunday bulletins from the first Sunday. They were mailed out to those who visited the services and those who sent their children to the summer Bible school.

Carolyn Harris was our first pianist, followed by Jonathan Gorst. They received a modest sum for their services. Bob Manning was our volunteer choir director. Others not named above who were leaders in the first months of the Fellowship were: Bruce and Sue Coulson, Chuck and Kathy Duncan, John and Sally Fletcher, Chris Grinde, Al and Joanie Norris, Nellie Pinnell, Randy and Debra Sollenberger, Mary and Duane Spaulding, and Jim and Vera Williams.

I had another important decision to make. On a nine-week fixed itinerary out of the state, there was adequate time to think about the future of my life. I was seventy-four years of age and a major decision loomed up before me: *"Do I want to remarry*?"

Lois had collapsed in 1986 and died in 1988 after being unable to move or speak for nineteen months. Now, eight months after all of that, I was free to look ahead. I remembered something a lecturer at the Hogg Foundation for Mental Health of Texas had said thirty years earlier at a month of training for twenty-five Air Force chaplains. Dr. Bernice Wilburn Moore told us that the best way to respond to the death of a beloved spouse was *"to reinvest that love in someone else."* The answer to the question above was, "*Yes, I believe I do wish to marry again.*" Now the question was "to whom".

Some of the widows in that huge church had invited me to special events. I had conducted the funerals of many of their husbands. But I could not tell who were among the few who might hope for me to take a special interest in them. Then I thought of Helen MacMillan.

She and her late husband were members of First Presbyterian Church. I had known her as the Executive Director of the Pikes Peak Association of Churches, as the fifteen-year person in charge of the television program "The Church Game," and as the manager of the famous Garden of the Gods Easter Sunrise Service. There was no necessity of seeking her friendship. It was already there. We had worked together in many ways. She and Stiles had been family friends.

As a matter of fact, in 1970 while President of the Association, I had responded to her letter of request to resign from her position. Her salary was grossly past due. I wrote as follows:

Dear Mrs. McMillan;

At its May 14 meeting, the Executive Board of the Council of Churches [name changed to 'Association'] voted to honor your tender of resignation as its Executive Director, effective on the 15th of June 1970. Attention was given to the fact that this was your second plea to resign within the last few months.

The above action was taken with regret and with great appreciation for the expertise, accomplishments and dedication which characterized your tour of office between 3 October 1966 and 15 June 1970. The board members express to you their thanks for a tremendous job—a job well done. Also, they moved that your arrears in salary be paid to you as soon as possible. We sincerely regret that we are unable to pay all of it at the time of your departure from the office.

I have ever been impressed with your great confidence in the Pikes Peak Council of Churches, your patience with the pace with which many of us responded to your vigorous leadership, and to your deep commitment to the work of the Council. Your ability to be aware of and promote a wide variety of projects simultaneously, has won for you a lasting place among the more gifted leaders in our community.

Only you and Stiles and God, and maybe God alone, knows the many overtime hours you both have put in because you took your work seriously. God bless you for this. Rarely does one find a husband with such understanding, and with such willingness, to support a wife in her dedication to the work of God's kingdom. This certainly indicates the kind of faith Stiles has for the work of the Lord. This also speaks eloquently of the love he has for you.

Perhaps the most outstanding work you did for the Council was in the area of the promotion of its projects and goals through the media of radio, newspapers, brochures, bulletins and television. The stature of the Council of Churches throughout the area is much more known and respected now than when you took office. The tenacity with which you have brought this about reflects great credit upon your appreciation for those things church people can and ought to do together.

Please know that we will be glad to recommend your name favorably to any Council of Churches, or to any employer by whom your immense capabilities are sought. In the meantime, we will appreciate your sympathetic understanding with the Council in its effort to find your successor.

Most sincerely yours,
Philip L. Green, President, PPCC

Helen resigned as the Executive Director but kept up contact with, and support for, the Council without pay. When Lois died after fifty-two years with me, Helen was present at the Service of Remembrance in a large sanctuary overfilled with loving people. She wrote this note following that event,

Dear Phil,

My love and prayers have been with you and your family as you have bid goodbye to another of the family. The funeral was very lovely. As all of you came up the aisle, you have no idea how magnificently beautiful you were. You reminded me of a great eagle whose strong wings were gently lifting and supporting its eaglets through the strong turbulence to smoother, higher currents and new visions.

My eyes were full of tears of both grief and joy, for I know that combined anguish of a love lost and yet a joy that there is release from that love to a new and beautiful new beginning. Head up, stay strong."

Signed,
Mrs. Stiles MacMillan

On the long itinerary, I called her up in order that she might know I was thinking of her. When I returned to Colorado Springs, I visited her in her office and invited her to lunch.

One thing led to another and soon I got enough nerve to ask her out on a date. As things worked out, she did not seem averse to a closer relationship. The answer to my question about marriage was affirmative. On June 3, 1989 we were married in her church by her senior minister, the Rev. Dr. John H. Stephens, assisted by the Rev. Dr. O. Gerald Trigg, senior minister of First United Methodist Church where I had been associate pastor.

Helen went with me for five of the six and a half years as pastor of Avondale UMC. Then decisions needed to be made by both of us. It was a bit tricky at first. She was a prima donna in her own right and I was a prominent minister, Rotarian, Shriner and community leader. There was the need for give-and-take on both our parts, but we did it. Four of the fifteen years we were married were marred by her journey down the road of dementia and death on January 5, 2005.

A major mental and emotional adjustment faced me in a return to ministry in one particular denomination—even though it was my own. For twenty years I had adjusted to a general Protestant service and ministry to an across-the-board smorgasbord of Protestant people. The military congregation was representative of many denominations worshiping under one umbrella. I had come to respect differences in faith and practice and even admire how some faith groups operated back home.

A deep question lurked in my consciousness. *"Could I return with an honest loyalty to the polity and practice of the Methodist denominations?"* The answer ultimately was *"yes."* And why not? Hadn't the Methodist Commission on Chaplains accepted me to be a Methodist chaplain for twenty years? Hadn't Commission supervisors read my monthly reports and visited me, encouraged me when ministry situations were difficult, scheduled retreats for Methodist chaplains in Europe and America where they asked people like Bishops Gerald Kennedy, Arthur J. Moore, and G. Bromley Oxnam, to be resource speakers?

I could only applaud the way my church had "followed me" to Germany, Spain and throughout America. I had invariably attended my Annual Conferences when stationed near enough to do so. Leaders in my annual conference had kept in touch with me by correspondence and were interested in my well-being. Under the Methodist banner, I was able to minister in difficult locations when chaplains of other denominations were not permitted by their church rules to do so.

A Heartbreaking Decision

A minister has more than his own decisions to consider. As a counselor, there was advice to be given to members who needed help in deciding what was best to do.

Below is a statement of a father, at the Custody Determination of his son, Joshua, before a District Court judge in Colorado Springs, CO.

> *Your Honor and members of this Court,*
>
> *Thank you for giving me this opportunity to say a final word regarding the custody determination of my son, Joshua. He is my son. I am his natural father. He is bone of my bone, flesh of my flesh.*
>
> *Thirty-one months ago I confessed my faith in God, joined a church and began trying to become a changed person. I am still in the becoming stage in this new life as there are no saints suddenly. I have made progress and I intend, through God's help and that of my pastor, my wife, and my clinician, to grow in my understanding and practice of what a Christian man should be.*
>
> *I would gladly fight to gain this court's decision to give me back my son. However, I have recently learned more of the meaning of a functional home and reluctantly yet rightfully admit that just now I could not give Gabriel the special care he so urgently needs. I am all too painfully conscious of the fact that he cannot wait for my progress to more fully arrive. He needs what others can give him now.*
>
> *I have been given one of the most difficult tasks in my life. I have been told that I must give up my son. How does one do that without a breaking of the heart? It is like ripping out a part of my body and throwing it away.*

> *My heart says "No, you can't." My mind says, "Yes, you must for his sake." I realize now that I might not have been all that a perfect parent should be. Still, I love my son with every fiber of my being. There is nothing I would not do for him. I have been told that a good family wants to adopt him. Perhaps they are good enough and strong enough to do a better job with him than I could.*
>
> *Your Honor, I ask that you accept my statement of no contest in the custody determination of my son, Gabriel. I am trying to understand the full consequences of doing this—that it means that I will be shorn of him as long as he is a ward of this Court. It does not mean that I will be unconcerned about him, that I will not still love him, that I will not continue to believe in him. I respectfully request that this entire statement I have made and am making today, become a part of the written record of this day's event.*
>
> *"My son, if you ever have the chance to read this transcript, there are three things that I want you to know, understand, and always remember. First, you must realize that I feel I am doing this for your sake. Second, Mom and I love you very, very much. Only because we love you so much do we let you go so you can have your chance to be the best you can be. Third, no matter where we are or what the circumstances may be, our door will always be unlocked and open for you.*
>
> *Goodbye, good luck, and God bless you, Dad."*

Some decisions are easy, others difficult or very difficult. While I was at the USAF Academy 1960-'62, I came to know and admire the senior minister of First United Methodist Church in Colorado Springs nearby. The Rev. Dr. Ben F. Lehmberg had built the church up from 3,000 to more than 6,000 members. He invited me to several of his official board meetings and we worked together on an invitation letter to the cadets and permanent party personnel. The letter contained a map showing the location of all the Methodist churches in the Pikes Peak area, and contained the location and hours of services in each. One day he surprised me with,

"Phil, I want you to be my Associate Pastor!"

I was most pleased that he thought highly of me. In a year, I would be retiring after twenty years from the Air Force (20 years was maximum for a reservist). That meant that I would need to contact my bishop in Western North Carolina, tell him I was retiring, and ask him for an appointment to a church. From stories of other chaplains who had returned from military duty, the bishop's answer would be something like this,

"Well, Philip, you have been out of line for twenty years, so you will have to start at the bottom of the list. Yes, we'll have something at land's end or last chance."

It was encouraging to receive the following letter from Dr. Lehmberg on March 18, 1963.

> *Dear Phil,*
>
> *Thank you for your letter. Also, thank you for coming to Colorado Springs and having the meeting with Bishop Phillips—and also for the fine lunch we had together. I am glad to know that everything looks satisfactory for you to have your retirement effective the 31st of July.*
>
> *Bishop Phillips has you down to be appointed as an Associate Pastor at First United Methodist Church. I presume that the appointment will be made at conference time effective the date that you stated. We are thrilled about this and are looking forward to having you. Quite a few of the men in the church who met you in the past have already expressed their tremendous delight in knowing that you will be here.*
>
> *We will be putting you on the mailing list for our church paper and bulletin. In addition, some time in the future I may be sending you some material. In the meantime it might be well for you to write to the Board of Evangelism at 1908 Grand Ave., Nashville, TN to ask them to send you some folders of excellent materials they have on hand, some of which you may find very helpful in laying plans for your services here at First Methodist Church. I am sending you a manual for the Commission on Membership & Evangelism. I am also sending you a manual for the commission on Missions.*

It's good to know that you will be out this way for the Annual Conference. Best wishes to your wife and daughter. Be seeing you.

Sincerely,
Ben F. Lehmberg

So the offer from Dr. Ben was both pleasing and heart-breaking-pleased because the thought of such an appointment was what I had hoped for—sad because I couldn't afford to take it. I said to him,

"Dr. Ben, nothing would please me more, but I have nineteen years toward retirement from the Air Force. I can't give that up."

What a decision to have to make!

So, I went on to Kincheloe Air Force Base in Upper Michigan from the Academy. Seven months later I received a letter from Dr. Ben saying:

Phil, I am still interested in talking with you about First Methodist Church, Colorado Springs.

My answer was,

Dear Dr. Ben,

Thank you for your letter of February 7, which was received with both pleasure and surprise-pleasure, because it revived a lost hope, surprise because I thought you had long ago filled the vacancy on your staff.

It was heartening to learn that he had not chosen other applicants for his staff. He actually waited a whole year for me to retire. On July 31, 1963, I retired from military service, returned with Lois and Mickey to Colorado Springs. Because Dr. Ben had waited so long for me, I gave up my month of accrued leave, and went to work on August 6. Lois had bargained with me. She would agree to the change if the Principal of Air Academy High School would rehire her to teach. She was hired and we both began to work. All was well, and I retired at the rank of colonel.

In 1980, another of life's turnings needed to be made. In consequence of my decision to attend the Congress on Evangelism at Oral Roberts University in Tulsa, January 1-4, I was in the valley of decision. I had announced my decision to retire from mandatory appointment from the Rocky Mountain Annual Conference at the end of the 1980 session. Then I noticed that Cal McConnell no longer needed me to help get his feet "under the table." At that time I changed plans to go until June and leave the staff at First Church at the end of February.

Little did I know that the wonderful Congress on Evangelism at ORU would put me on another track altogether. For five years, I had been Minister of Outreach, followed by twelve years as Minister of Pastoral Care. Suddenly, a new vista opened up before me. I felt a call, not to retire, but to seek an appointment as Pastoral Care Evangelist.

As I traveled along toward Colorado Springs with my son Phil Jr. and his wife, Elsie, I tried to formulate what such a ministry would look like. All through the next few weeks, I sought divine guidance, and on January 28, wrote a letter to the powers that be to change from "retire" to "leave of absence." I needed a year to touch all the bases for such an unfunded appointment.

A few paragraph's of that letter said:

> *The reason for my not retiring, as previously requested in my letter of September 19, 1979, is based upon a strong desire to be appointed in June 1980 to a special appointment under Category B-2 (with or without annuity claim upon the Rocky Mountain Conference) to a ministry toward which God seems to be calling me, that could best be described as: Conference Pastoral Care Evangelist. After twelve years in this church as Minister of Pastoral Care and five years as Minister of Outreach and Evangelism, I feel an inner imperative to tie the words Pastoral Care and Evangelism together, and try to develop an intentionality to pastoral care which will make it a more skillful ally to efforts to relate people more closely to Christ and the Church.*
>
> *I want to make myself available to pastors in local churches throughout the Conference to assist them and their lay leadership to do a better job of "shepherding," and in the*

> *process enhance such relationships of caring as will result in their coming to the Chief Shepherd and into his fold. I do not believe any effective pastoral care is ever wasted, but I believe the shepherding of the fruits of that caring is a harvest that can be more effectively garnered.*
>
> *This call, which burns so brightly within me, I have discussed with my senior minister, my District Superintendent, my wife, my colleagues on the staff here, my confreres in the Monday morning Sub-District meetings, Rev. Jim Cowell, as well as with a few trusted friends and groups to which I am close. There seems to be unanimity in affirming me in such a ministry. It is a new concept, to be sure, but I believe I can bring a special meaning to it, so that others may do a better job of caring and garnering.*
>
> *If I am granted an appointment as Pastoral Care Evangelist in June, I will immediately begin putting together (if I can wait) the co-conceptual and practical aspects of this new ministry. Hopefully, I would receive encouragement from others interested in making this idea get off the paper into appropriate action.*

So much of my future depended upon my decision to attend *that* Congress on Evangelism. I would have missed seeing the parade of the flags of all the world's countries during which evangelist Frank Routon Harvey prayed the prayer that Jesus prayed (John 17) in so dramatic a fashion. That was the time I saw Charles D. Whittle preside as national president over the most inspirational event ever. I would have missed hearing Charles Allen, pastor of the largest United Methodist Church in America, say about the controversial president of Oral Roberts University:

"If he would fly all the way from Tulsa to Houston to pray for my sick wife, he has my vote."

Allen Walker, world famous Methodist evangelist, gave the Harry Denman lectures. I would have missed them. I would also have missed seeing again such leaders of the National Association of United Methodist Evangelists as Maxie Dunham, George Hunter, George Morris, Sam Kamaleson, Whitney Dough and Jack Gray.

What If? What if I had not decided to go to the Congress on Evangelism in Tulsa? Would I have continued on the "road not taken?" Having decided to go, I invited Phil Jr. and Elsie to travel with me in my Oldsmobile, pulling a 29-foot Airstream trailer.

Truly, I had no idea there would be so many challenges on the way. First, we started late in the evening. Before sixty miles a rock flew up and ruptured the car's gas tank, leaving us stranded in a small town with no garage. We had enough fuel in the Airstream to make it through the remainder of the night. It took another day for repairs to the gas tank and we were invited to stay with a minister in the next county-seat town. On the way to Oklahoma, the trailer began to wobble because of a poor connection to the car. In short order I slammed on my brakes. The car and trailer swung all the way around but, thankfully, did not drop us down a steep bank or into oncoming traffic. A tire blew out and we had to change it and put another for a spare. We stopped overnight in a very rain-soaked field where commercial vehicles were parked because the local park for travelers was full. The next morning, we were hopelessly stuck in the mud until helpful young people came by in a truck and pulled us out. That truck threw a substantial amount of mud on the car and trailer. We had to dig it off at a carwash in town. What a mess!

Very late at night we arrived in Tulsa and hooked up in a motor-home park. In the wee hours of the morning one of the gas tanks ran empty. In order to connect to the extra tank, we had to get hot water and thaw the ice from the connection. Whee! What a trying trip! But we made it, thanks to help along the way and a very patient son and daughter-in-law. What if we had turned around and gone home? I'm so glad we didn't, but that we stayed to find inspiration and guidance for the years ahead.

An End and a Beginning

The inevitable result of my decision not to retire but to prepare for a new beginning was a goodbye to a church where I had been the associate pastor, and twice interim senior pastor, for sixteen and a half years. The final parting began with a farewell banquet of some 300 guests.

They gave us an album with the names of the many who had given love-offerings that paid for two tickets to the Passion Play in Oberammergau, Germany. Paul and Wanda Ballantyne played and sang one of my favorite songs and the whole crowd sang the Church's Centennial Hymn that I had written in 1971. (Our 'sorrow' was greatly mitigated).

The final sermon I was to have preached on March 2 had to be written and given by Cal McConnell because of a very sore throat. I was only able to croak the words of Bob Hope, "*Thanks for the memory.*"

27

AGING AND HERITAGE

When and where and to whom we were born account for the length of our lives. The society in which one's nearest forebears grew up stamps one with certain characteristics and susceptibilities, as well as the customs, beliefs and life styles of that society. Some people believe one's sex patterns predispose satisfaction or its opposite. Sociologists affirm that the number of offspring per family varies from place to place and from time to time.

I have been fortunate in the kind of parents and grandparents that were mine. My father was James Henderson Green, who was raised in the mountains of Western North Carolina of Anglo-Saxon parentage. He was born 6-21-1881 and died 5-23-1955, the son of James Tippit Green (4-11-1830 to 1902) and Mary Jane Cook-Green (4-1-1865 to 7-18-1930). He and his four brothers and two sisters were tall and strong and mentally healthy. Papa was a Methodist minister, as were two of his brothers.

My mother was Minnie Mae Grogan (7-28-1886 to 2-11-1962), Scotch-Irish, one of fourteen children of John T. Grogan and Elizabeth Wood-Grogan. She gave birth to ten children (three died in infancy). I was number eight, when my mother was only twenty-eight.

My father with his saddlebags

My father started out as a school teacher but early felt that his "calling" was into the ministry. A "calling" meant a calling, by God, to preach, teach or something special. It usually was a lifelong commitment. That's what it meant to my father and to me.

Papa became an interdenominational evangelist after being a pastor of churches. In 1932 he founded, and for twenty years was president of, a Bible college named John Wesley Bible School which later became John Wesley College and is now Laurel University in High Point, NC. He is the author of "Green Spots," which highlights his various ministries.

Growing up in a Christian home started me into a life on the road to right, happy and healthy living. In this chapter, I share a bit of Papa's early life in the ministry.

A Letter from the Past

The envelope carried a 2-cent stamp, and was postmarked August 11, 1915 from Iron Station, NC. The letter inside was in longhand, written with a pencil, and had the same date. It was from my father to Mr. George Gillespie in Leicester, via Asheville, NC.

Mr. Walter Gillespie, his brother, gave this letter to me in 1937 shortly after I had been appointed pastor of the six churches of the Sandy Circuit, with a parsonage in Leicester. George had received it less than a year after my father had completed four years in the Leicester parsonage.

I was born there September 15, 1914 and was now the new pastor of six of the ten churches my father had served. I have now completed 74 years in the ministry and treasure having the letter below as a memento of my legacy as a "preacher's kid." It was so good of Walter Gillespie to give me the letter my father had sent to his brother, knowing that it would be of inestimable value in the family archives. Here it is:

Dear Bro. Gillespie:

"I am in a meeting at Iron Station, 12 miles from home now. It is raining incessantly tonight. We have returned from

services. The congregations are so large we had a brush arbor built which gives room for hundreds of people, but it is not good for rainy weather. But it may seem strange to you when I tell you there is no church in this part of the state that will hold the folks that attend the revivals. I have seen nothing like it since, as far as I can recollect.

The County seems awake. Recently, I helped Bro. Modlin in a country meeting. The church was too small. They built a large brush arbor and hundreds gathered outside. There were present often from ten to fifteen hundred folks. Many came ten and twelve miles. There were over 200 professions, etc. At our Camp Meetings, what multitudes! There I preached to thousands of people. The great arbor 90 feet long was full and sometimes standing around it five people deep. Oh, how God did visit us! I can't describe the wonderful things that did happen. Such shouting, I can't tell it. No one knows how many were saved, but scores and scores were converted and many at the altar sought and found the second blessing.

You know, I am preaching the Second Blessing more this year and God is blessing my labors more. People are hungry for it. Everywhere they want help. I think I have since Christmas preached to eight or ten thousand people and maybe more. And there have been in all more than 1200 professions. Yet I have about 30 calls to hold meetings where I can't go before Conference. Many preachers and committees write and come to urge me and persuade me to help them—from county and town and city. One man said, "I will give you $5.00 per day for every one you will help us with." Bro. George, I can't tell you how I feel. I have not allowed this to exalt me yet. Rather, I feel too weak for such opportunities. I am so worn in body, but I can't rest—with so many needing help.

Yes, I am just plain Jim Green. Wife says, sometimes I don't "dyke" up enough as I appear before so many people but I am free from the folks—thank God, I am free. Jesus is more precious to me than all else. The Holy Spirit is my Comforter. My wife is almost a preacher now. At Camp Meeting the people said she beat me preaching one time. Oh, praise God!

> *Well, I am to go to Andrews Aug. 26 to hold a meeting. I want to come by and spend a night with you as I go, if I can, then I can tell you more. Oh, how I wish you could be with me some in these meetings! I have found no one I love better than you. Continue to pray for me. Say Godspeed to Walter for me. Love to all.*
>
> *Jim Green*
>
> *P.S. Three young men from my Circuit called to preach are intending to enter college to get ready. Three of my young ladies are giving themselves to become missionaries and nurses. Praise the Lord!"*

But my father grew in stature and understanding so as to be much more than a pastor and evangelist. In addition to founding John Wesley Bible School, he was the founder of camp meetings (at Avon Park, FL, and three in North Carolina), and of The People's Christian denomination. Copies of his sermons may be found in The People's Herald, the college periodical.

My father seated in front of some faculty and students of John Wesley College, 1936. That's my future wife Lois on the far right.

It is interesting that the Rev. Dr. John R. Church, D.D., wrote the following foreword to my father's book entitled, "Green Spots":

> *"It is inspiring to see how God can take men and women, save and sanctify them, and use them for his glory. Many years ago, God in His wisdom and grace reached down and picked up a mountain boy, in the hills of North Carolina, by the name of Jim H. Green, and down through the years God has used him in a mighty way.*
>
> *It would be hard to tell how much the life of Brother Green has meant to the cause of Christ, during these many years that he has preached the Gospel of Full Salvation. He has been recognized as one of the outstanding exponents of the Bible doctrine of Holiness. Thousands of souls have been saved under his ministry, and many others have been sanctified because of the stand he has taken for this great truth of Full Salvation from sin.*
>
> *Over twenty years ago, God led him to establish the People's Bible School at Greensboro, NC, and during these years he has been mightily used of God in teaching young men and women in the ways of the Lord. Many of those who have come under his influence are now on the battlefront for Christ, and are being used in a gracious way. Only eternity can reveal the full impact of his life on the cause of Christ.*
>
> *Through these years he has been a champion of the Bible doctrine of Sanctification, as a second work of God's grace in the human heart. In working to promote this great truth, he has been instrumental in establishing such works as Camp Free at Connelly Springs, NC. In connection with the work of the People's Bible School at Greensboro, NC, he started the Sunny South Camp meeting, and he also made a great contribution to the great camp at Avon Park, FL. For many years he was president of all of these camps, and God used him in all of these works.*
>
> *Brother Green has lived a long and useful life and has been used by God to bless many people. Some of them are still living while others have passed on to their eternal reward.*

> *Many people will rise up to call him blessed, and will thank God for His influence on their hearts and lives.*
>
> *Since his life has been so full and varied, it is very fitting that he should give to the world some of the highlights of God's dealings with him and through him. He is doing this in writing this book, "Green Spots."*
>
> *I feel sure that many people will want to get this book and read it, and then pass it on to others to read. This book ought to be a source of inspiration to many people, as they read how God has blessed and used this man.*
>
> *I am glad that I can have this little part in this book, and it is my earnest prayer that God will bless it to the hearts of many people.*
>
> *Brother Green's life has been rich and full, and now as he comes down toward the evening time of life, it is my prayer for him that his last days will be his best, and that at evening time it will be light for him. Through these years, we have been warm friends and I thank God for what this has meant to me."*
>
> *John R. Church*

An uncle of mine, who became a minister, married a woman of Cherokee Indian blood and bore five children. She spoke only English. I didn't know of her ancestry until later in my life. A niece married a man of Indian blood. Her daughter married a man of Afro-American blood whose son is of color. My oldest sister married a man of Greek blood. My son married a woman whose parents were from Puerto Rico. One of my daughters married a man from Persia (now Iran). A grandson married a Korean woman while on military duty there. At age ninety-five I find myself surrounded by an international family, now citizens, who love to get together often and lovingly, despite differences in cultures and complexions. I sit happily at the top of five generations and am the keeper of the Green Family Tree.

28

WATCH WHAT YOU SAY—TO YOURSELF

Written by my son, Rev. Dr. Philip L. Green, Jr.

Self-messages can make or break us. Some are positive, some are negative. But a lot are mixed messages and they are the ones that may be the hardest to unscramble to serve us positively. Take, for example, what we tell ourselves about keeping the law.

I found myself headed for a possible stint behind bars because I told myself that I didn't have to keep to the laws of New York City regarding the use of my car. A little excessive speed here and a little illegal parking there—everybody does it. The problem is, once you tell yourself that you are "above the law" in little things, it becomes easy to expand your parameters of breaking the law with the message to yourself, "Yes, I keep the law, but now and then I'm allowed to break it."

Here's my story. It was a blowy cold evening in Flushing, Queens. My wife and I had picked up our seven-year-old daughter at a friend's house. We had the small car and could not fit her bicycle in it. I proposed to bring my wife and daughter home about 10 blocks away, get the larger car jump-started and pick up the bicycle.

That simple errand earned me five carelessly broken laws in the space of a mere ten minutes. The car was cold and I was cold, so naturally I sped to pick up the bicycle behind the tree at my daughter's friend's house. I screeched to a stop, ran to pick up the bicycle, yearning to get home and out of the bitter cold. Racing home, I failed, quite noticeably, to do little more than a token stop at a quiet corner. Because the large older car was in disrepair, it had expired plates and an unrepaired taillight.

I decided to take a slightly illegal route home which required going the wrong way down a one-way street to get to my driveway, all the while not a car in sight, except behind me. He, too, went the wrong way down the one way street. He too pulled into my driveway. Only he (they) were in an unmarked police car.

I told them I lived in the house attached to the Church because I was the pastor. They didn't much believe me given the multiple ways

I had just broken the law. Challenging my statement that I had a key to get into the house, they said, "Well why don't we just go inside the house. Naturally, you have a key to get in." I did have the key. Going in and having full light, they looked me over carefully, and I looked them over carefully. They looked like street thugs and I looked like a mighty scared and freshly caught lawbreaker. When they asked to see my license, they announced that I was driving on an expired license. The mod squad looking police announced that there had been several bikes snatched in the neighborhood. They were assigned to catch the thieves and were pretty sure they had collared a likely suspect. They had been parked at a side street nearby when I had picked up my daughter's bike. They had seen everything. They observed that I had been (a) speeding, (b) driving without proper license plates, (c) driving with a broken taillight, (d) failing to use a turn signal, (e) driving the wrong way down a one way street, and now—the final insult to the traffic laws of the City of New York—driving with an expired license! One of them did some figuring on minimum fines and announced that a conservative amount would be about $600.

Just as I thought they would commence to write the tickets, they announced that they weren't there to write tickets but to catch thieves. They had neither the authority nor the time to write the tickets. The law had suddenly been replaced with grace. Thank you, Jesus. My bumper crop of careless law-breaking had been saved by grace.

I've tried to untangle the mixed messages I give myself about keeping the law. I'm not perfect, but I'm developing a much greater respect for the laws. After all, grace might not always be there to rescue me from my carelessness in keeping the law.

29

BETWEEN AGE SIXTY AND NINETY-FIVE

At age fifty I had become the associate pastor of a mega-sized church in Colorado Springs. There were other staff ministers and personnel assisting the senior minister, the Rev. Dr. Ben F. Lehmberg. He had wanted me to become his associate largely in order to have someone to whom he could say,

"Phil, I'll be doing preaching missions for the Air Force troops in Europe for six weeks, you're in charge of the ship."

Through the next 17 years, and two other senior pastors, the bishops kept me there "to be in charge of the ship" in the absence of pastors away on vacations or other events. At age 60 I was ten years down that busy track, 5 of which I was "Minister of Outreach" (Evangelism), and 5 years of the next twelve "Minister of Pastoral Care." After one year, the District Superintendent asked Dr. Lehmberg to spare me for an additional duty as Sunday night pastor of a small country church of thirty-five members fifty-six miles out on the plains. I filled that spot for three years.

Three years after I became the associate pastor, our beloved "Dr. Ben" had a heart attack in mid-August of 1966 and a fatal one in November. Bishop R. Marvin Stuart appointed me the interim senior minister. Four months later the Rev. Dr. Lawrence L. Lacour was appointed the new senior minister. The total of the seventeen years on that staff found me very busy, as may be seen below:

1. Interim senior minister Oct. 1977 to June 1978 and three other months running the ship while the senior minister was away except to preach on weekends.
2. Founder of: The Duo Class for young adults. The 7:30 a.m. worship service in the chapel where I preached for 17 years. Cowboy Church in a drive-in theater. Travel Club, PK (Preacher's Kid) Club, Fall Roundup at the Flying W Ranch.
3. Staff Representative: Membership and Evangelism Commissions, Pikes Peak Association of Churches, Missions Commission (and six Missionary Conferences).

4. Other activities:
    - Third Conference on Ministerial Excellence, a one-week event on Pastoral Care for ministers of large churches interfaith nationwide. Dr. Seward Hiltner was the dean.
    - Chair, Colorado Interfaith Counseling Center and Pastoral Care Institute for seven years.
    - Acting Chair of Host Committee, Rocky Mountain Annual Conference, 1971.
    - Member Host Committee, Council of Bishops, 1978.
    - Mission to Mexico 1970; to Liberia, West Africa, 1977.
    - One New Life Mission, one New World Mission with Bishop of Mexico.
    - Schuller's Successful Church Institute, at the Crystal Cathedral, CA.
    - Sub-District Ministries: Secretary, Board of Church Location and Building.
    - Chair, Grand Festival of Faith Celebration, Pikes Peak Region, USA's Bicentennial and Colorado's Centennial in Wasson High School Stadium.
    - Chair, Templed Hills Conference Camp Board and founder of the Aspenglow Camp for the elderly (1981-'84).
    - Convener, United Methodist Ministers' Fellowship Mondays 9:30-11:00 a.m., for which I prepared an annual roster and helped plan annual picnics.
    - Chair, Festival of Faith Bicentennial celebration of Methodism in America, 1985.
    - Co-Founder, Wilson Fellowship at the Flying W Ranch 1981. It became Wilson UMC.
    - Sponsor, Bill Peckham New Life Mission week, 1965, for Methodists and EUBs.
    - Member, Church Extension Society, Committee on the Ministry.
5. Before, during and after: Too many things to mention. They are to be found on pp. 255-262 in *The Mountains Are Happy*, (my autobiography.)

6. *A Veritable Storehouse of Memories and Life Experiences* is found in the document and photo albums I keep. Following is a list of only a few of them.

   "My Christian Ashrams"
   "Book of Philip I, II, III"
   "Book of Lois"
   "Book of Helen"
   "Military Chaplains Association"
   "My Worship Sites"
   "Church Camps, Retreats, Sites"
   "Our Travels Abroad"
   "Music in My Life"
   "Pastoral Acts, weddings, funerals, baptisms, etc."
   "My Cherished Friends"
   "My Extended Family"
   "My Schools, Sunday School, Vacation B S, Other"
   "My Scenes of Beauty"
   "Scenes in Germany, Austria"
   "Scenes in Spain"
   "First UMC, Colorado Springs, CO"
   "Edison-Leader, Avondale, Wilson UMCs"
   "Family Trees"
   "Pikes Peak Sub-District"
   "Examples, how-to, models, rules, rosters"
   "Prayer of Dominant Desire, 'Lord Use Me'"
   "A Fond Farewell"

At age ninety-five, I wanted to take a trip back to my native state of North Carolina. My only living sibling of the seven of us was Ruth Armstrong in Greensboro. She was ninety-two and in a care facility. It had been six years since I had seen her.

My son, Phil. Jr., said he would fly with me. My itinerary was by American Airlines through Dallas to Charlotte, then by rent-a-car to Greensboro there I saw Ruth and also had a luncheon with loved ones and cherished friends that was scheduled by my nephew, Kenneth Green.

Then we drove to Western North Carolina to the North American Christian Ashram session at Lake Junaluska. I took 150 of my books entitled, *Prayers Jesus Might Have Prayed* to give to others there in honor of Rev. Dr. William Berg, one of "The Four" leaders of United Christian Ashrams, who had received a test-marketing copy of the book about which he had written, "*The foreword and first two prayers are worth the price of the book.*" In May he had celebrated his 100th birthday. At the same address Phil and I visited the United Methodist Foundation for Evangelism in which I had been a member of "The Seventy" for twenty-one years.

I began my ministry near Lake Junaluska on two nearby circuits (1936-'40, 1940-'43), in Leicester and Franklin. The late Hal and Edith Wells had been cherished friends for a lifetime. When their daughter, Beverly, learned that we were coming, she offered her parents' old home as a place to stay for three nights, though it meant 320 miles of travel from her home in Wilson. Edith had lived with her during her declining years. So Phil and I were hosted less than a mile from where I had been born and where he had lived as an infant. Beverly invited several people to come together to meet us on Thursday afternoon. On Wednesday three people from the Franklin Circuit drove over from Franklin to have lunch with us, namely, Helen Carpenter and Bob and Jo Corbin, who were children when I was pastor there. They were pleased that I was the pastor who baptized them and brought them into church membership.

I am a nut about doing rosters, partly because I like to have readily at hand facts about colleagues, and partly because I always wanted to be inclusive of people who were usually not included or sidelined. For example, during the several years I was the convener of military chaplains in the Rocky Mountain Annual Conference, Bishop R. Marvin Stuart was strong against the Vietnam War but very affirming of his military chaplains. At his request, I prepared first copies of letters from him to three kinds of chaplains: Members of his Conference; Members from other Annual Conferences on duty within the boundaries of his Conference; and Conference Institutional Chaplains.

He wrote his version of these letters on his own stationery and had his secretary mail them. I researched and prepared a roster of the military chaplains. The Methodist Commission on Chaplains kept me up to date on these and sent a representative, some of the time, to present visiting chaplains to the assembly. The bishop's letter invited everyone to be at that presentation and to a luncheon afterwards. Often, in the absence of someone from Washington, he wanted me to make the presentation.

When I was invited to become the associate pastor of our large church, there was no roster of the Methodist ministers in the Pikes Peak Sub-District. At that time the Methodist Church had not yet united with the EUB (Evangelical United Brethren) denomination. That meant only ten churches. Only three of them had an associate. But the roster I prepared included the five EUB churches before the Methodist Church was renamed The United Methodist Church. It may be of interest that I also included the pastors' names, spouses, home and church addresses, and phone numbers. By 1969 I had added to the roster full-time professional staff members, retired ministers and spouses, widows of retired pastors, and Methodist military chaplains at three nearby bases. I became as inclusive as possible so that contacts and friendships could abound and blossom. At First Church alone there were ten retired ministers and seven widows of pastors.

John Stone was the executive of the Colorado Springs YMCA. Originally included was the YWCA for women. A building for single young women was located apart from the YMCA. In time, due to the cost of two separate organizations, the city recommended that they be combined. This was a disappointment to some, but the economics mandated the change. I knew John Stone as a member of First Methodist Church. He was a proven leader and added weight to the lay leadership of the Church. When his wife became ill, I visited in the home. When she passed away, John asked me to conduct her service. In retirement from the YMCA role, he grew in my estimation and I asked him to be a specialist in my retirement ministry, Special Care Ministries.

In that context, Rev. Dr. Clare Hoyt was the chairperson and Arnold Schneebeck was the treasurer. John was the secretary. All have finished their earthly race and gone on to a place in God's great tomorrow. After John's wife died, he married Ruth. And after my wife Lois died in 1988, the Stones invited Helen and me to dinner every Valentine's Day. I'll never forget level-headed, clear-thinking, predictable John Stone. He was an inspiration to me and to many others.

Bernard Vessey's diminutive body and curved spine made me wonder how such a small chest could produce such a tenor voice. Dr. Lehmberg put him in charge of the men's glee club. He also was the music leader of our Rotary Club. He was invited to sing at events all over the city and state. He was affectionately known as "the gospel songbird of the Rockies." A little more than a year after I was asked to join the staff of First Methodist Church, Bernard became suddenly ill and died. Because the law of the state required a mandatory autopsy for anyone who died that suddenly, his body was taken to the city morgue for the doctor to perform what the state required. The doctor knew Bernard Vessey. When he examined his pitiful little lungs, he said to his helper,

"If Bernard Vessey had not pushed his lungs to sing like he did, he would have died years ago."

Adding to the versatility and richness of the music at First Methodist Church in Colorado Springs was the talent of a violinist, Fritz Funk. He did not use an ordinary violin—he carefully unwrapped and tuned up a bona fide Stradivarius. Many times he played his instrument during the offering. People enjoyed hearing him play because he did it so beautifully. He had a shop at the famous Broadmoor Hotel. When the church honored me for the first forty years as a Methodist minister, through his shop he purchased an excellent heavy set of glass ware that went with Lois and me after the celebration. First his wife died in their home on North Cascade. Soon thereafter he died. I often wondered what happened to the Stradivarius. I know he had a son. He probably inherited it.

Many years later I discovered that Helen's father left a little-cared-for violin. I looked at the label and it said "Stradivarius." I took it to a shop in town for authentication. The owner said it was a fake, out of a Chicago firm that had made many fakes. I was very disappointed, and so was Helen.

30

ANYONE OUT THERE NEED ME?

My seventy-fourth birthday was coming up on the horizon. Many things of import had happened in my aging journey. I had retired from seventeen years as the associate pastor of a mega-church, and had been the Rocky Mountain Conference Evangelist for three years. Now I had just been retired from the mandatory appointment system—meaning, now I could say no to the bishop without fear of the consequences. My oar was out of the water, my robe in the closet. Now I was retired—again.

The Foundation for Evangelism of the United Methodist Church

When the Rev. Dr. Charles Kinder, President of the Foundation for Evangelism visited Lois and me in the spring of 1986, it was a sequel to our visit with him at the 1984 Congress on Evangelism in Kissimmee/Orlando, FL. Unveiled at that event was the now famous painting of John Wesley bidding Francis Asbury and Thomas Coke farewell beside a ship in England, with the words, "Offer Them Christ." The American artist was the Rev. Dr. Kenneth Wyant, a United Methodist minister. He made a special project of the painting, which historic masterpiece would be copied in quantity and sold to churches and people. The proceeds would go toward funds to put E. Stanley Jones Chairs of Evangelism in those United Methodist seminaries that requested them.

It was while we were hosting Dr. Kinder for dinner at the USAF Academy officers club that he asked me to become the Rocky Mountain area Director for the Foundation. I had recently resigned several positions of responsibility and said quite readily, "Charles, from now on I'm just going to do the things I really believe in," to which Lois interjected, "Phil believes in too many things already."

But Charles had my number. Evangelism was my fervent interest. I was ready to ask questions. What did the Foundation want me to do? The Cliff School of Theology in Denver had asked the Foundation to raise funds to establish an E. Stanley Jones Chair of Evangelism.

The immediate need was for someone to take on such a project. I told Charles I was interested, but that I felt uncomfortable with the title "Regional Director," and would he give me the title, "Regional Representative?" Almost overnight I found myself responsible for putting together a blue-chip committee of respected Conference leaders.

Could I, in retirement, form a strong effective committee of interested leaders?

The very word, "Evangelism" had fallen into disrespect, if not disdain, in the Rocky Mountain Conference. I was surprised that liberal Iliff School of Theology would even consider asking for a chair of evangelism to be filled by a professor of evangelism, and at a cost of something more than $250,000. But then, the trustees of the Foundation (through my committee), would raise that money. So, why not? The idea was for the Foundation trustees, in concert with the faculty and trustees of the seminary, to select the professor of evangelism to the satisfaction of all concerned.

With some uncertainty, and more than a little trepidation, I began this challenging assignment. Someone once said, "Fools rush in where angels fear to tread." I became that fool. But wait! Why shouldn't I? Hadn't I been the first approved Rocky Mountain Conference Evangelist ever to apply for and be appointed to that position? The thought strengthened my feeble knees. Every person I asked to serve said, "yes." The first brochure was made at my typewriter, after consultation with President Charles E. Kinder. Included were:

Rev. James E. Barnes, Pastor, Trinity, Denver
Dr. A. James Armstrong, Professor of Preaching, Cliff
Rev. Edward P. Beck, Pastor, Sunrise, Colorado Springs
Rev. Dr. Deanna M. Bleyle, Dist. Superintendent . . . .
Rev. James M. Calhoun, Pastor, Park Hill, Denver
Rev. Samuel S. Day, Dist. Superintendent
Rev. Thomas M. English, Pastor, Christ, Salt Lake City
Judge David W. Enoch, Colorado Supreme Court
Mr. Robert L. Gould, Builder, Colorado Springs
Rev. Aaron Gray, Pastor, People's, Colorado Springs
Mr. John H. Marshall, Dallas, Foundation Board Chair
Mrs. Maxine Marshall, Denver, Diagonal Minister

Rev. Dr. Donald E. Messer, Cliff President
Rev. Dr. O. Gerald Trigg, Pastor, First, Colorado Springs
Mr. Roy E. Warren, Denver, Foundation Vice Chair
Rev. John F. Willson, Development VP, Cliff

On the brochure also were Interested Church Leaders

Bishop Emerson Colaw, Minnesota Area.
"Tennessee" Ernie Ford, "Offer Them Christ" Sponsor.
Dallas Coach Tom Landry, Honorary National Chairperson, "Jesus and the Apostles" paintings.
Bishop and Mrs. James K. Mathews, retired, (Son-in-law of the late Rev, Dr. E. Stanley Jones.
Bishop Calvin D. McConnell, Portland Area.
Bishop Richard B. Wilkie, Arkansas Area.
Rev. Dr. Kenneth Wyant, artist for "Offer Them Christ" and of "Jesus and the Apostles."

Only one member of the working committee raised an eyebrow over all that "window dressing." In answer, I listed why each interested church leader was included (see above). Included only on the brochure were the names.

Almost immediately, we met and elected Rev. Jim Barnes, chairperson, Rev. Ed Beck, vice chairperson, and myself as secretary. Soon we had all our meetings at Iliff where we were sandwich luncheon guests of the seminary. It wasn't long until Dr. Don Messer offered the first $150,000 to establish the chair, at which time the committee began plans and publicity to raise $700,000 more to endow the same.

While I was out of the state for nine weeks in early 1989, there was "trouble in River City." As best as I can remember, the faculty would not support the plan to endow the E. Stanley Jones Chair of Evangelism in perpetuity. Then, without consulting with the trustees of the Foundation for Evangelism in the selection of the professor of Evangelism as originally agreed upon, Iliff selected its own choice for that professor. To say that the trustees of the Foundation were displeased would be putting it mildly. President Charles Kinder located me in early March in Nashville and filled me in on what had happened.

Upon my return on March 9, it was a "*fait accompli.*". The top-drawer committee was devastated for the most part and had disbanded. Charles Kinder retired and was replaced by retired Bishop Earl G. Hunt, Jr. as Foundation President. He and the Foundation members felt that it would be best to let the matter drop and to draw up clearer understandings for future seminaries that wanted the trustees to raise funds for such Professors of Evangelism.

I wrote myself a big question, "What does the Lord want me to do with the rest of my life?" I was sixty-nine and feeling great—and not ready to quit. So, I continued doing ministry under the incorporated name of Special Care Ministries. In 1984, another retired minister and I fulfilled the wishes of the sub-district Council on Ministries and formed a United Methodist Fellowship in the northwest part of Colorado Springs. In a short time it became Wilson United Methodist Church, with services in a small chapel that was loaned by Russ and Marian Wolfe, owners of the western eatery—the Flying W Ranch. They, and Russ's parents, had been hoping for a United Methodist Church in their area, and were willing to donate a site for it. At a reunion in 2007, to which all former pastors were invited and came, Russ Wolfe (now widowed) gave me a Bible in which he inscribed this message,

"Because of you, Phil, and the Lord, we are still on our way."

There are now some three hundred members. The second phase of the building plan has just been completed. Though the area called, Mountain Shadows is largely limited for many home buildings, it continues to grow. My ministry at the church was foreshortened two years later, due to the collapse of my dear wife, Lois, in the fall of 1986. For nineteen months, she was an invalid. After regaining consciousness and limited cognitive power, she still was unable to speak or move her arms and legs. She had been right in there pitching to get the new church growing. Chaplain, Col, Jack Richards, USAF, retired, took over and brought the fellowship into a Church in 1987.

At the Annual Conference of June, 1988, I was given the Harry Denman Evangelism Award for forming a new congregation. On the way from the platform, I picked up the mike and said, as any North Carolinian might say,

"I ain't done yet!"

Two months later, I spent five days at the Colorado Christian Ashram at the Horn Creek Ranch Retreat Center. Because I had lost my precious Lois on May 22, I was alone. During the "Hour of the Open Heart," I asked my Ashram comrades to pray that God would help me get my oar back into the waters of ministry. In less than a month, I received a phone call from Rev. Jan Sumner, Superintendent of the Sunshine District. She wanted me to consider, in retirement, being appointed the pastor of Avondale UMC in a village near Pueblo. Was it an answer to prayer? I didn't think so, because it was sixty miles from home and a small church with only slightly more than one hundred members. I had become accustomed to serving in a much larger situation.

It was not to my credit that, despite my 'I ain't done yet' statement at the Conference in June, and my request at the Ashram to get "my oar back in the water" in August, that I began equivocating. I told Jan Sumner that there were several retired ministers in Colorado Springs who would gladly fulfill her request. She countered by saying there were two retired pastors in Pueblo who were only thirteen miles away who could do it. She explained, *"But I want you!"*

No if's, and's or but's about it. She wanted me. As she twisted my arm, I made another excuse. She wanted me to begin in November, so I told her,

"I have a fixed itinerary for nine weeks out of the state beginning the day after Christmas. It wouldn't be fair for me to start in November and be absent for that long, that soon after the new beginning." She wouldn't let me off the hook. She said, *"I'll get someone to replace you while you're gone."*

Wow! She was really after me. It was only during the weeks away that I began to feel ashamed of the duplicity of saying one thing and doing another. As a matter of fact, I consented to go for an interview with the Pastor-Parish Committee members, "knowing" they wouldn't want a seventy-four-year-old pastor. But I was mistaken. They wanted me. "Wanted" was a key word with me. Many times I went "where they wanted me."

True to her promise, Jan Sumner asked retired pastor, Rev. William R. Obaugh of Pueblo, to fill needed duties during my preplanned itinerary between December 26, 1988 to March 5, 1989.

Upon my return to Avondale in March, it was time to get back to work. The church building, the parsonage and the grounds needed much upgrading. I married Helen McMillan in June and the partly-furnished parsonage needed improvements to accommodate my new wife on the days she accompanied me to the church—which was regularly. A nearly-lost tradition at the church was an Easter Sunrise service that had fallen to just a breakfast at the church. Helen had been in charge of the famous Garden of the Gods Easter Sunrise Service in Colorado Springs for many years. She offered to help restore the one in Avondale. The Richardson's took us to a high hill that we named Inspiration Point. It was a perfect site. We gained the permission of church officials to rename the event so as to be regional and inclusive. We called it, The Arkansas Valley Easter Sunrise Service at Avondale.

We celebrated the church's centennial year in 1993 with a great celebration the first Sunday in November. A grand dinner was served at noon to more than 200 members and guests. The new District Superintendent, Rev. Lonnie Eagle, gave a message of encouragement, with words of appreciation for the many improvements the church had made. New hymnals were purchased, and the roofs were replaced on the sanctuary and parsonage. I served that congregation for six and a half years—until I was eighty. As I was leaving in June of 1995, we received many kind and loving words of appreciation. Here is just one:

> *Dear Phil and Helen;*
>
> *How do we go about saying thank you for the past 62 years? We really don't know where to start. Six and a half years seems such a short time, yet it seems we have known you forever. We thank you for your faithfulness and leadership, not only in our church, but to us personally. You've been there for us in joys, excitements, sicknesses, troubles, and good times and bad and, for these, we are most appreciative. You baptized three of our grandchildren and took our son-in-law in as a member of our church. You've prayed for and with us, and cried for and with us, and we thank you from the bottom of our hearts. Please keep in touch. We love you dearly and will miss you terribly. God bless. (names omitted).*

We made the Sunday bulletin large enough to include a variety of subjects that called for special attention. The Sunday following the tragic bombing in Oklahoma City, we included this prayer:

> *Lord God of love and justice and mercy, we come to you for those who died so suddenly in Oklahoma City that they could make no preparation to meet you by either confession, or prayer, or repentance. How quickly a dastardly act of hatred cut short all their plans, hopes and dreams! How empty are the arms and hearts of those who will never hold them close again! How sad will be the homes which children once filled with laughter! How unfruitful are the work places that are destroyed and they that turn the wheels of industry in Oklahoma City.*
>
> *We pray now for the disconsolate survivors and families of those who have died, many of whose bodies still lie beneath unsearched rubbish heaps. As they face inconsolable days of loss and grief, please come to each one of them, in your own time and way. Enable them to recognize your sustaining presence in their pain. Let them know that they can bring their broken hearts, their anguish, and their sorrow to the feet of Jesus, and find through him their healing and restoring touch.*
>
> *We pray for the distorted minds of the perpetrators of this crime against people, little children, husbands and wives, and fathers and mothers. How deeply they must have hated, to have done such a cruel thing! If we, as American people, have pushed them in the direction of such hatred, please forgive us. Protect us from the violence of others. Keep us safe from the weapons of hate, and teach us to love one another in better ways. Amen.*

One reason I want to live longer is to minister to those in grief and shock and disbelief. Not everything was "sweetness and light" at Avondale those six and a half years. Because Helen and I took a strong lead in trying to make the church as beautiful as its name, we were sometimes guilty of helping do too many projects without a clear understanding of "who is doing what." The following letter of apology was written because I, Pastor Green, had trimmed two small evergreen bushes that I should have left in place. I suffered through arguable protests from a few members, and wrote to the board chairperson thus:

> *I write this letter with an aching heart-aching because my action in trimming the two trees at the front of the church has caused such a violent outcry from some members of the church. I knew that the trees east of the sanctuary were "hands off" by the action of the Council but I didn't remember that the trees trimmed were included. I am truly sorry to have caused so great a disappointment and am offering at my expense to either replace the trees or to landscape the space in a manner satisfactory to the wishes of the Administrative Council. With hindsight, trimming the trees is one thing I wish I had not done.*

Helen and I had a strong desire to leave Avondale United Methodist Church a more attractive place than when we came. To do this I, or we, have done, or have led the way, as follows.

[Key: (**) with Council approval; (*) without council approval; (#) at no expense to the church]

#** Purchased and installed a cross on the steeple, with appropriate ceremony and telecast coverage.

#* Planted and dedicated on Earth Day twenty (20) trees by the parsonage and along the west fence behind church.

#** Expanded, relocated and renamed the Avondale UMC Easter Sunrise Service to be area-wide and *now known* as the Arkansas Valley Easter Sunrise Service at Inspiration Point. Gained telecast service.

** Established our own Vacation Bible School, from Vineland UMC.

** Designated an evergreen tree in front of the church as an Advent Tree to be decorated and lighted with appropriate ceremony honoring the elderly members of the congregation, with lights to come on each night of Advent and Christmas. Electricity is the only expense.

#* Installed carpeting on the lower level of Fellowship Hall and the two stairways down.

** Found donors to pay for all but twenty of the new hymnals.

** Prepared the 1993 Centennial Directory with color photos, with very little expense to the budget.

#*With the hands of Helen and Philip, repainted the walls, ceilings and doors of the four Sunday School classrooms; redecorated and reapplied nursery and classrooms with new tables and chairs. Painted piano.

#** Converted the library to a multipurpose room.

#** Secured donations for the repair of the tower chimes, with enough money for present and future repairs.

** Added sod to the church and parsonage lawns.

#* Purchased and installed an adequate public address system because the chimes system could not be used with the church's sound system without detriment to the chimes system. I sold same to the church.

#* Had a set of mail distribution boxes installed in the library, to save postage. All members have boxes.

#** Added Ritual of Friendship pads in the pews for members and to make visitors known.

#** For over a year, furnished a copier for Sunday Bulletins. A small amount for this came out of the budget.

#* For five years, purchased bulletin covers for Sunday Bulletins, etc.

** Mailed Sunday bulletins to the elderly and shut-ins, as well as to prospects and chronically absentee members. Most of the postage for these mailings came from personal expense.

#** With the acquiescence of the Council, prepared weekly Sunday bulletins that included news, keeping the church aware of weekly program events. The quality of the bulletin compares favorably with those of large churches.

** Have taken in thirty (30) new members; baptized 17 infants and children, and eight adults; conducted 14 funerals.

#* Paid my own way to Annual Conference most of the time.

#* Scheduled ministers, laity and special speakers for most of my absences on vacations, conferences, retreats, etc., and paid most of them.

#* Furnished invitation cards for our church's Centennial Celebration on Nov. 5, 1993 and for other special events.

I was upset with what I considered nit-picking over nearly nothing. I told no one I had seriously considered walking out or resigning. I was nearing seventy-nine and had been overly generous with them in gifts from myself and Helen. But why quibble? I knew most of the members thought well of me, so I pleased the District Superintendent by not saying a word about taking my oar out of the water. My Prompter whispered to me, "*I want you to stay.*" I never had quit anytime, anywhere.

SECTION VII

What I mean by challenges in my life can be summed up by my facing difficult and challenging career assignments—like a super-challenge at the Sixteenth Air Force in Madrid, Spain 1954-'57. I knew I had been chosen by the Chief of Air Force Chaplains for the task of developing "from scratch" a full-blown Protestant chapel program in a Catholic country—and that all alone for three years. An even greater challenge came with my election as the national president of the Military Chaplains Association during the time I was the associate pastor in a church of more than six thousand members.

Have you ever been so happy you could cry? Lois D. Ritter was a teacher in my father's Bible college. Even though she was seven years senior to me, I found myself in love with her. Nearly everyone tried to break up a relationship with such an age difference. My father tried to get me to transfer to a college in another state. That didn't work. It took awhile before I got my first kiss. Then I claimed her as my own. When she agreed on a marriage date with my father to officiate, I could have "cried for happy."

I pray because I believe there is Someone up there, out there, over there, down there, who is greater, holier and infinitely more understanding than I am. Because of my faith, I believe that that Someone loves me and has chosen me to be his heir. My prayers, and those of others, have seen me through many difficult times in my life.

A major contributor to my longevity has been my participation in out-of-doors active sporting events. Tennis, golf, volleyball, basketball, touch football, hunting and fishing and the "old swimming hole" have kept me out of doors a lot. Getting away to church camps and retreats has softened the grind of heavy duty.

31

CHALLENGES IN MY LIFE

Most challenges I have met and mastered. One of my weakest assets as a public speaker has been the ability to do a little more than passable. Between one major thought and another needs no hesitation, but easy connectives. I greatly admire speakers who are free of notes. I have never reached that stage of perfection. All the senior pastors of my large church have had doctoral degrees and the ability to speak without notes. My greatest skills have been pastoral and relational. On military efficiency ratings, I have been glad to have words such as:

"He is a very sincere person and mixes well."

"His performance of duty has been superb."

"Your creativity level continues to amaze me."

"Chaplain Green is held in high esteem by everyone"

"Chaplain Green is particularly gifted for pastoral work. He ought to stay in day to day contact with the people. The Air Force, as well as Chaplain Green, would be the loser if he were to be assigned to a job which was largely administrative in character."

And with such comments came descriptions of my successes. How satisfying!

Challenge at the USAF Academy

One of my assignments was at the USAF Academy. There I was expected to be a top speaker in the pulpit. I had tried to do better by being a member of Toastmasters Club and was making progress. Six years earlier in Madrid, Spain, I was in charge of the only English-language worship service. During those three years, the congregation was tolerant of my imperfection and threw around me a large contingent of able volunteers for duties that might have been done by additional chapel personnel. During the last half of my time there, I finally had one enlisted helper assigned. This do-it-yourself stance made people accept each other's shortcomings—even the chaplain's.

Now, I was in a spot where expectations of me as a preacher lecturing to cadets was high—too high for me. I had come from three years at Whiteman AFB in Missouri, where my ER's were very high. When another Chief of Air Force Chaplains was leaving from a highly successful opening ceremony of our new chapel, he had thrilled me by getting me aside and saying, "Phil, Carp wants you at the Air Force Academy."

"Carp" (Charles I. Carpenter) was the former Chief of Chaplains who wanted to stay on after that duty and be assigned at the Academy. He was told that as a Major General he couldn't go there because he'd outrank the Superintendent. So he took off two stars and put on the eagles of a colonel and was assigned and sent for me. The fact that he wanted me was exciting, and I went there with great expectation. [He wanted me and the other assigned chaplains to make the worship services and Sunday School to be together at the beautiful new chapel with the cadets.]

But that was not to be. The professors and other permanent party personnel rebelled. Shortly after my arrival, it was my painful duty to break the news to Carp that most people were against that arrangement. They said, "We work with the young cadets all week. We don't want to be tied to them on Sundays, too. Our hope is to have a family service for our wives and children."

So the "Chief" and some of the chaplains developed separate worship services for cadets and others who chose that place of worship. The community center chapel was still on the drawing board and would not be constructed for a few years. Where to have the community services? The only place available was at a large lecture hall in the cadets' classroom area. From that platform, professors lectured to groups of cadets. Those were professionals. Their lectures were standardized and, after being put together and often printed, they were plus-perfect. That meant that my sermons, which were different each time, had to compete with perfection.

The real heroes were Chaplain Carpenter, and the other cadet chaplains. Carp was a star in his own right, a baritone soloist, and coach of football for the new cadets. This did not displease me because Chaplain Carpenter had been a role model of mine for nearly two decades. But it put me in a spot where my weaker abilities in the pulpit could not compete with those professional lecturers.

A Super-Challenge in Spain

Sometimes in a lifetime a door opens to a very challenging chapter in one's life journey. During twenty years as a chaplain in the Army and US Air Forces, there were a couple of times I felt that I was in over my head. As the only Protestant chaplain in Madrid, Spain, and responsible for the only English-language chapel worship service and chapel program, there were many facets for which there was only one sergeant the last eighteen months, plus a secretary. All religious activities needed to be developed from scratch. Because Spain was a Catholic country, I even had to purchase and carry with me Sunday school literature. There was only the unfurnished American school auditorium, hidden from Catholic eyes, as space for worship services. No church building that looked like a worship site, (except for Catholics) was permitted.

All equipment had to be ordered, including chairs, drapes, speaker system, communion set, pulpit, Bible, hymn books, etc. On top of that, volunteers were needed to be recruited, trained and assigned for teachers, bulletins, adult and youth choirs, ushers, alter guild, correspondence and others. There were no colleagues in civilian churches with whom to share fellowship. When I went on vacation, it was necessary to secure a chaplain from West Germany to fly down and fill-in for me. Whee! My hands were full.

First Protestant Chaplain in Spain

It became obvious to me, that this would be a highly sensitive assignment requiring more than ordinary caution. "Spain is more Catholic than Rome," so it was said in Madrid in 1954. This did not mean that everyone was a "good" Catholic, only that they were nearly all at least nominally Catholic. In much the same sense we say that America is a Christian nation, knowing that the statement is not literally so.

As already mentioned, I was the only Protestant chaplain in Madrid for three years and the only one in all of Spain for about eighteen months. Chaplain Charles I. Carpenter, Chief of Air Force Chaplains in Washington, DC briefed me thoroughly as I passed through there on my way from Parks Air Force Base, CA to the Aerial port of embarkation. He indicated that the influx of thousands of American service people—a majority of whom were non-Catholic—was a threat to Catholic unity in Spain. My task was to develop a meaningful and satisfying chapel program of worship and services for liberty-loving Americans who would be inclined to resent having no other English-language service they could attend, and to do it privately.

The rationale and need for caution was based in the tenuous position of the new bases our military leaders had received permission to build from Generalissimo Franco. If the Spanish people (mostly Catholics) became aroused about all those Protestants in their country, plans for military bases in Spain might wash out. America's need was to have Air Force bases in that part of Europe, because of the "cold war" with Russia (see above).

To make American GIs less conspicuous, for three years we were ordered to wear civilian clothes only rather than military uniforms (on or off duty). All Americans were asked not to attend services led by denominational missionaries from the USA nor invite Spaniards to attend our Protestant worship services. A few defied that order. My wife did not attend any of those services, but I found out later that she co-hosted one of the missionaries.

As to religious literature, my challenge became apparent in Chaplain Carpenter's office when he told me that Catholic Chaplain Raymond Stadta (already in Madrid) had phoned to alert me to bring Protestant Sunday school literature—because such literature would be hard to get in Spain. That was a masterpiece of understatement, as none was available.

What! No Chapel!

I was to discover that there was no chapel, no pulpit furniture, no piano or organ, no communion set, nor any ecclesiastical furnishings when I arrived in early September. My family was delayed a week in Frankfurt, Germany, awaiting a flight to Madrid. During that week I learned that there was a small Anglican church in Madrid where a few Americans could attend an early "family" service. The Anglicans served cocktails after services—to the delight of some, and the dismay of others. It didn't take long to gather a cadre of interested American men and women and begin planning for space, chairs and a Sunday school. We began the Sunday school before we were well organized. Colonel James O. Frankowsky, a Lutheran, volunteered to be the superintendent. He gave me a fright the following week when he and his wife made an appointment one night to talk about that leadership position. He said he had attended the adult class the previous Sunday where the lesson was about alcoholic beverages. Some in the class thought religious leaders should not drink alcoholic beverages. He confessed that he drank some socially, but that he never drank to excess. He wanted to let me off the hook by resigning if I thought that was the right thing to do. Although I am a teetotaler, I would not accept his offer to resign. He turned out to be the very leader to head the Sunday school. Before I left three years later, we were averaging more than 400 per Sunday in the school, which proved him to be an outstanding organizer and supervisor.

By this time the Armed Forces Chaplains board had developed what was known as a "Unified Curriculum" of literature for Sunday schools at military bases. We were users of this curriculum. It was departmentalized for age groups. It is of interest how the curriculum was chosen for each quarter and age group. Representatives of the Air Force, Army and Navy scanned the materials planned by several denominational publishing houses in advance of their printing. Orders were then placed for the quantities thought to be adequate for orders from chaplains at bases. When families moved to new bases, they found that the literature provided continuity and eliminated unnecessary repetition of materials by the children. Our teaching staff found this continuity of lessons very helpful. This made it easier to recruit teachers and stand-by teachers. The 400 plus in Sunday school each week the last year was a tribute to the dedicated efforts of a large and dedicated volunteer staff.

The Dynamics of Restricted Choice

A disaster could have occurred as a result of telling a group of Americans that there was approval for them to attend only one Sunday worship service for three years. Such a situation could have angered any hot-blooded independent Protestant. The wide mixture of worshipers from little-structured Pentecostal to ritualistic Episcopalians, including Baptists, Lutherans, Methodists, Mormons, Nazarenes, Presbyterians, and many others made my task as the only preacher and spiritual leader extremely challenging. There were many occasions for adjustments in worship style without compromising essential convictions.

For nine months after arriving in Madrid, there was no grape juice in the small commissary where Americans shopped, nor was any for sale in any Spanish markets. This meant that we had only wine for communion services. There was no outcry about this because everyone understood the problem. We almost had a problem when a VIP member of The Women's Christian Temperance Union from the USA visited us on Communion Sunday. She confronted me with the question,

"Chaplain, do you mean to tell me that you serve wine in all your Communion services?" When I explained that there was no grape juice in our commissary yet, she cooled down fast and left in good humor. When grape juice became available, we changed from wine to grape juice, but then another problem surfaced. Some denominations regularly use wine in Communion services. What was a chaplain to do? It was finally solved by placing wine in the small circle of the trays and grape juice in the two larger circles. Everyone was happy with that.

The director of the youth choir and later President of United Chapel Women called my hand for announcing "Holy Communion" in the bulletin. She said Southern Baptists did not have Holy Communion. The next time I inserted "The Lord's Supper" in the bulletin. Smiles, again. Later, she took exception to "The Apostles Creed" in the bulletin for the same reason—"Baptists have no creeds," she said. I changed the entry next time to "The Affirmation of Faith," and all was sweetness and light once more. There was no rancor either time.

I thought the millennium had come when the Baptist teacher of the adult class said to the Mormon postmaster, "Bill, will you lead us in prayer this morning?" At another time he said to him, "Bill, I'll be working on the pipeline from Rota to Zaragoza next Sunday. Will you teach the class?" And this coming from a wonderful Christian whose provincialism was clear when he said to me one day, "Chaplain, I never take Communion anywhere except in my little hometown church in Texas." Navy Captain Bob Sparks and his wife, June, were and still are cherished friends even after forty years. I learned humility and adjustability from them. They were staunch supporters of the chapel program in Madrid. Serving Communion to such a diverse group of worshipers prompted me to preface the invitation with these words: "Everyone is invited to partake of The Lord's Supper and place upon this act of worship whatever special meaning seems in keeping with your prior teaching."

Sharing the Chaplain's Load

At times the load grew heavy. There was not another chaplain with which to communicate, to share joys and concerns. At one vacation time, the USAFE command chaplain in Wiesbaden, Germany, sent a chaplain to give the sermons while I was away—Chaplain Joseph Sides. Others came later.

The enormity of the possibility that failure on my part would impact negatively upon those who looked to me for leadership in such a sensitive spot spurred me on to work harder and longer to please the chief of Air Force Chaplains. The possibility of falling prey to a reduction-in-force at some time during the last six years of active duty quickened my pace to fulfill this solitary duty with flying colors.

To achieve desirable goals in the Madrid ministry necessitated the help of a maximum number of volunteers in chapel duties. In one way or another, some 150 persons put their shoulders to the wheel in committees, choirs, visitors to the sick and troubled. Trusted volunteers kept me informed as to needs. Because of all these helpers, I held onto having an attractive printed Sunday bulletin. Many Sundays, in the evening, I'd get a call from Colonel Frankowsky about how Sunday school went that day and any problem that needed my attention. How faithful he was!

Lois took a major load off by being the director of the Vacation Bible Schools each year. She had oodles of helpers. Rear Admiral Short headed up the Men-of-the-Chapel group. June Sparks was president of Women of the Chapel, and Raymond Reistad, Lydia Ruiz, and Kenneth Fish directed the chancel choir in turn. Mary Peterman was our faithful pianist. Others took on the ushering staff and the altar guild. S/Sgt. Noel Gaerttner was the Protestant chaplain's assistant and Maria del Carmen Gallego kept the chaplain's fund. Several others assisted with correspondence. We had a Social Night for Chapel Workers that spun a square dance group called "The Madrid Squares." When it came to the Christmas parties of 1954, '55 and '56, children of all religions were invited. A strong committee of persons within all organizations helped plan it. We had to camouflage the annual chapel picnic in a public park in the metropolis, to keep the populace from knowing it was a Protestant chapel picnic. If they had known that, we could have had an ugly public relations problem. A joint committee of Protestant and Catholic leaders planned the Easter egg hunt.

Our Hidden Protestant Activities (through Spanish eyes)

Americans in Madrid were informed that they were not to invite Spaniards to attend or visit our Protestant services and activities. Even the place where we worshiped (in the school auditorium) was not publicized. Most Spaniards had never met a Protestant Christian. A few people came to know that I was the Protestant chaplain. Though the media knew I existed, my role was downplayed in the news. Example: when the Catholic chaplain and I appeared in public while escorting plane crash victims, he was referred to as a lieutenant colonel and I was referred to as a sergeant. This was one of the realities in a country with monolithic Catholicism.

We had a Spanish live-in maid named Teresa. She must have been all of twenty-one years of age and a good worker. She observed us, a Protestant family, for many months, and knew I was the leader of the Protestants. She finally spoke her evaluation of us. She said in Spanish:

"Senor Green, I know you and your family are Catholics, but not Roman Catholics."

That was such a compliment that I will never forget it. I was never introduced to a local Catholic priest. It might have started unwelcome inquiries. Cardinal Segura might have heard about it.

Until the commissary became more adequately stocked, I did most of our family shopping at a large *mercado*, or open air market. There I bought the best fish I could find. Fish came iced down by fast train daily from the north coastal towns to Madrid. One had to get to market early to buy the freshest and best fish. In 1954, Spanish merchants had no frozen meats. Each day, meat was butchered and sold the same day. This meant a rush to the market to get our daily bread—"el pan nuestro de cada dia,"—as the Lord's Prayer says. I felt conspicuous as a man among mostly women, and the tallest one there. Lois didn't know enough Spanish "para la defense" (to shop without being taken advantage of.) Madrid was full of small shops, little more than holes in the wall, each selling one or two specialties, shoes, hats, scarves, tableware, and the like. While we were there, a large store opened up, a near equivalent to one of present day American K-Mart stores. Numerous sidewalk coffee shops were available all day and evenings to sell *café con leche* or whatever.

Our 1947 Road-Master Buick followed us to Spain—not so much that we wanted it with us—there just was not time to sell it in the USA because mine was a rush trip from California to the port of embarkation in New Jersey. Five years of travel had added many miles to the odometer and, though it was in fairly good shape, I would have been better off to have traded it for a new one. Once in Madrid, it looked better by comparison with beat-up used cars on the streets there. In Spanish hands, a car like mine would have been shined up, decorated with mistletoe or baby's breath in the rear window, and used to pick up brides and grooms and others for a wedding. Nevertheless, the engine was leaking oil onto the spark plugs, requiring their frequent removal for cleaning. Taxi drivers sped (raced is too strong a word) around with horns blasting as though they had the right-of-way over all other traffic.

While driving with my family in a nearby city, I was involved in an accident in the downtown area. I was waiting in a line of traffic at a stop sign and the car in front backed into us. There was a hubbub as a crowd gathered around. The driver in front was at fault, but who would believe that I didn't run into the other car? It took three hours in the traffic court to affect the release of our vehicle. I was lucky that witnesses in our car were able to verify who really was at fault. Spain seemed to favor the one who first said "*La culpa es suya!*", meaning "It is your fault!"

When I first arrived in Spain, my vocabulary was very limited. One day I saw a sign over a store that said "Hello, Americans!" At least that's what I thought the sign said. Later on I discovered I was mistaken. In

Spanish, the sign read, "Helados Americanos." Those words translated meant, "American Ice Cream." That wasn't the last time I goofed.

During the first eighteen months, there were no resident Air Force chaplains at Sevilla and Zaragoza where two other bases were being opened up. It was my duty to visit the US troops there from time to time. On these visits, there were no worship services, as there were no chapel locations. I met in homes, where invited, and served Communion.

32

I COULD "CRY FOR HAPPY"

Who knows how much time happiness adds to one's life? The amount of happiness could be directly related to longevity. Happy people appear to have fewer serious worries and concerns, factors that shorten life spans. Happy people have a sense of direction and purpose that motivates a forward motion. Satisfaction with one's self, one's appearance, one's personality and one's accomplishments carries a message—a message that puts a smile in one's heart and on one's face.

"I Could Cry for Happy," comes from an Oriental movie in which a woman is very happy, and says to her beloved, "I could cry for happy" meaning "I'm so happy I could cry!" I have chosen that expression for this chapter because I firmly believe happiness has added years to my life. I want to share with my readers just how happy I have been throughout these four-score and fourteen years. That is not to say that all has been "sweetness and light." Elsewhere in this book one will discover that there have been times when my heart and mind have been loaded with the kinds of burdens any one of us might have. But this is my time to ask you to say "yes" or "no" to the fact that I had a super abundance of experiences that made happiness come my way.

I was chosen by a loving heavenly Father to become the third son of the Rev. James Henderson Green and his wife, Minnie Mae Grogan-Green. I was chosen to become the father of a son who was born on the same date I was, September 15, twenty-three years after my mother delivered me. How glad I am that Phil has followed in the footsteps of his father and paternal grandfather. He is the third pastor in a row. I was chosen to be the eighth child of my mother who, at age twenty-eight, helped me to see "the light of day," in a parsonage in Leicester, North Carolina. So, at the leisurely age of a nonagenarian, I wish to reflect on some of the times when I have been chosen (selected, asked for, and wanted). All have made me happy.

Lois D. Ritter was a teacher in my father's Bible College in Greensboro, NC. Later the school became John Wesley Bible College and moved to High Point. I heard Lois' beautiful contralto voice before I ever saw her. She was practicing in a home nearby. When I saw her spare 5' 2" body, I could hardly believe all that resonance came from such a small body. She not only began to teach in the fall of 1932, but sang in the college musical groups (duets, trios, quartets and small groups) that traveled throughout the state to advertise the new school. I was glad to have a part in some of those groups.

It was my good fortune to get to know her quite well. I lived on the campus of the school while attending Guilford College near by. We often sang duets while visiting care centers and nursing homes. She accompanied me to a small church in north Greensboro where we worshiped many Sundays. I became the director of the youth choir that competed with other youth choirs in the churches of the Greensboro District. "Miss Ritter" was a part of that also. In that context, we began to care for each other to the point that others began to "talk." It soon became an open secret that we were fond of each other. At that time, and in that place, such a relationship was a no-no. She, a teacher and seven years my senior, and I a college student, found ourselves in an awkward position. Besides, it was against the rules of the Bible College to become emotionally attached to students of the opposite sex. And here I was, the son of the founder and president, breaking the rules. It was to our credit that we were discreet. But my parents and others were vocal about what most people called "mismatched." Remarks such as, "she's too old for you," and "it won't last," were common.

One summer my father took four singers with him for a revival in Todd, NC. Miss Ritter and I were members of that party. The two women were billeted in the home of Ed Blackburn, a religious leader in the community. It was cherry-picking time and we all picked and ate our fill. One afternoon I made my way toward Ed Blackburn's house, hoping to get a glimpse of you-know-who. As I walked along below a prominent ridge, I heard Lois praying aloud. She was wrestling with the Lord about whether or not to terminate her relationship with me. My heart sank within me for fear that she would get the wrong answer.

And so later that day, Lois ate too many cherries and came down with what was called "cherry-itis." I missed her at the tabernacle service and, after the song service, I slipped out and went to see about her and found her better. She was glad to see me and felt well enough to spread a blanket on the grass under a full moon. We sat and chatted there. I had never kissed her before, but I braved the odds about what God's answer was to her prayer on the ridge might have been, and kissed her.

From then on we claimed each other. Years later I remember a song from a play called *South Pacific* that mirrored my happiness,

Once you have met her, never let her go.

Three years later, after Lois and I had been married six months, we visited in the home of, "God-bless-your-heart," Ed Blackburn. It was cherry-picking time again. We enjoyed a kiss once again in that same spot. Nine months after that visit, Marcia was born. How happy can one man be? Those who said, "It won't last" were wrong—the marriage lasted fifty-two years.

I am happy to be sitting at the top of five generations—three children, eight grandchildren, twelve great grandchildren and thirteen great-great grandchildren. You can bet that I'm smiling with happiness and holding on for dear life. My Family Tree extends from my grandfather, James Tippit (canoe) Green—a veteran of the Civil War (1864), through my five generations (2008). That is a lesson in history—fourteen decades of it.

I was chosen by the bishop of the Western North Carolina Annual Conference to be the pastor of the Sandy Circuit in the Asheville District of the Methodist Episcopal Church (1936-'40). The parsonage was in Leicester, NC and its six churches were found in the mountains of northwest Buncombe County. One of those churches, Old Brick Church, had been closed for two decades. While pastor, I made it my business to resurrect it during my second year. Hal and Edith Wells were a newlywed couple who attended the first worship service. Because I knew no one present that night, I was at the pump organ for the first hymn. In the middle of it, I paused and said, "I wish I knew someone who could play this organ." Edith spoke up and volunteered to play it. That couple became among the first to join that new congregation. Edith became the organist (and later, pianist)

They became close friends across many decades. Six years after I left that circuit, a letter came to Lois and me. It warmed our hearts. It said:

Dear Rev. Green and Lois;

Old Brick Church and community suffered a great loss when you two left. Others have come and gone, several, and

we have loved them too. But there is a place in our hearts that you filled and still remains.

In all sincerity, I tell you this, that during your stay here, Brick Church grew and blossomed as it never has done since. Even the non-church members of the community discuss it. They say, 'Philip Green did more for that church than anyone else has ever done.' I know you feel, as we do, that what you did, God did through you.

How happy we were to receive such a loving letter. Hal and Edith remained close friends and, though we mostly communicated by Christmas cards, letters and phone calls, after Lois' death I sent widowed Edith a copy of my autobiography, *The Mountains Are Happy*. Late in her life she began to slowly go down the road of dementia and moved in with her daughter, Beverly. That daughter did more than read every Christmas letter I sent. Edith asked her to read a page or two of my book every day until she had heard and commented on all 385 pages. I only met Beverly late in my life. After her mother died, I sent her a letter of condolence. At the next Christmas she was upset because my usual letter was late in being sent. She thought I had decided that, after her mother died, I didn't consider her someone close enough to be a dear friend and get a Christmas letter such as the one she read each year to her mother. I closed that gap quickly. I was happy that she wanted to be a close friend still.

In 1940-'43, the bishop had us in Macon County, on the Franklin Circuit of six more churches. World War II came along in 1941. Lois and I were on our way to visit a family near the Iotla church when, over the car radio, we heard President Franklin D. Roosevelt announce that the Japanese had bombed Pearl Harbor. Because so many of our young people were conscripted, near the end of my third year, I volunteered to become a military chaplain. The editor of the local newspaper, not one of my members, wrote an article along with my picture that sent us away happy. She said, in part:

"Rev. P.L. Green leaves to become Army chaplain. Lieutenant Green was assigned to this field as pastor of Franklin Circuit composed of Bethel, Clark's Chapel, Iotla, Louisa, Salem and Snow Hill. To this work he has

> *devoted himself untiringly, and it may be safely said that no more beloved pastor has ever served in this county. His service to the community has gone far beyond the bounds of his churches, always reaching out to those who needed his spiritual ministrations or need in time of trouble." He served as County Red Cross chairman, 1940-'42, and was elected County Chairman at the annual meeting. Since his becoming chairman, this chapter has received the distinction of becoming a direct contact Chapter. He also organized and directed the Franklin Choral Club that had to disband because of the war*

Looking back over those three years, and six churches, my happiness was complete to have ended with a job well done and an editor who was so pleased with my work in Macon County.

Another most happy and satisfying day was Thanksgiving Day, Thursday, November 27, 1997. By this time I had been married to Helen for 8 years.

This Thanksgiving Day was special in that Helen's daughter, Sara Jensen, of Coeur d'Alene, Idaho, was with us. This visit was a tremendous satisfaction to Helen, as well as to me. Sara's struggle with leukemia for several years was still going on but she looked better than during her previous year's visit. Three of us went to a union Thanksgiving service at First United Methodist Church that was led by seven pastors from downtown churches. The service was inspirational, what with the chancel choir from First Presbyterian Church singing the anthems. Helen was a member of that congregation until our marriage, at which time she became a United Methodist preacher's wife.

Another factor that made this day a time of happiness was the Thanksgiving dinner in the home of my daughter, Mickey, and her husband, Bruce Salimi, in the afternoon and evening. Before that sumptuous meal, Helen, Sara and I drove out to the airport to meet a Northwest Airlines plane that brought my daughter, Marcia Thompson, here from Minneapolis, Minnesota. Her oldest son, Allen Thompson, and his Korean wife, So Pun, were at Mickey and Bruce's dinner, along with their two daughters, Lisa and Jackie (8 & 10) of Colorado Springs, CO.

Last, but not least, at the dinner was my son, Phil Jr., with his wife, Elsie, from Denver. They brought with them Christy and Cindy from Denver and Carolyn (Newman) from the Washington, D.C. area. Carolyn brought her two sons, Joshua Philip and Matthew Alexander, (2 & 4). Her husband, Neal, was at the bedside of his father in a Pueblo hospital, where he was having a serious operation.

During the visit with so many treasured loved ones, I had a serious conversation with my granddaughter, Cindy Green (age 30). She hardly looked more than a teenager. As we sat alone at a table, she asked about my lineage—who was I? She was looking for the roots of her own identity. Who was she? I explained that my first wife and I were white Caucasians of English/Irish descent and that her father therefore had the same bloodline. She knew, of course, that he had married her mother, Elsie DeJesus who was of Puerto Rican descent, since Elsie's parents were born in Puerto Rico before they immigrated to New York City.

When I stated proudly that mine was an international family, Cindy's eyes grew large as she waited for more information. My daughter, Mickey Salimi, was married to Bruce, a student from Iran (Persia), whose father was Iranian and whose mother was of White Russian blood. Then I pointed out her first cousin, Allen Thompson, who had married So Pun, a Korean woman, while he was on duty in Korea. Their two daughters, Cindy and Jackie, were Korean Americans.

Cindy was so proud to be a part of such an international mixture that it showed in her face the remainder of the evening. She seemed pleased that her less-than white complexion was as acceptable as that of anyone else in the room. We left that night happier being one big family than we were before we came. I was so happy I could (and did) cry.

That night, I sat at my computer, thanking God that I had been with my three children, Marcia, Phil, and Mickey, their spouses, a grandson and his wife, and four of my great grandchildren, as well as Helen's daughter, Sara.

"Bless the Lord, O my soul, and all that is within me, bless His holy name."

33

WHAT GOOD IS PRAYER?

Why I Pray

I pray because I believe there is Someone up there, out there, over there, down there, in there, who is greater, holier, and infinitely more understanding than I am—who is interested in me, and who cares what happens to me. I believe I belong to him by his creation and redemption of me. God loved me so much that he gave his son to save me from the law of sin and death. I believe that I have been chosen (at my option) to be a member of the family of God, his very heir, and a joint heir with his beloved Son. I believe God intends the best for me even as my earthly father yearned and worked for the best for me—that wherever my journey of faith leads along the road of life, he wants to transform it into something good and beautiful. I believe that God will answer the last recorded prayer of Jesus for his followers, and for me, to be where he is—that the last chapter of my life has been written in victory—and that I *will dwell in the house of the Lord forever*, if I remain faithful.

I pray because it is natural to do so—as natural as it is for sparks to fly upward. The way I pray, and what I pray for, are far less than perfect. In one way or another I pray when the answer to my prayer may seem in doubt. At times, I feel that I cannot help but pray. Is that feeling universal? If the answer is yes, then all pray in one way or another. If I were deprived of the tendency to pray, a vital part of me would be cut off and I would wind up less a human being than I was intended to be. I am an nonagenarian who admits openly that I have never outgrown the desire to pray.

I have to say in all honesty that I have not developed prayer and praying to the degree that I feel adequate and effective. But I pray on because I know He is there, either far away, or *closer than hands or feet*. If God gives food because we are hungry, air because we need to breathe, knowledge and truth because of our inquisitive minds—because there is prayer, He gives Himself, and *fills our cups to overflowing*.

I pray because I want to learn how to make God more real, to receive his grace and His guidance in difficulties, and to become a seasoned veteran in prayer. In my ancestral home we had a plaque that read, "Prayer changes things." I like answered prayers, and not because I need to feel God's availability and action upon each *pull of his chain*. Rather, that I see things happening in my life and in my world. I readily admit that the trouble often lies in me, the pray-er, and not with prayer itself. The psalmist wrote, "If I regard iniquity in my heart, the Lord will not hear me." I have not always been willing to place my heart and soul under severe scrutiny. There could be found acts and habits that I didn't wish to amend or give up. Some sins are still sweet savors that are enjoyably "rolled under our tongues." Sins of commission are easily camouflaged by sins of omission. Ever so reluctantly am I willing to face up to the cost of a discipleship all the way. The road to complete sincerity comes with a sobering scripture that says, "The heart is deceitful above all things, and desperately wicked." Honesty has often found me in the slow lane.

I pray because it is more than a universal instinct. It is a God-given privilege. It offers me the chance to overcome all hindrances that would keep me from getting to know and to commune with my Maker. Through more than four scores of years many privileges have been mine. My mountains have been happy! I've had the family love of wife, children, grandchildren, great grandchildren, great-great grandchildren, and of multitudes of friendships, of laughter aplenty, great books, wonderful music, art and of travels at home and abroad to see God's beautiful earth and its peoples.

But, when I have neglected my prayer life, I have robbed myself of life's supreme privilege—that of friendship with God. No, prayer offers more than an obligation. It offers a journey into the beautiful garden of prayer, even into the innermost Holy of Holies where all sins are seen, confessed and forgiven. There comes the overwhelming fact that there is nothing between the soul and the Savior. That feeling is expressed in the words of John Newton, written before his death in 1807:

How Tedious and Tasteless the Hours

How tedious and tasteless the hours,
When Jesus no longer I see;
Sweet prospects, sweet birds, and sweet flowers,
Have all lost their sweetness to me.

The midsummer sun shines but dim;
The fields strive in vain to look gay;
But when I am happy in Him,
December's as pleasant as May.

His name yields the richest perfume,
And sweeter than music his voice;
His presence disperses my gloom,
And makes all within me rejoice.

I should, were he always thus nigh,
Have nothing to wish or to fear;
No mortal as happy as I;
My summer would last all the year.

Do prayers really change things? At age 19, I came face to face with a need for an answer to my own prayer. In the fall term at Peoples Bible School, a glorious freshet of revival swept through the student body. All students not formerly Christians gave their hearts to Jesus except two. One of the two was my sister, Ruth, four years younger. I was impressed to pray especially for her conversion. It is difficult to pray for a sibling—especially when one has not set a perfect example. So I didn't let Ruth know I was praying for her.

Early in my contract with the Lord, he let me know that what I asked might not be easy. Ruth might be quite resistant to making such a life-changing decision. Would I be willing to give up a few meals to accent my sincerity? Rashly, I said I would fast. And more rashly still I said,

"Lord, I'll not eat again until Ruth becomes a Christian."

At this point, the Evil One got into the conversation. He said,

"Philip, don't you know that people are never saved against their will?"

I knew that. I knew that the Lord stands at the door that has no knob and knocks. For Him to enter, the one on the inside must open the door. At the enemy's challenge, I stood stalemated. But I went to classes, came to my room, read my Bible, prayed and meditated on the situation. My roommate was the only person who knew I was fasting on behalf of my sister.

That day I happened to be reading in my Bible about the prophet Jonah and his reluctance to take God's message to the sinful people of the city of Nineveh. I was among young people who earlier had made humorous cracks about Jonah and the whale. And I found the idea of a human being living after being inside a whale altogether unbelievable. However, that was missing the point of the story of the prophet who finally did what God wanted him to do. There was something in the story that related to my present impasse. What was it? Very clearly it was revealed to me that, though Jonah ran away from his mission to Nineveh, God made the road in that direction so undesirable that he decided to take the divine message to that city. The people repented and were saved from God's punishment. So I took courage and prayed that God would make Ruth's path away from Him so disagreeable that she would take a second look at her decision

The next day my sister found out I was fasting in her behalf and sent a discouraging word,

"Philip, you might as well go ahead and eat." Said the Evil One, "See, I told you a person has to want to be saved. Now, you'll starve to death."

By the third morning without food, stomach juices entered my stomach with a bang. The enemy suggested that I should take Ruth's advice and eat. After all, hadn't I made a rash youthful promise not to eat again, when the Scriptures taught that God could not save a person without that person's own decision?

I made it as far as the school kitchen where a large oven took the frost off a very cold morning. Sitting beside the cozy warm oven, I heard the pleasant sounds of breakfast being eaten in the dining hall. As I sat, I took a stern stance not to break down and go eat. I would not go back on my promise to God. It occurred to me that I had not given God time enough to make Ruth's path away from salvation distressful enough to make her want to change her mind.

Just then the door opened from the dining room and someone came up behind me. I was surprised to feel feminine arms go around me from behind, and in wonderment, felt tears fall upon my face. It was Ruth. She said, "Philip, you can go ahead and eat now. I've made my peace with God."

Hallelujah! Prayer does change things. Fasting does, too. Thanks be to God!

34

RELAXING AND RECREATING

Sunshine and Fresh Air

A major contributor to my long life includes entering into outdoor sporting events. I began playing tennis as a pre-teenager and continued through age fifty. In high school I played touch football and was on the race team. Most everywhere I went I was afoot unless my father was driving that way. When a vehicle was available I was allowed to drive at age fourteen. As a teenager, I became a caddy at the local golf links. As an adult I played golf until age eighty-five. The first golf course I played on was in Franklin, NC. There were nine holes and the greens were on sand. The golf pro gave ministers free rounds on Mondays. My golf partner was Rev. Dr. J. Len Stokes, pastor of the downtown church. I was pastor of six churches in the County for three years. Although he was diminutive, his game was better than mine.

While I was good at croquet, I enjoyed games that called for more strenuous exercise like touch football, basketball, tennis, and volleyball. Hunting and fishing took me many miles into the forests and on streams and lakes. I took one skiing lesson on top of a high mountain in Austria and found that the rule of putting weight on the downhill leg was too risky and gave up that sport. I did learn to put on the skis unassisted and get up by myself when I fell.

A Thrust into Checkers

During three years as pastor of the Franklin circuit in Macon County, NC, one of my other enjoyments was that of playing checkers under a mighty tree in front of Broady Pendergras's store on the main street of Franklin. That's where would-be county champions vied with one another. With two small books on the game, I entered into competition and gained some note as one of the best players around.

The game of checkers did not require near the brainpower that chess did. One had to stand in line to get a crack at whoever was winning, but having won yourself, you stayed with it until someone could unseat you. There were times when I spent too many hours playing in public view and took just criticism for the same. When that happened, I often went into the back of the store and played with the owner.

One day I drove over near Asheville some 75 miles northwest to visit Cousin John Henry Green, a patient in a hospital in Oteen. The visiting hours were not until 2:00 in the afternoon. While waiting to visit him, I inquired about local checkers players and was told there was a good player nearby and was given directions to his house. I followed the pavement to an unpaved road, to a narrow lane through the woods to its end. There stood, or leaned, a house, seemingly on its "last legs." On the porch a man dressed in well-worn bib overalls minus a shirt. I introduced myself reluctantly as a checker enthusiast. He said he played some and invited me to a game. The board was overly used and scraped by the use of Coca-Cola bottle caps with one set inverte—so that one could be known as the defender.

I was surprised that the man was such a good player. He won nearly every game. With my "tail between my legs," I finally beat an ignominious departure. I learned an important lesson. To be a top checker player one had to live at the end of the lane, far from neighbors, in a house in sad need of repairs, dressed in the scantiest of attire. Right then and there I decided the price was too great. I still know and like the game but no longer look for the best players to come up against. It is consoling to remember that I was the champion of Macon County, in Franklin, NC.

I'm still able to do the following at age 96

Chew gum
Eat corn on the cob
Swallow meat
Brush teeth
Shave, electric
Brush hair
Use bathroom
Hear without aids
Phone friends
Send E-mail
Do mailings
Send 100 Christmas letters
Sort medications
Two-finger typing
Author books
Sing many songs, tunes
Play a few card games
Pay bills, tithe
Speak clearly
Live purposefully
Share my faith
Ride church bus
Enjoy memories
Accept life changes
Tolerate differences
Make new friends
Make decisions
Travel, auto, flights
Prepare for life's end
Give all now. No Will
Be loveable, radiant
List things yet to do
Share prodigally

Unable, now

Play my piano
Do magic tricks
Whistle
Drive car
Pick up medications
Doctor visits alone
Go for haircuts alone
Walk without help
Prepare meals
Keep my balance
Scratch my back
Shower alone
Reach my toes
Put on socks, shoes
Climb stairs

Barely Able

To hear well
Put on shirt, coat
Take phone messages
Get up from falls
Dress myself
Control weight at 175lb
Stay humble
Accept criticism
Move in carrier-chair
Walk with a walker

35

SPIRITUAL LIFE RETREATS

A Christian Ashram is a spiritual retreat and is distinguished from secular Ashrams. The word Ashram comes from Sanskrit and means "apart from labor." The Ashrams of India are fresh schools conducted by Gurus (teachers). Their disciples sit at their feet and learn from them. The late missionary to India, Rev. Dr. E. Stanley Jones, founded the Christian Ashram and placed Christ in the center as the guru. To help the Kingdom of God to become a part of the group, barriers of race, class, denomination, titles, and others are minimized. Barriers within people include resentments, impurities, jealousy, guilt, self-preoccupation, fear, anxieties, etc. Christian Ashrams are intended for the elimination of these barriers. Ashramites call each other by their given names and any other titles are omitted. So I became "Brother Philip," and my wife became "Sister Lois."

As a young pastor in the late 1930s, I heard of "Brother Stanley" from a variety of sources, because he was a world figure. Some called him "the greatest missionary since St. Paul." I began reading his first books, "Christ of the Round Table," "Christ of the Indian Road," "Christ of the American Road," "Christ of Every Road," and later, "The Divine Yes," "Abundant Living," "A Song of Ascents," and many more.

He graduated from my wife's alma mater, Asbury College, but a number of years before she was a student there (1928-'32). I heard some of his inspiring messages in Pueblo, CO, and was happy that he was the Colorado Ashram Evangelist in 1971, my first one. It was his last full Ashram before declining health slowed him down. His death, two years later, finished his phenomenal ministry on earth.

The Foundation for Evangelism came into being by a famous lay evangelist, Dr. Harry Denman, who saw the need for more funding than normal channels gave for this important emphasis. While he was the leader of the Board of Evangelism in Nashville, he used the prestige of that office to establish a foundation, to which individuals and churches could voluntarily contribute. In 1986, in retirement, I became interested in that foundation when its president, Rev. Dr.

Charles Kinder, came to visit me. He asked me to become the Rocky Mountain Regional Director of the Foundation.

Among the many facets of the foundation was that of raising funds to endow an *E. Stanley Jones Chair of Evangelism* at all our thirteen seminaries. That meant that I needed to form a blue chip committee within the Conference to obtain enough money to endow a chair at the Iliff School of Theology in Denver. It was a challenge for me because I had been in retirement for five years and, at the request of the Bishop, was serving Avondale UMC sixty miles from home. Fortunately, the response to my efforts was almost 100%, and included the seminary president, a district superintendent, the pastor of our largest church, and other strong conference leaders. With such a committee, we were able to fill that chair at Iliff.

There were times when I needed what an Ashram could do for me, more that what I could do for an Ashram. At times, every busy person needs time away from it all. In the seventeen years as the associate pastor of a mega-church, the load became so heavy that it was "get away or burn out." How did I ever get myself into so many things?

After that first Ashram in 1971, I saw a light "at the end of the tunnel." Let the Ashram be the time to get away for four or five days. Enjoy others. Slow down. Get your second breath. Dr. Lehmberg had died at age fifty-seven. Why? The expectations of a six-thousand-member church were unreal. What! All the sermons, baptisms, weddings, funerals, hospital visits—because "if the senior minister hadn't been there, you had not been visited." After his death from a heart attack, I took advantage of four months as interim senior minister to spread the duties out more evenly.

The Christian Ashram has an interesting beginning. *The hour of the open heart* is a time for one to say aloud needs hoping to be met at that Ashram. The leader, or someone appointed, keeps a written record of what the people lift up. Someone might say,

"My brother won't speak to me unless I apologize for what I did. But what I did was the right thing to do at the time. I'm trying to decide what to do next."

Another might say, "My mind is full of doubts about my standing with God. Would he forgive me for using his name in vain? I didn't mean to say it. It just slipped out."

In the last morning, the Ashram includes *the hour of the overflowing heart.* In that period they share joyfully what God has done for them there.

In 1971, I felt led to plunge into those waters at the Colorado Christian Ashram. My first one was held at a retreat center at the Horn Creek Ranch near Westcliffe, Colorado, 85 miles from home. Brother Stanley was the evangelist and it turned out to be his last full Ashram before his health began to fail. [Sometimes called the greatest missionary since St. Paul, he died a few short years later.] I was asked to be in charge of the music at the first one I attended. In 1973 yours truly was elected the director of the one that year, and two others. The Horn Creek Ranch was an ideal site place to meet. It was at the foot of the Sangre de Cristo mountain range.

After the death of Brother Stanley, his son-in-law, Bishop James K. Mathews, became the President of United Christian Ashrams, International. He had traveled in India with E. Stanley and had married his daughter, Sister Eunice. The Bishop conducted our Ashram in 1983, at which time I enjoyed getting to know him personally. I picked him up and took him to Horn Creek Ranch. Afterward, I brought him back to Colorado Springs to get a flight back to Washington, D.C. He enjoyed crossing the highest bridge in the world at the Royal Gorge. A stiff breeze rocked the bridge as we were crossing it. That gave us a feeling of temporary uncertainty.

I have attended every Colorado Ashram since 1971, either as a member of The Twelve, Director, or supporter. At my request, I was approved to be an Ashram Evangelist and was invited to conduct the Arizona Winter Ashram in 1987. It has been my happy privilege to know and serve with many outstanding Ashram evangelists and workers, namely, Mary Webster, who traveled and witnessed with Brother Stanley; Earl Tyson, founder, and his wife, Director of Emmaus; Roberto Escamilla who toured South America with Jones; Samuel T. Kamaleson, President-at-Large of World Vision, Int'l; Maurice Culver, Missionary to Zimbabwe; Bishop Richard Wilke, co-author of the Disciple Bible Study; William E. Berg, Lutheran Pastor, Minneapolis, MN; Charles E. Blair, Pastor of Calvary Temple, Denver; and many, many others.

At the end of the 1987, Lillian Sheets, the Ashram Secretary, penned the following report about the 1987 Colorado Christian Ashram. This will give you a good idea of what the Ashrams are like.

Report:

1. Date: Colorado Christian Ashrams began—1971.
2. Directors: On a list provided by Brother Phil Green, Sr.
3. National speakers I would recommend: I have enjoyed the three main speakers I have heard: Rev. Dr. Paul Wagoner, 1985; Rev. Edward P. Beck, 1986; and Bishop James K. Mathews, 1987.

   I personally thought Rev. Beck was especially dynamic, effective preacher. I thought Bishop Mathews was a warm, personable man, and I was impressed with the way he included the youth and children, making them an integral part of the services, in a very natural and relaxed way.

   I think Rev. Willis Goettel, who has served as Director of the Ashram several times, expressed the feelings of most of us when he said he had enjoyed all the speakers, and has felt that each Ashram is even better than the last.
4. Regional Speakers: In the three years I have attended, I have enjoyed the local people who have participated in the different areas as each has an individual, unique approach to the music, Bible study, Church-in-Action, etc.
5. Other views: I think the 1987 Colorado Christian Ashram was inspirational and fulfilling. As more than one said, perhaps the best ever. From its beginning, the Colorado Ashram has been held at Horn Creek Conference Center, hosted by Rev. Paul Zeller. The accommodations are comfortable and the food is good. The location, set among trees, streams, wild flowers, deer, squirrels, and other interesting flora and fauna, just at the foot of Horn Peak, is itself an inspirational experience and a constant reminder of God's glorious creation.

   In addition to all this, we had excellent leadership, including Director Cliff Johnson Evangelist Bishop James Mathews (son-in-law of Brother E. Stanley Jones); Church-in-Action Rev.

Dwight Zeller, Bible Teacher Rev. Elwood Bartlett; Music leaders Cliff and Kathy Johnson; Youth Leaders Rev Randy and Sue Jessen and Children's Leaders Rose Saunders and Ruth Novak.

My husband and I had an opportunity to become better acquainted with the Children's Leaders this year, as our eleven-year-old grandson attended the Ashram with us. This was a special blessing.

6. Overall: We thought the 1987 Ashram was well directed, well organized, and conducted according to Ashram guidelines. The round-the-clock Prayer Vigil schedule was completely filled in one-hour segments. The book table offered a variety of selections, including several of Brother Stanley Jones' books. The Prayer and Share Groups were a very special time, providing a close, caring fellowship in a loving atmosphere. The discipline of silence was observed from the end of the evening fellowship hour until broken by Brother Jim Mathews during the morning devotions. The afternoon period of Recreation, Rest and Fellowship gave adequate time for a variety of activities, or inactivity, as each one chose.

   To me, each year's Ashram is a unique and inspiring experience—busy, yet relaxing, uplifting, but stabilizing—giving new meaning and purpose to bring back to our daily lives, with a renewed love of God, and closeness to our fellow man.

The Christian Ashrams in Philip's Life

- Member, Council of the Twelve, 1971-1987
- Director of Colorado Christian Ashram, 1973-'75, 81-'82, '85
- Became an approved Ashram Evangelist, 1982
- As regional representative, attended Conference, Jackson, MS, 1974
- Attended Nat'l. Exec. Committee 1974, Leesburg, FL; and near Minneapolis, MN 1987
- Attended most annual Colorado Ashrams at Horn Creek Conference Center through 2006
- Attended Florida Ashram, 1987-present

- North American United Christian Ashram, St. John's University, MN in 1989 and another in Estes Park, CO in 1998
- Evangelist for Arizona Winter Ashram, 1987

From time to time I assisted directors in finding and selecting principal leaders at Horn Creek Ranch, YMCA of the Rockies at Estes Park, and at Saint Malo Retreat Center.

In 1980 there was a need for the history of the first nine Ashrams. I did that and recently put together a 150-page album of *The Christian Ashrams in My Life*. Looking through it gives me a spiritual boost, and a keen desire to keep on keeping on.

SECTION VIII

When one of my cherished friends suggested that memories helped people to live longer lives, I had to pause and ask, "But what kind of memories?" The lives of some people are filled with sad and unhappy memories. They are not turned on about memories. So, this chapter is about remembering good memories. If you remember a good time along life's road, cherish it, tell others about it, add good memories to it. Multiply and hoard all the good memories of your life.

Correspondence sounds so common-place and unimportant. Yet, remember that note a friend sent to you, thanking you for your kind words. Recall how you felt the first time you sent a note off by e-mail or on-line. Until my ninety-fifth year, I (or my wife and I) sent a newsy Christmas letter to more than a hundred and fifty cherished friends and loved ones. This year I cut the number down to a hundred letters. It is a chore, but a pleasant one. Receiving replies is a great joy. Many years as an Air Force chaplain, I accumulated the birth and marriage dates of servicemen and women who passed through my office. When they received a call on one of these dates, many were both surprised and pleased.

Knowing and being known, caring and being cared for, and loving and being loved has been deeply ingrained in me. Across the decades I have loved many friends and some of them still love me. Others have preceded me across "the river." Love is one of those things that cannot be seen or measured, but it adds years to your life.

In our busy, busy daily living we are prone to ignore paths to tranquility. There is soothing music available, a path to tranquility. For me, watching a golf tournament is so restful that it is easy to drop off to sleep. When I talk to my loving heavenly Father, and listen for what he would say to me, the hurry and scurry of life are put in the right perspective.

It has been said that a picture is better than a thousand words. If that is so, then the multiple albums I have in my possession don't give me time, in one lifetime, to hear it all again. Among the many photos I have is one showing the twenty-six chaplains on occupation duty in Germany at a retreat center in Bavaria. I took the photo and was able to run and get in it because I had a lapse-time camera. I am spending too much time now trying to remember the names of the faces in my photos.

36

ENJOY A FEW GOOD MEMORIES

Most everyone possesses a few memories that are cherished and available when needed. Sometimes they are hidden or camouflaged among memories that are best not revealed. Good memories are worth their weight in gold and are happily shared with others. The more often they are shared, the more precious they become. A certainty: Repetition deepens impression, per William James.

Happy are they who accumulate and treasure life's good memories. I have in mind a close aging friend who suggested a name for this chapter, *Enjoying Memories.* Three years ago I sat through a multitude of eulogies at her husband's funeral and thought about how rich in memories had been her sixty-some years with him. For many years our families had been friends. Rev. Dr. John M. Vayhinger and I had founded the Colorado Interfaith Counseling Center and Pastoral Resource Institute. We spent many Monday morning sessions together with other clergy colleagues. Many Sunday mornings we sat on the same pew at worship.

A copy of my annual Christmas letter to some 150 cherished friends and loved ones was sent to her. In it I told about my Lord's mandate to write the book entitled, *Being Young at Ninety-four.* (then it was changed to *Much Alive at Ninety-five*). On the back of the letter, I included more than twenty suggested chapters and asked readers to make other suggestions. She did that and gave many written suggestions for the book. We became closer friends after John's death, and she asked me often about how the book was coming, and whether I received her suggestions. I did receive them and was able to include a few in the book.

When she died, her brother was in charge of her service of remembrance at the church. He came down to where I was sitting in my wheel chair and asked me to make a few remarks. I was unable to get up the steps to the pulpit and sound system but, thanks to the thoughtfulness of an associate pastor, a sound system was carried down to my chair. It was a precious memory to get to say a few words about our joyous relationship, even in my diminished body.

In the summer of 1930, my grandmother Green lay dying, surrounded for weeks by her two daughters and five sons. The day before she passed, she asked them to promise to meet her in heaven. The next day, she asked all her grandchildren to come to her room. Because I had come to be close to her, and loved her so much, I knelt close to her bed, where she placed her hand on my head, and said, "Phip, make a good preacher." I've carried that precious memory close to my heart through eight decades.

My preacher-father never once told me that he loved me, but I knew he did. In the bedroom next to mine, I often heard his vocal prayers for all his children by name—including me. How peacefully I fell asleep even before hearing his prayers for others. What precious memories!

I was graduated from Valdese High School in Burke County, NC, in 1932. During the closing days of that school year, students were writing messages in each other's autograph books. After so many years since then I have misplaced my booklet, and the name of the classmate whose cherished words I shall always remember. She wrote,

When your work on earth is ended,
And its paths no more you've trod;
May your name in gold be written,
In the autograph of God.

37

THE MINISTRY OF CORRESPONDENCE

If it is spoken, or oral, the message you wish to convey can be underestimated and sometimes misunderstood or misconstrued. Words of censure or praise are more lasting if conveyed in writing. They become incontrovertibly a record that can be seen, saved, filed and acted upon. What one's supervisor thinks of you is important. What you think of those who work for you is also important.

With a pastor most messages are oral, from the pulpit to worshipers. As an Air Force chaplain for twenty years there were times when I wanted to convey a personal message to one particular person. Doing this massively to troops in my outfit would be virtually impossible. But, at Vance Air Force Base in Enid, Oklahoma, I found a way to do it. It became a part of my ministry to the troops. How? All troops who reported to a base were required to do certain things while "clearing in" or "clearing out." One step was an interview with the chaplain.

During each interview, I made it a practice to obtain that person's date of birth and, if married, date of wedding and name of the bride. It was an extra chore to accumulate and keep a useable file of those dates. In those years (1949-'51), I purchased thousands of appropriate birthday cards that could be mailed for one penny. In post offices across America anyone could afford what was known as "a penny postcard." Earlier in life when a phone call or a three-cent stamp cost too much for a college student to send a letter, I sent messages to my sweetheart on such a card. The more intimate messages were written in French so nobody else could read them. We sent many such messages on penny postcards.

It took some doing to arrange individual names and dates of birthdays across the 365 days of the year, and mail the cards so as to arrive before a GI's birthday, but I did it. You may be sure that the troops appreciated it. Wedding anniversaries were much fewer, so I phoned each GI three days before the wedding anniversary and, as one of them said, "Thanks a million, Chaplain, you saved my life. I had forgotten that date."

Our senior chaplain at Vance Air Force Base attended a Strategic Air Command chaplains' conference in Omaha, Nebraska. He recommended such a plan for other chaplains to copy. They laughed at him and said that it could not be done. He told them, "You say it can't be done. But at Vance AFB, Chaplain Phil Green is doing it."

Chaplain Glen Shaffer wrote a letter of commendation for my 201-file in which he said,

"Your pastoral services through the ministry of correspondence have merited the recognition of higher headquarters due to its unique and effective contribution to the spiritual phases of morale."

Shortly before the end of three years as the only Protestant chaplain in Madrid, Spain, I received a thank you note from Mrs. Anne Dawson on May 28, 1957. She said,

> *Dear Chaplain Green,*
>
> *I cannot thank you enough for your anniversary card. It meant so much more to me than you'll ever know.*
>
> *As a matter of fact, our family has had so many occasions to thank you—for your birthday remembrances, and Christmas and Easter—to say nothing of the wonderfully inspirational talks that we have heard Sunday after Sunday.*
>
> *I am sure that you must know that your thoughtfulness of others means so much more than words will adequately express. Thank you again.*

Correspondence is a two-way responsibility—a message and a response. I was a military chaplain for twenty years during which time I had to live by strict rules. It was up to me to know and live by those rules. The rules were written and available to all the troops. Most efficiency ratings (ERs) were written by commanders and communicated through channels to all levels of command. I rarely was given a copy and had to wait until after retirement to send for copies—which I did.

Most of the time, I knew that my ratings would be outstanding or excellent, and I had no reason to be concerned. After my twenty years, I got copies and included them in my autobiography, *The Mountains Are*

Happy. For my relatives, cherished friends and professional colleagues, I gave a copy. The 250 copies I had printed are long ago gone, except two or three I keep as "loan copies."

Some responses to *The Mountains Are Happy*

May 15, 2001
Dear Brother Philip,

It's a great book packed not only with your story but with His Story. The cover is incomparable. The title brings happy anticipation as one prepares to read. The mountains indeed tell of our Lord's awesome creation in nature. But the story tells of a far greater miracle, the miracle of what He can do with one's life fully dedicated to Him and His service.

Your Foreword was an excellent introduction. I quote, "I hesitated at the cost of discipleship, that is, until I discovered that solid joys and lasting pleasures were worth the price."

There are few pastors who could match the diversity of your ministries. We read of a fruitful Parish Ministry, of a brilliant military record, of a beautiful family life, of your extensive Christian Ashram Ministries, Evangelist, Circuit rider and others. And your closeness for this Amazing Grace Ministry is the gift of our Lord according to John 15:16 (Note: "You didn't choose me. I chose you. I appointed you to go and produce lovely fruit always, so that no matter what you ask for from the Father, using my name, he will give it to you.")

Congratulations on a unique and comprehensive autobiography. And God bless you for not retiring.

Sincerely,
Bill Berg

(Note: Rev. Dr. William E. Berg, Lutheran, of Minneapolis, MN—one of four top leaders in the International Christian Ashram Movement.)

May 30, 2001
My dear Phil,

This will be brief but full of love. Arthritis has just about crippled me. I can't walk even a block—without a cane. I have lost 6 inches in height, and 40 pounds of my life and normal weight. I cannot write very well, and my sight is gone in my one eye, and failing in the other.

I was delighted to receive that wonderful book you sent to me. I know how much work that was. You ought to get the Nobel Prize for literature—and be very proud of the book. Thank you for all of the credit you gave to me. If I helped, I am glad. I'll read all I can (and look at the pictures). On Sunday 1 June '01, I'll be 89.

Our love, Karl and Eileen Justus.

(former Executive Director, The Military Chaplains Association)

May 9, 2001
Dear Phil,

Thank you for sending me The Mountains Are Happy. They are indeed, and I read your story with interest. Some of it I knew, but most I did not. Your Ashram interest I well recall Justus. I also knew Lehmberg, Lacour, Stuart, McConnell, Wheatley and many others. I commend you on a book well written and worth telling. Yours has been an outstanding ministry.

Sincerely,
Bro. Jim

(Bishop James K. Mathews, Washington, DC, President, United Christian Ashrams, Int'l., and son-in-law of the late Rev. Dr. E. Stanley Jones, "Brother Stanley," founder of the Christian Ashram.)

May 5, 2001
Dear Phil,

I am asking my son, Rob, to print this letter on my behalf being my "right-hand man," as I cannot write or type with my right hand after a stroke a year ago December. I am glad that my mind remains sharp—though, at ninety-one, I do have my "senior moments."

Thank you for your book, including a notation of a page on which there is a picture that included Mary Ella and me. It was very thoughtful of you to send it. That is a "mountain" of a work, in itself, and I congratulate you on doing it. You have had a very rich ministry, and it is good to reflect on it. I am glad our lives touched during my years in the Denver Area. Communications like yours brighten my life greatly. Thank you for that expression of regard. Again, I congratulate you on the publication of your book.

Gratefully,
Marvin

(Bishop R. Marvin Stuart, Palo Alto, CA)

He also added: *Mary Ella is largely out of touch with the world around her, but still recognizes me and Rob. We pray for her to be released from her worn-out body and mind and freed to go on to the "other side," by God's grace. It is no fun to be confined to a wheel chair, but I manage to have some mobility, nevertheless. Friends push me down the street to the First United Methodist Church, for instance, which continues to be an important part of my life.*

May 3, 2001
Dearest Uncle Philip,

I finished your book while I have been away since Friday. [NOTE: She is an airline stewardess.*] What a treasure! As I was reading it on the airplane, my co-workers kept asking what The Mountains Are Happy was about. Of course, I was* *most willing to tell them. Sunday I spent about an hour with Aunt Ruth before driving to Charlotte to go back to work. She was not having one of her better days with her arthritis but was still the sweetest inspiration I could ever hope for.*

All through the years, Uncle Philip, I have watched and admired you. You have been one of my most important "Light Houses." I can remember once during my teenage years, while in a crisis, that I felt that you were my only lifeline. You have always made me feel loved and special and that positive input has kept me hanging on many, many times. That is why your book is so important to me. It has and will inspire, instruct, comfort and direct me until we are together forever with Our Loved One. Thanks with the great love I feel for you.

Rachel "Rae-Rae"

Some responses to the book
Prayers Jesus Might Have Prayed

"A good work that has the potential of blessing many lives"
(Rev. Dr. John H. Stevens, Jr., Pastor, First Presbyterian Church, Colorado Springs, CO)
"I had misgivings about putting words in the Savior's mouth, until I saw the inspiration of what was written"
(Rev. Dr. J. Lem Stokes, University President)
"A highly original approach"
(Bishop James K. Mathews, Int'l Pres, United Christian Ashrams)
"It is too good not to be saved for the centuries to come"
(Rev. Dr. Kermit Long, Peoria, AZ)
"The inner spirit of Jesus is revealed in a new and compelling manner"
(Bishop Calvin D. McConnell, Portland, OR)
"The *Foreword* and first two prayers are worth the price of the book"
(Rev. Dr. William E. Berg, Lutheran, Minneapolis, MN)
"A book of deep spiritual refreshment"
(Bishop Benjamin J. Oliphint, Houston, Texas)

"Profound yet simple"
(Rev. Dr. O. Gerald Trigg,
Author, "Hinges of the Judeo-Christian History")
"An interesting and inspiring book"
(Harlan L. Ochs, President, Acorn Petroleum)
"A wonderful book of prayers"
(Bishop Richard B. Wilke, Winfield, KS)
"A Masterpiece"
(Rev. Dr. Charles E. Kinder, Murphreesboro, TN)
"We felt the master present with us as we prayed with Him"
(Chaplain, Col, John F. Richards, USAF, Ret'd)
"The book was, and is, a blessing to me"
(Bishop Mack B. Stokes, Lake Junaluska, NC
"I was impressed by the deep spiritual insights that were stirred in my heart through the behind-the-scene looks into the heart of Jesus"
(Rev. Dr. Randall Jessen, Senior Pastor, First United Methodist Church, Colorado Springs, CO)

For the past 45 years I have sent about 150 copies of our annual Christmas letter to relatives and cherished friends. Perhaps I am a bit vain to keep doing so, just to let people know what I remain able to do at age 95. How glad I am to be able to share the blessing that one of my books has been to readers.

38

LOVING AND BEING LOVED

Love is one of those powerful things that cannot be seen, yet is quintessential to a happy life. A happy life is conducive to a longer life. One can love in any kind of broken-down body. There are several kinds of love. Only one kind is non-fulfilling—self love. But, by being surrounded by the love of God and significant others, love can give inner strength sufficient to meet extraordinary challenges. The ravages of stress can be greatly mitigated by the knowledge that others share in love and are shouldering part of our load. It is sad when there are those who are reluctant to let others know of, and accept, help from anyone.

The love of God, the Creator, for us is known as grace—unmerited and eternal. It is the disposition of the Creator toward the creature. He made all that is and saw that it was good. One need not ask, "Where is God?" He is outside the fold, seeking his lost strays and mavericks, or yearning at his gate for the welcome sight of a returning prodigal son or daughter. He loved us so much that "he gave his only begotten Son, that whoever believes in him should not perish, but have everlasting life," in the Father's house. The greatest commandment he gave to us was that we should:

"Love the Lord thy God with all thy heart, thy soul and mind, and strength, and thy neighbor as thyself."

Do that, and forget about keeping the Ten Commandments, for "love is the fulfillment of the law" of "do this" and "don't do that." The consciousness of that kind of love can then be your guide. Love begets love. In all my travels in this country and abroad I found people responsive to being understood, cared for and loved. It tears down walls of distrust and alienation and builds an attitude of mutuality. I tried it in occupation duty in Germany and Austria after World War II and felt reconciliation taking place. In Catholic Spain, the little housemaid who cared for Lois, my three children and me, after observing our feeling of acceptance of her and watching our family prayers and scripture readings, insightfully said to me (the only Protestant chaplain with the US Air Force in Madrid),

"I know. You are Catholic but not Roman Catholics."

We were accepted. My insurance policy later took care of her need for an appendectomy. How pleased she seemed that we considered her a part of our family!

Throughout my ninety-five years on earth, I still yearn to know the extent of God's love for the human race—and for me, His oft times erring sheep. It is enough for me to know that he sent His only Son to take on the form of my humanity, in human flesh, in order to die—in my place—for my sins. My vocabulary could never adequately express what that means to me.

I once heard a song entitled, *The Love of God* written by F.M. Lehman (date unknown), whose daughter, Claudia Lehman Mays, arranged the words first written in Aramaic, later translated into many languages. The lyrics are based on a Jewish poem. I had heard it sung, and loved it, before I found it in a Korean English Hymnal of which I was given a copy. At the time, 1995-2000, I was the English-language pastor of that Korean Christian (nondenominational) Church.

The Love of God

The love of God is greater far
Than tongue or pen can ever tell,
It goes beyond the highest star,
And reaches to the lowest hell;

The guilty pair, bowed down with care.
God gave His Son to win;
His erring child He reconciled,
And pardoned from his sin.

Refrain
O love of God, how rich and pure!
How measureless and strong!
It shall forevermore endure
The saints' and angels' song.

Could we with ink the ocean fill,
And were the skies of parchment made,

Were every stalk on earth a quill,
And every man a scribe by trade;

To write the love of God above,
Would drain the ocean dry.
Nor could the scroll contain the whole,
Though stretched from sky to sky.

In Linz, Austria, I had a man working as a clerk who lived in a Displacement Camp nearby. He spoke fairly good English and was after me often to learn to speak German. One day after lunch, I surprised and pleased him by getting his attention and repeating, in German, one of the beatitudes of the Bible:

"Selig sind, die da hungert und dürstet nach der Gerechtigkeit; den sie sollen satt werden." Which translates to:

"Blessed are they that hunger and thirst after righteousness, for they shall be filled."

I was eating peanuts at the time, so after I finished that Bible verse he held out his hand and said, "Mit peanuts." and smiled his appreciation for my "special" effort.

The year I was on duty in Upper Michigan, I attended the weekly meeting of the Kiwanis Club in Sault St. Marie. It had some members from Canada, so we sang the Star-Spangled Banner as well as *"O, Canada."* That bit of international contact helped me receive another Commendation Medal at the end of my twenty years as a chaplain in military service. And I learned to sing the Canadian national anthem and enjoyed the reciprocity. The Canadian chaplains asked me to visit one of their meetings and share with them the story of the United States' Military Chaplains Association. After all, they were our next-door neighbors.

Getting back to "Loving and Being Loved"—throughout my adult ministries my life has been blessed with much love. Because my father had been loved during his circuit-riding years 1910-'14, when I went to serve six of those ten churches, the old-timers transferred some of that love to me. At the end of my time in Macon County in 1943, the editor of the local paper (not one of my members), announced my departure for military service that included these words, "and it may be safely said that no more a beloved pastor ever served in this county."

As I left to become a chaplain, I felt a few inches taller. And it was doubly pleasing that the words came unsought from an unexpected source.

As I was leaving to return to the USA after three years of occupation duty in Austria and Germany, my commander in Wiesbaden penned these words:

The chaplain has been most active among all personnel assigned and has been accepted by personnel of all faiths as an exceptionally friendly and likeable individual and, through his efforts, the tasks and difficulties of all personnel have been considerably eased.

Those words mitigated my disappointment over not being approved by my denomination for a regular commission. The military headquarters did approve it. I left determined to get the seminary degree that prevented the Methodist Commission on Chaplains from giving its approval.

As I was ending my last duty station at Kincheloe AFB, Michigan (and twenty years in the armed forces), the commander included the following words of affection:

"Chaplain Green possesses a highly pleasing personality, a warm approachableness and an outstanding sense of humor. These traits made him one of the friendliest, most loved chaplains the base ever had."

For twelve of my seventeen years as the associate pastor of huge First United Methodist Church in Colorado Springs, one of my main jobs was to develop a caring system for the elderly, and that without letting anyone drop through the cracks. As the Minister of Pastoral Care, I was in charge of between seventy and eighty funerals a year. In that capacity I went all out to bring comfort to grieving families. Often loved ones asked for a copy of my part in the funeral. That was virtually impossible, because my sketchy notes were augmented with much else, such as poetic expressions and remembrance of unwritten notes.

It pleased families that I initiated tape recordings of each service and gave families a copy to send to loved ones not present. I had visited, in the hospital beforehand, many of those who were dying. My practice also was to visit the home of bereaved families where I took notes and went into some detail as to what the deceased was like. Obituaries in newspapers completed the picture.

There was one elderly couple I will never forget. The man was a retired minister. I had made many visits in the home during their declining years. I listened to things they said. She died first. When he died, I did an interview with his three children—one of whom was a minister. I now share with you what the family thought of my final visit before the funeral. The senior minister had the service with the help of a pastor who had been close to the family earlier in life. But I did the interview and other necessities. After the funeral, the preacher-son wrote the following letter to Dr. Lacour. He read it and gave it to me. Here it is,

> *Dear Dr. Lacour,*
>
> *Our father's life was full and he worked relentlessly on the side of The Almighty. All of you fine ministers honored him for that and also for the many other attributes on the occasion of his funeral. In doing so, you eased the pain in our hearts and helped us remember that Dad is on the other side—filled with all joy—as he unites himself with loved ones who preceded him there.*
>
> *His faith was endless and because of that our faith in the renewal of life is strong. We think that the eulogies were deserved. He truly earned all the things that were said about him. Hearty thanks to you, Dr. Lacour, and to Rev. Glen Barney, a longtime friend.*
>
> (Then he changed the subject and began talking about me). He wrote,
>
> *In all my observance of ministers of all denominations of the Christian Church, I've never met a man like Rev. Philip Green. He painstakingly drew each one of us out as he took notes on the telling of our experiences living with and knowing our Dad. The 'talk' session proved to be therapeutically valuable. We discovered that we could laugh again and know that Dad approved of it. We leaned on Phil Green for other details attendant to the funeral, and he not only didn't lose patience with us but walked the extra distance to bring about solutions. He's miraculous.*
>
> *Please tell Rev. Green that we hold him in very high esteem for his love and tenderness to both our parents and*

to us when we needed his special brand of love. Thanks to you all.

Sincerely,
Harold, Jim and Carolyn Dryden

Words of love and approbation like those were sufficient for me to face the heavy duties in a church of six thousand members. That's one of the reasons I survived those challenges for seventeen years. It is quite understandable, then, that my philosophy of life is found in the expression, *Knowing and being known, caring and being cared for, loving and being loved.*

Such words open one's heart and life to others—great and small—to whoever yearns for what we have to share. Some people have been given much and, therefore, have much to share. But whatever we are, or have been given, we all have something to give—a smile, a friendly nod of acceptance, a phone call, a letter of encouragement, a visit, a gift—something of value to share. Every one of us hears what is being said around us and—in response to what others know we hear—is attached to an opportunity for some act of kindness. Write a note to someone and say something gracious or loving. It won't be long before a response will come back to you. Try it.

LOVE

by Emmet Fox (copied from an old document)

There is no difficulty that enough love will not conquer; no disease that enough love will not heal; no door that enough love will not open; no gulf that enough love will not bridge; no wall that enough love will not throw down, no sin that enough love will not redeem.

It makes no difference how deeply-seated may be the trouble, how hopeless the outlook, how muddled the tangle, how great the mistake, a sufficient realization of love will dissolve it all, if only you could love enough you would be the happiest and most powerful being in the world.

39

PATHS TO TRANQUILITY

Tranquility is a satisfied state of being. Ideally, it is a quiet time, a time of peace and unruffled waves upon the waters of life. Jesus was asleep aboard the ship in the midst of a storm on the Sea of Galilee so threatening that his disciples were terrified. He said to them,

"Why are you fearful?" Then he quieted the winds and the waves (and their fears).

I remember a poem that addresses our troubled waters but not the name of the author. Here it is (I think):

I met God in the morning when the day was at its best,
And his presence came like sunshine, like a glory within my breast.

All day long his presence lingered, all day long he stayed with me,
And we sailed in perfect calmness over a very troubled sea.

Other ships were tossed and battered, other ships were sore distressed,
But the storm that seemed to wreck them brought to us a perfect rest.

So I think I know the secret, learned from many a troubled way,
You must meet God in the morning, if you want him through the day.

Many years ago there was a plaque. My wife had found it somewhere and placed it in the upstairs bathroom so as to be seen before anything else. I think I can still quote it:

The kiss of the sun for pardon, the song of the birds for mirth.
One is nearer God's heart in a garden than anywhere else on earth.

Those words made me want to finish shaving and other things and hurry through breakfast to get my hands in the dirt of a flower garden. One is so tranquil doing the more pleasant things needing to be done. But, during those years of my ministry, I was very busy—preparing a sermon each week, having an average of eighty funerals each year, making visits to hospitals and nursing homes, counseling those who needed to make difficult decisions, and a myriad of other things.

Lois and I often softened the blow of too much work by sharing the events of the day, hers in the classroom of School District 20, mine at the church with people in need. One Friday night I asked her to go with me to a nearby town and spend the night in a motel where no one could reach us. Another time I varied my day by going to the church and returning home a different way, just to break the grueling routine.

I guess I saved the day by a few minutes in the flower garden, or playing hymns on the piano, or yet by finding a quiet place somewhere in the house or yard to let my soul catch up with my body.

My album named *Christian Ashrams in My Life* shows how one can get away from the regular grind for most of a week—with no mail, telephone calls, or distractions—during which one's own tranquility is only topped by intimate conversations with the One who created me, and who is pleased to have my undivided attention. Then, it is possible for anyone to build and defend "a secret hiding place," where you intentionally meet one another.

I was well into my 40s before taking an increased interest in growing flowers. Moving around in short-term military assignments was not conducive to a long-term commitment to growing things. That is, until we had a three-year tour at Whiteman Air Force Base near Warrensburg, Missouri (1957-'60). The commander launched a home beautification contest for those who lived on the base. We lived on the street where he drove by several times a day to get to his house, so we gave ourselves to the project to such an extent that our iris, verbena, salvia, petunias, calla lilies, Lombardy poplars, and well kept lawn, won for us the first prize, two years in a row.

After military retirement, at 2215 Condor Street for more than two decades, we had oodles of time to grow trees, fix flower beds and beautify our fairly new home in the "bird farm"—or Audubon section of the city. Each year saw challenges to move from annuals, as colorful as they were, to perennials that came up each year with less muscle power needed. Wintertime always wiped out the annuals and we longed for an indoor growing area. We met this challenge by glassing in our back porch and using a heater to keep the temperature up to 40 degrees. That made an ideal place for red geraniums. At times we had a glory of blooms for months at a time. We were fortunate enough to have found a Hoya vine, and it grew around half the porch, giving scented clusters of triple stars for months. Our grapevines did well. Each year we had a bumper crop. I especially enjoyed eating the Concord blue grapes because the commissary carried only imported grapes from California. They were good, too, but I longed for the grapes of my childhood back in North Carolina.

We had good luck with Lombardy poplars. In time (10 to 12 years) they needed to be replaced with elms, maples, linden and evergreens. The kitchen garden eventually gave way to flowers when we found that vine-ripened tomatoes were nearly impossible to ripen before frost. Our perennials did well—achillia (yarrow), chrysanthemum, clematis, columbine, creeping phlox, day lily, delphinium, gladioli, hollyhock, honeysuckle, iris, peony, plantain lily, rhubarb, rose, and Shasta daisy. These were added through the years.

Because the soil in our yard was resistant to cultivation for flowerbeds, we added new space each year until as much as we wanted was transformed into arable space. Early on we purchased a number of wooden flower boxes. These resembled those we had seen in Bavarian windows while assigned in Germany (1946-'49). From time to time, either in the back yard or the front, we had the following annuals—ageratum, calendula, cosmos, four o'clocks, geranium, larkspur, lobelia, marigold, pansy, petunia, ragged robin, salvia, snapdragon, sweet pea, verbena and zinnia. Beyond the back fence was 18 inches of growing space between the fence and the paved alley. One year, in that narrow space, we planted pumpkins and trained the vines up the fence. It was something to see a large pumpkin anchored to the top lap of the fence. Wow! How much tranquility we had!

During Lois' incapacitation with around-the-clock nursing care in a nearby nursing home, I had a lot of free time at home alone outside the three visits a day I usually made to her bedside. I planted rose bushes in the front yard in her honor. Also, I extended the flowerbeds along the driveway and all the sidewalks and took photos in color, had them developed for the projector and displayed them on the ceiling above Lois' bed. She was able to open her eyes and see them. Though largely unable to communicate, she did seem to enjoy looking. She had been a lifelong partner in helping to choose and plant our flowers. In 1959 we purchased from Readers Digest a 14-volume encyclopedia of flowers and techniques of growing them.

Some kinds of music are soothing. The hymn *Abide with Me* that is sung in solitude, brings into my being a tranquil peace as nothing else does. Watching the last rounds of a golf tournament on television puts me into a contemplative mood.

Reading the 23rd Psalm reminds me not to worry about the "valley of the shadow of death." If ever I am in need of a peaceful reminder, I find and read the words of John Greenleaf Whittier in *Dear Lord and Father of Mankind.*

Sometimes I quote from *The Ancient Mariner* the words of a stranded seaman,

O sleep, it is a gentle thing, beloved from pole to pole. To Mary Queen the praise be given, she sent the gentle sleep from heaven, that slid into my soul.

40

PHOTO MEMORIES

To say that I have a trunk full of photographs is to put it mildly. In fact, I have 25 albums chock full of pictures and saved writings. Each is named elsewhere in this book. Here is a small sample:

- Book of Philip I, II, III
- Book of Lois, Helen, Extended Family
- Travels Abroad, Germany, Spain
- Music in My Life
- Military Chaplains Association

There are a sufficient number of memories in those albums to bring happiness for the remainder of my long life and, please God, into the next. I have borrowed from them liberally for this book. Included among them is an album of Christmas letters. At age fifty, Lois and I began sending long letters (sometimes too long) on Christmas stationary to some two hundred loved ones and cherished friends, instead of cards. We ran out of space on cards, wanting to say more than the space allowed. After Lois' passing, later Helen and I kept up the letters. Since 2005, I send them myself—but to an ever-declining number. I have outlived most of the friends, but picked up a few new ones.

When I was on occupation duty in Germany and Austria 1946-'49, I purchased a camera in order to capture some of the extraordinary scenery, cathedrals, and people. The film speed was the slow kind, even in black and white. The Germans had invented a three-way camera that took three different colors at the same time. The films were put on top of one another to make a complete color picture. On a lottery, I won the privilege to purchase a Leica camera. Because of the rarity of photo reproducing shops at that time, I began developing and enlarging my own photos in black and white. Sometimes I would over paint the black and white in color, but it was never like a real painting. My dark room was in basements of the buildings in which we lived. I learned a lot about how to minimize the graininess of enlargements.

During the seventeen years as associate pastor of a mega-church (1963-'80), we became friends of Paul and Marie Pearson who were both artists. We paid Marie to take several choice photos and 'copy' them in color paintings. I cherish the paintings as well as the memories of Paul and Marie. I have kept copies of enlarged black and white scenes taken and enlarged. With the ability of a Leica, I have several scenes in color from Germany and Spain.

One album I view from time to time is entitled *Scenes of Beauty.* It is full of many photos I have taken in color and black and white. Lois and I grew beautiful flowerbeds around some of our homes. At Whiteman Air Force Base in Missouri, we won first place in having the most beautiful flowers around our house—two years in a row. At 2215 Condor Street in Colorado Springs, we turned clay into friable soil and had a wealth of beauty in our yard. Another of my albums is entitled *Cherished Friends.* It is a limited edition because of space in the album and the absence of photos of many friends.

One picture is worth a thousand words. In August 1946, I arrived by troopship in Bremerhaven, Germany. World War II had ended the previous year and there were selected troops still in Germany with the occupation forces. On the ship with me (along with other troops) were a few chaplains to replace those who were coming due for rotation back to the States. This photo includes the twenty-six who were onboard the ship, or who were already there in USAFE (United States Air Forces, Europe), with headquarters in Wiesbaden. We were on retreat at Garmisch, and I just happened to have a lapse-time camera at the time. So I put it on a tripod, clicked it on, and had a few seconds to get in the photo (far left end).

All 26 chaplains on occupation duty in Germany from 1946 to 1949, during a retreat in 1948.

My father and his family of 7 children, 1921, on the front porch of our newly built home at Rutherford College, Burke County, NC. (front row, from left) Ruth, Papa, Lois, Mama, Philip (back row, from left) Mary, James, Kilgo, Chessie

Our family at MacDill AFB Tampa, FL 1946. Baby Mickey was born July 4th that year.

My family in Madrid, Spain 1955
Marcia, Lois, Philip Jr., Mickey, Me

Lois and I with all our family.
50th Wedding Anniv. 1986

Here I am with only some of my great AND great-great grandchildren!

A few of my many, many family photos

SECTION IX

The way I tried, ever so hard, to bring comfort to the sorrowing hearts and minds of the many surviving family members across the decades, is found in this chapter. Every pastor tries to do the same. But I have my own way of doing so.

There are all sizes of satisfactions immense, mid-size and diminutive ones. Each relates to the size of one's desire and the difficulty of its attainment. I have my own desires, wishes, hopes and expectations. A look at the nine and a half decades of my life reveals that my path has been lined with many, many satisfactions.

When someone you know very well merits special recognition or honor you can give, say so or write them so. They may not need it on top of what others may have given, but you may be sure that they will appreciate what you say, write or do. If they have died, family members and close friends will put what you write with their keep-sakes.

Just as there are great health factors at work in the process of forgiveness, even so there are avenues to ill health in that of being unforgiving. Grudges wrinkle the mind, clutter the disposition and close doors.

The parsonage in which I was born September 15, 1914 was literally on what had been a religious camping ground, a half century before I was born. All that remained of that campground was a marvelous spring of fresh, cool running water. Such grounds were plentiful in the 1800s and 1900s. My father founded two of them in North Carolina and one in Florida. Church camping has been a regular part of my life.

41

GOOD GRIEF

Funerals and Grief Situations

The stance of our church until November 17, 1966 was that the senior minister would have them all, except when out of the city. When Dr. Lehmberg died of a heart attack at age 57, it became clear that it was impossible for a senior minister to have all the funerals, all the weddings, all the baptisms, all the hospital visitations, most of the sermons at the two major Sunday morning services, most of the counseling, all of the above and more without a serious health threat, especially in a church with more than 6,000 members.

It was not realistic for the congregation to expect it. Sure, it was a comfort to know that the headman would come in a crisis, at their individual time of need. But multiply this by several times a week and the picture is untenable. Dr. Ben tried to do it all, and even after his first heart attack when his cardiologist warned him to slow down, he told a friend, "I don't intend to be half a preacher."

In view of the obvious fact that any future senior minister would need to have some protection from the unrealistic expectations of the congregation, with the concurrence of the Pastoral Relations Committee while I was the Interim Senior Minister-in-Charge, the policy was established that when a member asked for a particular minister for a pastoral act, that minister would perform it, unless there was a serious reason not to. On March 17, 1967, Dr. Lacour became senior minister and, much to his credit, he accepted this policy. As it turned out, the minister of pastoral care caught the greater load of funerals and grief situations. I had been on the staff for forty-three months and it was rather natural for members in grief situations to seek the minister who knew the family best. Wish it or not, I became the staff minister most often called upon for funerals. Most of the years from 1968 until 1980 I conducted between 70 and 80 funerals a year. They were not scheduled neatly like one or two a week. In fact, in one ten-day period I had seven funerals. One was a suicide and another was a crib death. That stretch of duty almost plowed me under.

In the midst of so many funerals, a colleague asked if I didn't routinely conduct these numerous funerals without much emotional involvement. I needed to be honest in my answer, because it was a question I often asked myself. In truth, each funeral hurt me, some more than others. As I sat talking with a distraught widowed mother, she told me that her son had a very painful cancer. She had stayed by him day after day, but had slipped away for a few minutes to the grocery store on that fateful day. During that half hour, he had found the family pistol, put it in his mouth and pulled the trigger. She found him lying on the floor in a pool of blood. I felt her grief deep in my own heart. My words of consolation at the funeral were baptized in the waters of my own identification with her life situation.

As a matter of fact, I can't remember a funeral at which grave-side I didn't feel that "this could have been my mother, my brother, my wife, my child"—even when I stood by the grave side of a lone tradesman from the infirmary of Union Printer's Home, who had been shipped there from Chicago, St. Louis, or San Francisco only a week earlier, to die without a loved one near.

It was my determination that I never would conduct a funeral without first sitting down with members of the family of the deceased if he had one, and (1) get to know something of the life of the deceased, (2) get to know those he knew and loved, and (3) help in this way the bereaved with their loss. At the service, after the obituary, I asked, "How else do we want to remember him?" Sometimes the only remaining ones with whom to talk were neighbors, an attending nurse, a bank power-of-attorney, or an official personal representative. In each case I took the time to get to know as much as possible about the deceased, and to reflect that information in my notes.

Without fail, I honored the memory of the one deceased. And never did I make diminishing statements about his lack of church attendance, any bad habits, or any failures. Regardless of known evidence of not being affiliated with a church of choice, I would surround his family and friends with Scriptures of hope and comfort, and undergird the service with the assurance that God was walking with them "through the valley of the shadow of death."

To give the next of kin something tangible, I taped each service and gave the tape to the family. In many cases, I wrote a note to the next of kin on the first anniversary of the service in which I offered to meet with them in case they were having extended grief.

My overall intention for each death situation was to visit or phone the next of kin upon hearing of the death, setting a day and hour when a visit with members of the family could take place. Then the visit with the family at which time the wishes of the family could be known about the type of service; the music (vocal or instrumental) desired; any special Scriptures chosen; and an in-depth profile of the deceased. The family would be met at the church or mortuary or grave side and the service conducted. In most instances, a follow-up visit in the home a few days after the funeral was made.

With variations, most services included: Prelude music, opening sentences and an invocation, hymn, scriptures, prayer (with The Lord's Prayer), special music, pastor's message and/or eulogy, benediction and postlude. Sometimes a family member or friend gave or read a eulogy or poem or music. Most of the time the length of the service was limited to 30 minutes or less, a fact most families appreciated.

The pastor's part in the service began with these words:

> *Dear Friends, we are gathered here to pay our offices of faith and love to (or to honor the life and mark the passing of his/her name). Let us be together as family and friends and neighbors. But also let us be together as members of the community of faith, (if the deceased were known to be a person of faith), as we turn to his God and ours for an invocation.*

Beyond the requested scriptures the family made, also included were scriptures I added. To keep within the time frame of the service, I often telescoped long familiar passages, as follows:

> *The Lord is my Shepherd, I shall not want—Yea though I walk through the valley of the shadow of deZath, I will fear no evil. Thy rod and thy staff they comfort me. Surely goodness and mercy shall follow me all the days of my life, and I shall dwell in the house of the Lord forever.*

OR

I would introduce the passage from John 14 with this preface: *One day Jesus found his disciples sad. Sad because he had told them that he was going away and, for the time being, they could not follow. He said,* (A free partial translation of parts of John 14, by PLG)

> *You must not let yourselves be distressed. You must hold on to your faith in God and to your faith in me. There are many rooms in my Father's house. If it were not so, I should have told you that I am going away to prepare a place for you. It is true that I am going away to prepare a place for you, bit it is just as true that I am coming again to receive you unto myself, that where I am, there you may be also I am not going to leave you alone in the world; I am coming to you. If you really love me, you will keep the commandments I have given you, and I shall ask the Father to send someone else to be with you, to be with you always. I mean the Spirit of truth. He is with you now, and shall be in your hearts.*

Most of the time I began the message with a poem such as, *It Is Not Death to Die* by H.A. Cesar Malan, in part: (from p112 in *A Service Book)*

> *It is not death to die—*
> *To leave this earthly road,*
> *And, 'midst the personhood on high,*
> *To be at home with God . . .*

If the deceased were quite aged and suffered much and wanted to go, I often used a part of John Oxenham's poem entitled *Nightfall* from *Bees in Amber*, in part:

> *Fold up the tent,*
> *The sun is in the West.*
> *Tomorrow my untented soul will range*
> *Among the blest, . . .*

Before the benediction, another poem was used, such as *The Tenant* by Frederick Lawrence Knowles, especially if the deceased were a member of a Masonic order.

Now and then I closed with a poem by Roselle Montgomery entitled *On the Death of an Aged Friend.* I first heard it at a funeral I was conducting in Forest Lawn Cemetery, Glendale, California, in 1944. Hollywood actor Edward Arnold quoted it. Here it is in part: (from p138 in *A Service Book*)

> *You are not dead—Life has but set you free.*
> *Your years of life were like a lovely song,*
> *The last sweet poignant notes of which, held long,*
> *Passed into silence while we listened, . . .*

An oft-used committal service included the following:

Let us hear the words of Jesus, spoken at the grave of Lazarus:

"I am the resurrection and the life," saith the Lord: "he that believeth in me, though he were dead, yet shall he live: and whosoever liveth and believeth in me shall never die." "Peace I leave with you. My peace I give unto you. Let not your heart be troubled, neither let it be afraid." John 11:25-26

These words comfort our hearts, as do the words of John Greenleaf Whittier, who said:

"God calls our loved ones, but we lose not wholly what he has given. They live on earth in thought and deed, as truly as in his heaven." (from p174 in *A Service Book*)

Coping with Death and Dying

Many people are reluctant to come to grips with their mortality—even many of the elderly. Like Vivian Leigh in *Gone with the Wind*, they say, "I'll think about it tomorrow." Seeing a need to help our members think about, talk about, and plan for their deaths whenever they might come, I set up a series of death and dying seminars with eight separate sessions. The general public was invited also. They were well attended and the evaluations were good.

One man waited almost too long before his death. He was a retired professional who had brought his second wife to live in our city. The couple attended our church and, because he was in declining health, I visited in his home several times. One night about 11 p.m., I received a phone call from a doctor I knew. He was at a hospital attending to our member and said that he was in critical condition with heart trouble. He doubted that the man would last through the night. He said the couple had been playing games with one another, reassuring each other that, "everything was going to be all right" and would I come over and help them face up to the fact that he was dying? He responded well to one question, which was,

"Joe, if you should die tonight, is there anything you wish you could do before that happens?"

He asked me to try to get an attorney to come to the hospital. At 2:00 a.m., a friend of mine responded to my emergency call. The patient dictated to him the contents of what he wanted to say in his will, and he signed it, with nurses as witnesses. He seemed very relieved that he had taken this action. If he had died that night, his present wife would have been left completely out of consideration. He died the next day. I am thankful for that doctor who saw that a man and his wife needed to have a quick and serious talk with his pastor.

Dr. Elisabeth Kubler-Ross Comes to Town

Famous Dr. Kubler-Ross came to Colorado Springs for a few days of lectures at the invitation of the medical staff at Penrose Hospital and some of the ministers of the city. Dr. Lacour asked me to do all I could to represent our church during this event. There was no auditorium at Penrose Hospital that would come anywhere near being large enough to accommodate the expected crowds. Corpus Christi Catholic Church across the street from the hospital invited the event to happen there. One of the specialties of Dr. Kubler-Ross, author of *On Death and Dying*, was her ability to talk to dying patients and to get more than monosyllables in response—children and adults. When she expressed the wish that a dying patient from Penrose Hospital be brought across the street to the Church, I thought of Mrs. Adams, mother of the building superintendent at our Church, who was expected to die very shortly. I told Dick Adams the situation and asked whether or not he would allow his mother to be taken to the event. He said that it would be all right, unless she objected. She did not object.

A blizzard was blowing that day, but she was wrapped well and the ambulance drove right up to the church steps. At that session, a church full of interested community doctors, ministers, nurses and church people watched and listened carefully as Dr. Kubler-Ross talked with Mrs. Adams. She elicited answers that all could hear over the sound system. Near the end of the interview, a man from our congregation, who himself was dying gradually over a few weeks time, arose and asked permission to speak. He wanted a few people to gather around the bed of Mrs. Adams and pray for her. There was a hushed crowd as a few of us gathered around her bed for several spontaneous and fervent prayers.

After Mrs. Adams was returned to the hospital, Dr. Kubler-Ross was perceptive enough to know that there needed to be a time of response to what had happened—especially about the prayers for the patient. There were those who favored the interruption. Others were vocal against what happened because of the wide range of religious backgrounds represented in the audience. I was happy that the Jewish Rabbi stood up and defended the idea of praying for Mrs. Adams, a dying woman. Sentiments leaned in his direction as he spoke of the courage and love of one human being who invited believers to gather sympathetically, if not personally, around a woman who was not long for this world.

42

SATISFACTION'S GUARANTEE

The feeling of satisfaction is the culmination of desired achievements and attainments. That feeling has a price tag. The cost of getting what we want, going where we wish, becoming what we want to be, depends upon the relative depth of one's desire and the difficulty of its attainability. Another factor relates to the amount of time fulfillment of the desire takes. An impatient person wants what he or she wants, and wants it as soon as possible—or as "right now" as possible.

"I'll not be satisfied until . . . ." is limitless, if it means "until I get my way," for one may never get one's way.

There are immense satisfactions, middle-sized satisfactions and minute ones. The degree of satisfaction depends upon the size of the desire times the difficulty of its obtainment. Some philosophies of life call for the death of all desire, as in Buddhism. I am not that kind of person. Like millions of normal persons, I have desires, wishes, hopes and expectations. A review of my 95 years of life shows that my path has been blessed with many satisfactions. They have guaranteed my desire to keep on letting God fulfill my prayer of dominant desire, *Lord, Use Me.* I have Him to thank for using me as a country preacher for seven years, as a military chaplain for 20 years, as an associate pastor in a huge church for 17 years, and in retirement for the last 25 years.

When a member of my church said, as I was leaving at age eighty, "You have made a difference in my life", I was satisfied with my six and a half years there.

Beyond the halfway point of my duty of 17 years at our huge church, I received the following note from Dr. L. Ralph Chason, Ph.D.:

Dear Phil,

On behalf of the Pastor Parish Committee and the congregation, I want to take this opportunity to tell you how much we appreciate you. We are continuously aware of the good and faithful work that you do for us with such dedication and energy. You have gone beyond the successes of your first career [as a military chaplain] to make a deep and lasting spot for yourself in the hearts and lives of the members of this church. You have met the needs of so many of us in a way that only you can provide. Ralph

Satisfactions such as these encourage me to push the end of my life of service in the church, and in life, a little farther down the track—in fact, 37 years. And I am still young at 95.

Satisfying Moments and Events for Philip

When my new senior pastor said to me, "Phil, Bishop Stuart wants you to stay on my staff."

When Chaplain, Major General Terrence Fennigan said to me, "Phil, 'Carp' (Chaplain Charles I. Carpenter) wants you at the Air Force Academy." Carp was the former Chief of Air Force Chaplains.

When Lois (D. Ritter), my sweetheart, said she would marry me within two weeks after I had put a modest wedding ring in her hand.

As I directed the 700 plus gathering of Air Force personnel at the first Spiritual Life Conference at the Baptist Assembly Grounds, Ridgecrest, NC (1953).

When I was chosen to be the first Protestant chaplain with the 16th Air Force in Madrid, Spain (1954-'57).

When the presiding Bishop of the Western North Carolina Conference of the Methodist Episcopal Church, South, read the name of the Sandy Circuit, Asheville, District with my name as pastor-on-trial of the six-point circuit—my first appointment (Oct. 1936).

When my sister, Ruth, came to where I had been fasting for three days, praying that she would become a Christian, put her arms around me with tears in her eyes and said, "Philip, you can go ahead and eat now. I have given my heart to Jesus."

When Clarence Correll said to me as I struggled the last steps through a blinding snow storm into his yard, "Preacher, what are you doing out in this blizzard?"

When my Grandmother Green put her hand on my teenage head on her dying day and said, "Phip, make a good preacher!"

When my longtime Air Force chaplain friend phoned me at Spence Field, Moultrie, Georgia and said, "Phil, I need you at Parks Air Force Base (California)."

When the threat of the Russian Bear during the Berlin Airlift motivated the Air Force policy to let military personnel with families to send them back to the USA, my wife said, "Let the Russian Bear come and let other families go home—I'm staying with you!"

When the Military Chaplains Association elected me to be the first Air Force chaplain to be their national president.

When Helen Thompson MacMillan said she'd be happy to share the remainder of my broken life. (Lois had died the year before, following 19 months of incapacitation).

When I stood beside Grandmother Green's grave in Burke County, NC in 1999, I said to her, "Grandma, I'm still trying [to make a good preacher]."

When I was invited to preach Sunday, October 17, 1999, in Big Sandy United Methodist church after 59 years as pastor there—an elderly woman told me she had found Christ as her Savior while I was pastor (1936-'40). Most of the others were already in the church cemetery nearby.

43

HONOR WHERE HONOR IS DUE

"A Tribute to a Fallen Hero of the Pulpit" who died at age 57
by Philip L. Green
Rev. Dr. Ben F. Lehmberg—"A Man to Remember"
(See chapter 5, Models, for text)

A Debtor: I owe so much to so many others. However did I get from being a towheaded freckle faced preacher's kid to the ripe old age of 98 without you and you and you? Looking back over the years, I am amazed to remember the many wonderful turnings of my life brought about by others. I have been led, and often kicked in the pants, by a provident heavenly Father who helped me see that his way was the best way, and worth every sacrifice to stay on that way.

When I contemplate the many who have perceived in me the promise of a faithful follower of my Savior, I am deluged with "Where shall I begin and with whom?" Then I begin to realize that it will take volumes of pages and decades of time to give justice to all those who have helped me. At this late time, I don't expect to have decades, just a few remaining years of faltering beginnings before "the silver cord of life snaps, and the golden bowl is broken, and the pitcher is broken at the fountain, and the wheel is broken at the cistern, and the dust returns to the earth as it was, and the spirit returns to God who gave it." The quote is from the Living Bible, paraphrased—part of Ecclesiastes 12.

My greatest debt is to my heavenly Father who knew me in my 28-year-old mother's womb. She was married to my father, a minister of The Methodist Episcopal Church, South. I was a happy replacement for my brother Andrew who had just died of diphtheria at age two. It was fortuitous that Papa and Mama were devout followers of Jesus Christ. My father was a pastor/evangelist who possessed and proclaimed the blessing of sanctification, or being filled with the Holy Spirit.

Worthy or not worthy, I look across the decades of my life and see God's hands guiding me, sometimes a reluctant follower, through the decisions of a bishop or military authority. I see doors of opportunity opening along the way that turned out to be best for my developing hopes. My first appointment to Sandy Circuit of six churches where I was able in four years to do my church work and, at the same time, complete the four-year Conference Course of Studies for becoming a traveling Deacon and an Elder. Under the guidance of the Holy Spirit, I revived Old Brick Church that had sat empty for a score of years. [I could have been moved in less than the mandatory four years at the end of which the fixed rule was "four years" only.]

I was transferred to the Franklin Circuit of six more churches in the northernmost part of Macon County, NC. Here I was able to develop fully the pastoral care part of my preaching ministry. Three fruitful years were followed by my volunteering to become a military chaplain. In 20 years of service in the Army and U.S. Air Force, I was blessed by the friendship of Chaplain Charles Wesley "Dri" Marteney, American Baptist; Chaplain Charles I. Carpenter, Chief of Air Force Chaplains; and Chaplain Glen C. Shaffer. All helped keep me on the straight and narrow with overseas assignments in Austria and Germany and Madrid, Spain.

44

FORGIVENESS AND SPIRITUAL HEALTH

I should have known better, that there would have been a better time to tell the truth. But I thought that the truth was the truth anytime, anywhere. I chose the wrong time to tell the truth in my message to one of six congregations in 1940. The truth about which I write was that everyone should forgive. To me nothing seemed more central to the teachings of scriptures than that. In five of the churches, the message of forgiveness was well received.

In one church, there was a woman who carried a grudge against another woman in a different church. What made it hurt so deeply was that it was public knowledge and that woman knew it. She "knew" something else too. She knew that someone had told the new pastor, so that the pastor could "load his gun" without fear of missing. But she was mistaken. No one had told me about that bit of bitterness. It is possible that, during my three years there, she always held it against me and whoever she thought spilled the beans.

There is a physician who always wants to know what's wrong with a patient. Every doctor wants to know that. But this one probes behind the up-front cause of the visit, in search of hidden causes of the malady. If he finds a grudge in the life of the patient, he begins by working on that. His past experience tells him that unsolved broken relationships lie behind a multitude of physical manifestations. In short, he knows that one cannot stay well and harbor ill-will against someone else.

So, turn to the Good Book where wellness and wholeness are to be found. In no uncertain words one finds that it is impossible to be right with your Maker and at odds with your fellow man. Over and over again the scriptures lift up the importance of forgiving others. In The Lord's Prayer Jesus makes that the precondition of receiving divine forgiveness.

As a matter of emphasis, Jesus taught that when we are praying and, remember a broken relationship with someone else, we interrupt should our prayers by getting up right then, and if possible go to seek reconciliation with that person before continuing to pray. Forgiving others is the key to unanswered prayer, yours.

45

OLD TIME CAMP MEETINGS

I was born in 1914 in the parsonage that was previously the Turkey Creek Campground in the 1800s. It was at Leicester, Buncombe County, North Carolina, twelve miles from Asheville, the county seat. When I was born, all that remained of that camp was a wonderful, ever-flowing, spring. Twenty-two years after I was born, Sandy Circuit, which is now where Turkey Creek Campground used to be, became my first appointment in 1936. The six churches on the charge were part of ten churches that my circuit-riding father served 1910-'14.

Thus, began a lifetime of love for camp grounds and church camps. In 1921, Papa founded Camp Free at Connelly Springs in Burke County. I grew up a quarter of a mile from it and spent many midsummer days helping him and others ready the camp for ten days of services. At the three services a day, people from throughout the state enjoyed outstanding evangelists and Bible teachers. For me it was a time for the renewal or my commitment to God.

In 1939, my father was asked to found White City Camp in Avon Park, Florida. As a young pastor, it was my joy to direct the music the first year. I attended ten days there in 1986 long after its name had been changed to Avon Park Camp Meeting. Because there were changes of leadership after my father's death in 1955, except for a few old-timers, I was asked to write a history of the camp from its beginning. The title was *Grace Abounding in the Orange Groves*. It has grown to be a very large camp with dorms and motor home sites.

As a chaplain in the US Air Force for 20 years, it was my happy privilege to have interesting experiences at retreat centers at Berchtesgaden, Germany in 1948; at the Baptist Assembly Grounds, Ridgecrest, NC in 1953; Asilomar retreat center, CA, in 1961. Never to be forgotten have been numerous times at Lake Junaluska, NC. In 1977, during a month in Liberia, West Africa, I attended a church camp for native clergy and key lay persons.

At the YMCA of the Rockies at Estes Park, CO, I benefitted at several retreats and conferences. Church camping during the past forty-five or so years was plentiful. The church had a camp in the mountains called John Wesley Ranch and we used it a multitude of times for retreats, skiing, snowmobiling, parties, and whatever.

The Rocky Mountain Conference had a camping site known as Templed Hills near Woodland Park. The facilities included buildings for overnight and all-summer youth and adult camps. I had the responsibility, and honor, to be the chairman of the board of control several years. In 1981, for four years I founded and supervised a retreat activity for adult seniors. I named it *Aspenglow Camp* because it was scheduled in late September when the aspen trees were at their most beautiful yellow glory. At other times there were picnics, steak fries and a host of good times with congregants and friends from throughout Colorado. It was my honor and privilege to chair the Templed Hills Camp Board for several years. Thankfully there were staunch supporters who backed me.

A 1914 Camp Meeting

My father's book entitled *Green Spots* describes Rock Springs Camp Meeting in the bounds of Rock Spring Circuit where he was appointed the pastor in November. I had just been born September 15. It was typical of many camp meeting sites in that day. When he was appointed to that circuit, he did not like it. The people were divided over whether or not the camp should continue and he felt caught in the middle between the opposing sides. Both sides wanted to know on which side the new pastor stood. He postponed his answer for many months and condemned both sides for being uncharitable with each other.

In January, he announced a revival in one of his churches. In January, of all unlikely times! Whoever heard of a revival meeting in the winter time? He asked no one for permission to conduct a week or more of morning and evening services in that church. Gradually, attendance improved and the hopes of some were dashed when he announced a second week of services. It succeeded wonderfully. Another and another and another revival was announced and resulted in people being revived and sinners converted. By the time for the big camp meeting to begin, he asked both sides if they would accept the pastor's decision on the matter. They agreed.

The camp area was laid out in a huge rectangle with the tabernacle in the middle. A hundred yards separated it from two rows of cabins and shacks and tents. Between them was a wide walkway which the people used to promenade. Saint and sinner, husband and wife, relatives, neighbors and strangers, sweethearts, adventurers and adventuresses, children and family pets, all mixed together there. Outside the perimeter was a wide assortment of horses, mules, buggies, wagons and surreys. To one side was a large spring of bubbling cold water that adequately met the need of everyone and, in addition, cooled many a watermelon.

Due to the success of several revival meetings in the local churches nearby, Papa announced the beginning of the camp meeting. Those who had not lost their zeal stood with him for the ensuing battle. Five prayer bands were organized. Thousands of people came and filled all billeting areas, with many sleeping in their wagons. Thus, the merry-go-round began as in former years. But this time they were in for surprises. A prayer band formed at each of the four corners. With clocks synchronized, they met as planned. At 7:00 p.m. they began singing. The gay, worldly, thoughtless crowd came parading along, ran head-on into a prayer meeting, made an unmilitary about-face, only to come upon another group at the next corner. They turned to the spring—the only other gathering place outside the tabernacle—and there found another prayer group.

Stunned, they staggered and surrendered and turned toward the tabernacle. Hundreds knelt at the altar and were blessed. The bishop kept my father there two years during which time 239 people were added to church rolls.

In 1998 at the North American Christian Ashram at St. John's University in Minnesota, an elderly woman saw my name tag and wanted to know whether or not I was related to Rev. Jim Green. I told her he was my father. She said that her grandmother used to rave about Pastor Jim Green who was in charge of the Rock Spring Camp Meeting. What a small world!

Tabernacle at Camp Free

Camp Meeting Preachers

Forceful proclaimers of the gospel were engaged each year to preach and teach at morning, afternoon and evening services. I list some of them: Dr. Henry Clay Morrison, twice President of Asbury College in Wilmore, KY, and longtime editor of the Pentecostal Herald in Louisville, KY, who was elected a bishop but decided against serving in that capacity. He did not like long prayers. At a service at Camp Free, a minister was using up too much time praying for people and things all over the world. Dr. Morrison stood it as long as he could, and finally was heard to say, "Shucks! God help us! Somebody start a song while this brother finishes his prayer."

In old age, as President Emeritus of Asbury, his health had become so poor and his heart so weak that his doctor had given him a very short life expectancy. It was his daily custom to shuffle to the college from his home nearby and be a part of a before-breakfast prayer meeting. One morning, he was late and someone was already praying aloud for him. "O Lord, bless Dr. Morrison and give him three or four more years."

When he heard this prayer he broke in with, "Lord, make it fifteen years anyway!"

In a sermon about Abraham offering up his son, Isaac, on the sacrificial altar, he was so dramatic with his arm uplifted and his hand holding a knife, that a woman cried out, "Don't kill him!"

Rev. Dr. John R. Church, General Evangelist of The Methodist Church, was often a camp-meeting preacher. Later in life I got to know him and his wife, Lola, more personally while I was a young pastor. They endeared themselves to Lois and me by defending our right to love and get married despite the fact that Lois was seven years my senior. Dr. Church was for many years Chairman of the Board of John Wesley College where my father was founder and President. He preached Papa's funeral in May of 1955. I was an Air Force chaplain in Spain at the time and did not arrive in time for that service.

My father was the founder of Camp Free for summer camp meetings one mile west of the hotel. He used funds coming out of a powerful revival meeting in Thomasville, NC to purchase land and, with the influence and help of like-minded clergy and laity, he built, organized and scheduled the camp meeting annually in late July through early August. The tabernacle was open on three sides so as to admit people from those directions. One wall was located behind the participating speakers, musicians and special guests to give a bit of privacy from anyone walking by. In those early years there was no sound system.

SECTION X

A short while ago I asked a physician what he thought would help a person to live longer and more healthily. His ready response was, "ATTITUDE." He left it for me to differentiate between a good and a bad attitude

It is true that we all have our own attitude toward nearly everything. For the elderly there is the attitude toward doctors, Medicare, growing old and what to do about this and that and everything else. There is an attitude toward others and an attitude toward one's own self.

To get an adequate work salary there may be times when we find ourselves in job situations or places that are much different from what we would like them to be. Moving from a rural to a city area could cause a major adjustment, a shocking one. When I was finishing my sophomore year in high school we moved from a small town to St. Louis, MO. There I enrolled in a high school with a building that had three floors, including a front area and two side wings. The rooms on one of the side wings had even numbers, and the other wing had odd numbers. For a shocking few minutes I could not find my room number because my room number had an odd number.

Many times our bodies heal themselves, as with a cold. Patent medicines can help us recover from minor ailments. A diet can cure obesity. Hospitals are often needed as well as doctors, nurses and care attendants. I believe in the efficacy of prayer—yours and those of others.

My prayer of dominant desire is for the Lord to use me whenever, wherever, however and as long-ever as He may wish. A daily translation of that prayer is, "Lord, make me a blessing to someone today, and in this situation."

I like the popular song that goes,

. . . accentuate the positive, eliminate the negative, latch on to the affirmative . . .

46

THE ATTITUDE OF GRATITUDE

When I finally felt led to write another book with the title, *Much Alive at Ninety-five,* I began scrambling to find sources upon which to draw. As I was being examined by my kidney doctor a short while ago, I asked him to give me two things that contributed to a longer life. Before he had time to speak, I told him one that nearly everyone agreed upon—the body given by your forebears, what you inherit. He agreed, and gave me one more—attitude. That fit right in with a Thanksgiving sermon I had heard years ago on the topic of the attitude of gratitude.

My preacher father often included in his always audible prayers with the family, "Lord, we thank you that everything is as well with us as it is."

He banked his past, present and future on the fact that things could be, or have been, worse and the future could be even better. Of late I have been teaching two of my twelve young great-grandchildren something the shepherd king David wrote some two thousand and five hundred years ago, "It is a good thing to give thanks to God in the morning, and offer praise to him every night."

They have memorized it. Hopefully, they use it at breakfast, even when I'm not there to smile approval. When one tries to live biblically, all he needs to do is to turn in his concordance to "thanks", "thankfulness", "thanksgiving", and find throughout Holy Writ, an enormous number of references to that thought. One of them reads, "In everything give thanks, for this is the will of God concerning you." (Eph. 5:20)

At first, I had difficulty with that one. Everything? Good AND bad? Then I began to realize that trouble is a teacher. Pain is an alert that one needs medicine, a doctor, a hospital. Twenty years ago a doctor discovered that I had diabetes. One of the results of that has been a marked decrease in the feeling on the bottom of my feet. My podiatrist must be careful to examine them betimes, to make sure there is no cut or wound because such can happen without my feeling it. At this writing, the heel of my right foot is taking a long, long time healing from a peeled blister. Weeks and weeks have passed while it gradually responds to the special attention of my Right-at-Home helpers. They medicate and wrap it daily and, I hope, will save my foot from disaster. I can't see it, for I'm unable to bend my leg far enough to view it. They assure me that it is healing. My daughter and physician agree it is getting better. I do hope nothing will happen to prevent me from finishing this book. I thank God, "that everything is as well with us as it is," to quote my father who died at age seventy-four in 1955.

Living with a hopeful attitude brightens the future, puts a light at the end of the tunnel, and makes for a positive outlook. Hope is one of those realities of "things unseen." One sacred writer put it in these words, "We look not at the things that are seen, but at the things that are not seen: for the things that are seen are temporary; but the things that are not seen are eternal."

(2 Cor. 4:18 KJV).

The right attitude toward wealth, or lack of it, gives one comfort or pain. If we hoard it, we deprive others of what they need, and rob ourselves of the joy of sharing. In the story of the good shepherd there were four attitudes toward possessions:

(1) What is mine is mine, I'll keep it. (2) What is yours is mine, I'll take it. (3) What is yours is yours, just keep it. (4) What is mine is yours, I'll share it.

Let that Samaritan, so looked down upon by the Jews, be a noble example for all of us. We will live longer.

The right attitude toward relationships with others makes for happiness or discontent. Knowing and being known are met in different ways by different people. Some people spread their feathers like proud peacocks to be sure that they may be known as really somebody. Others are approachable and open, easy to meet. They are the ones whose lives are enlarged and enriched because their expanded knowledge brings self-fulfillment and insights unobtainable otherwise.

Then there are those who are like tortoises. They are difficult get to know. Others shy away rather than gather around them. Who wants to pry open their shells? Why are some so reluctant to be known? Some have a feeling of inferiority and are reluctant for that to be known. Some have weaknesses and short-comings they wish to keep unknown by others.

47

CULTURE SHOCK

Along the continuum of life you might, and could, be brought you face-to-face with work or employment in an unfamiliar and unwelcome situation. On the other hand it could be just what you wanted. I chose to apply to become a chaplain in military service in 1943. I didn't realize at that time that I'd be the spiritual leader of a smorgasbord of many Protestant servicemen and women. In some assignments, I was the only chaplain. Regardless of who the chaplain was, service people had no other choice but to accept my pastoral leadership. At first it was a shock.

I had been raised the son of a minister and my wife had graduated from a rather strict college. All of a sudden we found ourselves among people of all kinds of moral upbringing, or none. We had been taught that dancing, going to movies, drinking alcoholic beverages, and profane language were unbecoming for a Christian. We found ourselves in the position of being among people who did one or more of these things. It was my responsibility to minister to all of them, and accept them, without approving of their life style and conduct. It was a culture shock.

I attended most of the cultural events on the bases where I was assigned. I distributed invitations to chapel worship services, but I also visited GI's at their work places and sports events. At their clubs I was most always present, without doing the things I had been taught were wrong. I only ordered "double ice and Coke." Only twice did anyone ever try very hard to get me to drink beer, wine or whiskey. I did break over and attend a few movies that were considered better than most.

Many of my commanders, in their regular evaluations, wrote words similar to these:

"Chaplain Green is held in high regard by everyone. His pleasing personality, military bearing and polite mannerisms are the best. He has furthered the religious program by meeting people socially and joining the various social activities of the base. He mixes well and yet maintains the dignity of a religious leader."

Having been surrounded by ultra conservatism in my youth and growing-up years, I began my emancipation after choosing to answer the call into the ministry. No longer could I continue measuring one's piety by strictly arbitrary human standards. That is the kind of culture in which I was raised. To cheat in school was so out-of-bounds that a good Christian would not dare, nor steal, or defame the name of God. But this is not to say anyone is at liberty to do these things without some kind of guilty conscience. No one in my former time, or now, believes that it is right to skip most of the Ten Commandments. But one of the saintliest women I knew dipped snuff. For her that was all right because she had her own rules by which she lived.

Even so, it was a far cry from serving congregations in civilian life. Chaplains were expected to visit with the troops wherever they were found. What about in their barracks, in their mess halls, in their social clubs? Some chaplains, because of their convictions, would not visit the NCO or Officers Club because they were against smoking and dancing, smutty stories, profanity and, sometimes, nudity by entertainers. Most troops were respectful in the presence of chaplains by cleaning up their language and acts.

But sometime things get out of control. In one party in Austria, a female dancer performed so vigorously that a strap fell from her shoulder and revealed a bare breast. My wife, Lois, had just arrived overseas. She had "culture shock" at that moment. As a result she rarely wanted to accompany me to a club even though we would leave early. I braved the worst and helped her to find satisfaction by singing in chapel choirs, opening up Sunday schools, and supervising vacation Bible schools. She never complained. I was so proud of her, when the Russian Army threatened to over-run our allied forces in West Germany, military families were given the privilege of returning to the USA, or staying put, she chose to stay with me, no matter what. Oh, joy! That made me happy!

The culture shock came after I stopped being pastor of local churches and volunteered to become a military chaplain in 1943. My first orientation was at the Chaplains' School for a month at Harvard University. World War II was in full swing. At that one of many months, there were 443 ministers, priests and rabbis. That was an eye-opener at which time I realized that my military congregation would consist of a smorgasbord of many religious faith groups, such as Assembly of God,

Baptist, Christian, Disciples of Christ, Episcopal, Lutheran, Evangelical, Methodist, Mormon, Nazarene, Presbyterian, Seventh Day Adventist, Unity, Wesleyan, etc. I soon learned that most of them were partly unified by The Apostle's Creed that many groups repeated regularly.

A military chaplain's duty was to introduce young men to God and God to young men. Later that included young women. After the end of World War II, military families joined their spouses, at which time chaplains expanded their ministries to provide worship and Christian education for the whole family.

A General Protestant Worship Service, constructed by a consortium of denominational leaders, was a service seemingly agreed upon. It followed no format commonly used elsewhere. The liturgy was acceptable to most Christians. In some large military installations where there were many chaplains of differing faiths, denominational services were allowed provided they did not conflict with the time and space of the general Protestant Service. Such an arrangement was new to me. In the mountains where I was pastor, most of the churches were either Methodist or Baptist. Now and then there was a Presbyterian congregation.

After 20 years as an Air Force chaplain, I retired and went through the shock of the transition back into one denomination. The two decades with inter-denominations ended in 1963. I had been a United Methodist chaplain for those years, and representatives from the Methodist Commission on Chaplains in Washington, DC, had surrounded me with many visits and retreats so that I felt a loyalty. In my new assignment in a large congregation, I exhibited a continuing interest in the ecumenical movement.

Pastoral Prestidigitation

What a name! What a title! And what has it to do with Rev. Philip L. Green, Chaplain, Col., USAF, Ret'd? It is a way of saying that, included with my other activities, I learned and used simple tricks of magic for the many children in my first churches. (1936-'43). At that time I was the pastor of rural churches in the mountains of Western North Carolina. At the age of 22, I began my ministry as a Methodist circuit rider. A circuit is a group of several churches served by the same pastor.

My Pastoral Prestidigitation began soon after I became a pastor. I discovered that a better way to gain the interest of the adults in my congregations was through their children. The children were taught to be respectful of their pastor. I found them too respectful. When I went to visit them in their homes, the children were largely absent from conversations with their parents, as though their spiritual care were secondary or unimportant. Often I invited them into the room for a time of informal talk. I made up stories that neither they, nor anyone else, ever heard of. They were enchanted (sometimes). I soon discovered that they were pleased to have me play simple games with them in the yard. They were even more pleased with a trick of magic. On purpose, I learned several tricks with strings. They eagerly watched each one, hoping to learn how each was done. Other sleight-of-hand tricks left them mystified, as were their parents.

It was not surprising then that the children often spoke to me after the sermon, and asked when I would be coming for another home visit. I was pleased that they wanted more time with me, or at least another opportunity to learn my secrets. My informality made it easier for them to respond at church to my invitation to Christian discipleship. Even after seven decades, I received a letter from one of them in which she thanked me for helping her to become a Christian, when she was young.

When I left the civilian pastorate to become a military chaplain, during and after World War II, I was unable to fill my pockets with the gadgets that my magic tricks required for the children. What to do? Would the GIs respond to a minister in uniform? They would, and they did. I needed simple equipment and a deck of cards, so often available. That turned out to be just the ticket. When I didn't have a deck with me, someone almost always had one, and that was better. My own deck was considered suspect anyway.

Cards were taboo for some preachers in civilian life. In my father-preachers' home, Rook cards were the only ones ever used, and then only when he was not at home. I needed the mental and manual dexterity to work with cards now, in a military setting. Fortunately, in a small shop near Hollywood and Vine, near my airbase in Glendale, California, anyone could purchase all kinds of equipment for feats of magic. On Friday nights, local skilled and unskilled would-be magicians gathered to show each other their dexterity. As I watched them, now and then, it gave me an opportunity to learn to build up some card and other tricks.

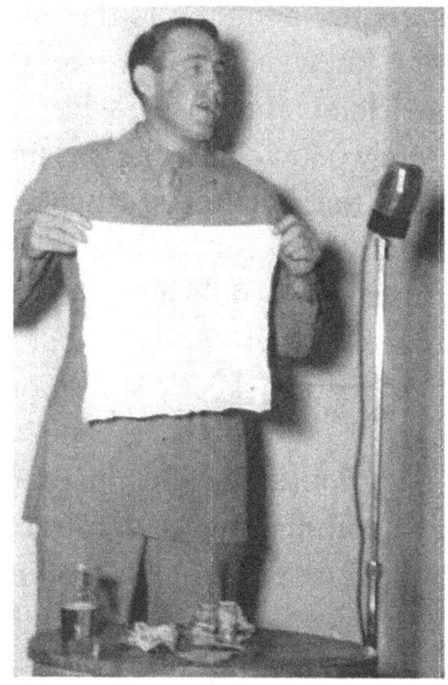

The Magic Handkerchief

Take A Card

At the USO Club nearby in Glendale, Bud Abbott and Lou Costello came over from Hollywood once in awhile. They also sent a magician. From them I learned a higher degree of disciplined skill with the cards. Soon I was able to enter a barracks at night where troops often played cards, even poker games. With ease I could interrupt a game and surprise them with a trick or two.

48

DIVINE HEALING

During the years of my youth and young adulthood, the only references about physical healing that I knew about were in the Bible. There were notable present day claims made by what we non-charismatics called "Holy Rollers". Many people held these claims to be suspect if not fraudulent. It was not that Methodists, Baptists, Lutherans, Presbyterians, and others did not pray for healing of the sick. It was just that there were very few claims of people being healed. The Catholics had a history of "healing sites" where people went to be healed. Even about these sites there was great skepticism among Protestants.

While my father was the pastor of Lighthouse Mission Chapel in St. Louis, MO (1929-'31), he discovered he had diabetes. A devout but eccentric woman of German descent offered to pray for his healing. He resisted submitting himself to her special prayers—held back by pride and unbelief. Finally, after reading about how the leper, Naaman, resisted following the direction of the prophet to go bathe in the river Jordan, he asked her to pray for his healing. He was healed, completely healed, and never needed to seek further treatment of his diabetic condition. I wish my father had witnessed more often to the power of God to heal.

While on the staff of at First United Methodist Church, I was Minister of Pastoral Care. As such, it was a primary duty to visit and minister to the hospitalized and chronically ill. Most patients were willing for me to pray for them. With my hand in theirs, or on their head or shoulder, my prayer was similar to the following; "Father God, I lift Brother Sam up to you for his stay in the hospital. Bless the doctors and nurses and all those who minister to him while he is here. Beyond their skill and knowledge and that of all our human hands, we ask for your special blessing, healing and strength until he is well and home again. Bless his roommate, and all those who need you and turn to you. Be to him a very present help in this time of need. We pray in the name of your Son, Jesus Christ, the great Physician—whose joy it was, and still is, to heal the sick. Amen." The prayer changed from time to time depending upon whether or not the patient was known to be dying.

There were unspectacular healings claimed by some patients. Six months after a woman went home from the hospital with cancer, her daughter said to me one day,

"Rev. Phil, when you placed your hand on my mother's head in Penrose Hospital and prayed for her, she was healed. She is well now."

I told her that God was gracious and good to her mother and that I did not do the healing. Who knows where the faith of the patient, or the efficacy of medical intervention, or both end, and God's healing begins?

I have been a leader in the Colorado Christian Ashram since 1971 when "Brother Stanley" (E. Stanley Jones), the founder of the Christian Ashram, led ours at Horn Creek Retreat Center near Westcliffe, Colorado. A part of every Ashram is a healing service at which people are invited to come forward for the healing of body, or of memories, or of broken relationships, or whatever. At one of our Ashrams, the Rev. Paul Leaming came for the healing of an unusual growth on his vocal chords. He said he was due for surgery the following week. When he went for the surgery, the doctor made a final examination of the affected area and declared, "The growth is gone. You will not need surgery." The condition never returned and he continued in full-time ministry. Praise God!

I have always felt unworthy to include healing as a major part of my long ministry in the United Methodist Church (1936-present)—or has it been lack of faith and trust in One who said, "all things are possible with God"? I sometimes wonder whether or not I have depended too much upon modern medicines and skilled physicians to continue my life in reasonable good health to my present age of ninety-five.

49

MY PRAYER OF DOMINANT DESIRE

The process of developing one has helped me to focus on my purpose in life. As a youth growing up in the home of a devout, serious, earnest preacher-father, I heard many messages that included invitations to make commitments for right living. I gave my heart to the Lord early in life and tried with limited success to live as a Christian should. As with many others, there was the need for many returns from waywardness. There were sermons during camp meetings and summer revivals that pictured God as a stern judge who required a readiness to be chosen for those on his right hand, or the lost ones on his left hand. When I heard a message about how Jesus, God's Son, loved me enough to die for me, my heart melted and I chose to follow one who would do that for me. During those times when I was a stray, I never wanted to become a maverick.

There was a song that appealed to me called, *The Old Rugged Cross* that highlighted the love of Jesus and brought me back "on track" ever and anon. The Methodists believed in and practiced "back-sliding" without turning their backs on God and religion. Other denominations practiced it without naming it as such. In those early days, Methodists drew a rather strong line over which a "good" Christian would not step.

In high school I felt a special call, a call to become a preacher. It was God's call—a definite call to enter the ministry. Two of my father's five brothers had been called into the ministry and were pastors of Methodist Churches. Whether into the ministry, or teaching, or whatever, there are people who feel they are doing God's bidding. Sometimes some people misjudge that call and seek what they feel is the "right" one to follow. When a person feels what is right for him or her, it is a good feeling. Finding oneself a misfit makes for unhappiness, and that estrangement tears down one's gusto for life.

The late Rev. Dr. Harry Emerson Fosdick wrote the book *The Meaning of Prayer* in 1915, a year after I was born. When I was young, I found it in my father's library. Papa must have used it heavily because it was well-worn and had many scribbling in the margins and blank spaces. I inherited that book and have worn it further until the binding has come loose in places from many readings. I have under the glass on my desk the titles of its ten chapters. Here they are:

- The Naturalness of Prayer
- Prayer as Communion with God
- God's Care for the Individual
- Prayer and the Goodness of God
- Hindrances and Difficulties
- Prayer and the Reign of Law
- Unanswered Prayer
- Prayer of Dominant Desire
- Prayer as a Battlefield
- Unselfishness in Prayer

All have spoken meaningfully to me many times across the decades. The one that has impacted my ministry the most has been, *Prayer of Dominant Desire.* Fosdick said that such a prayer was "your demand on life, elevated, purified, and aware of a Divine Alliance."

The prayer of dominant desire is costly. It puts us in the position of helping God answer our prayers. Across human history great saints have been those deeply committed to Christ and willing to hurl *their lives after their prayers.*

In 1818, James Montgomery wrote the words of a hymn that describes that kind of prayer:

> *Prayer is the soul's sincere desire,*
> *Unuttered or expressed,*
> *The motion of a hidden fire,*
> *That trembles in the breast.*
> . . .

I am far from putting myself beside the great men of prayer and faith. Nonetheless I have made my prayer of dominant desire, *Lord, use me, whenever, wherever, however and as long ever as you may wish.*

It took some years for it to formulate and integrate into a paramount intention. This book is about how God has been, and still is, answering that prayer. A peek at the bird's-eye view of my life speaks volumes about how many ways, places and years God has used me.

It was in my father's footsteps (and his two minister brothers) that I began to receive nudges during my childhood and youth years. Add to that the fact that I was the only one of three sons who chose to go with Papa at the time he was ready to go somewhere. If you were not ready when he was ready—you didn't go. He wouldn't wait for any of us except my mother. I went with him to church services where he preached, the only one of seven who wanted and was ready to go. I enjoyed going with him for more than one reason. He was invited to eat in the homes where he went—a big incentive. Food at the parsonage was not that good or plentiful. Conversations between Papa and others was interesting, at times, especially if it related to young people or eating.

This may seem unusual but one reason I liked to go with him was that I enjoyed the stories (illustrations) in his sermons. In different locations he often preached the same sermon. I was alert when he began a story and noted that the same story was repeated slightly in a different way each time. I would tell Papa he didn't tell it right, and he'd tell me he'd get it right next time.

Rudd Newsome was often engaged by my father to lead the music in his revival services. He was tops, with his excellent baritone voice, and led the congregation while he pumped and played the organ. Country churches hardly ever could afford more than a piano or self-pump organ. One of the enjoyments with him was that—following a service—he'd come over to me, put his hands on my shoulders and exclaim, "Philip, the evangelist!" It very well could be that his words influenced me later to respond to God's call into the ministry.

Other motivations along my youthful pathway kept me on track. On her death bed, my Grandmother Green put her hand on my head as I knelt thereby and encouraged me to "be a good preacher."

I had a rough time getting started as a minister. My college years were preceded by an overload of studies and activities during the senior high school year. I had changed schools four times (from North Carolina to St. Louis, to Kentucky, and back to North Carolina), and my required subjects became arranged so that as a senior, I had to take six solid subjects (French I, French II, Ancient and Modern History, Mathematics, and English Literature). During the year I played center on the school basketball team, I had a character part in the junior play and in the senior play, and sang in the school chorus (singing also a duet and in the quartet).

Exhausted, the family moved 125 miles to Greensboro, NC where I sang in commencement exercises at the Bible College, and played *To a Wild Rose* on the piano in a recital. During the summer months I was called upon to sing in revival services as a quartet member before "new" congregations of strangers. The challenge and excitement was too much. I wound up in the fall unable to wind down. Enough about my excuses or reasons for not making a better academic showing at Guilford College, where I was not a resident student on campus and missed most college activities except that of being a member of the A Cappella Choir as a senior.

During four years of college, I had given my musical talents in several ways. I had directed a youth choir at Newland Street Methodist Church in Greensboro. I had sung in mixed and male quartets throughout Western North Carolina and adjoining states (as I represented my own faith but also in benefit of Peoples Bible College), and had brought some musical pleasure to shut-ins in hospitals and health centers. I had been exposed to my father's sermons during childhood and youth, as well as to a plethora of the best camp meeting preachers of the day, including the Rev. Dr. Henry Clay Morrison, twice president of Asbury College, the Rev. "Brother" Bud Robinson, the Rev. Hezekiah Ham (under whose ministry the Rev. Dr. Billy Graham found Christ).

On two different occasions, it was to my benefit to have heard the famed Rev. Dr. G. Campbell Morgan, great expository genius who came from England two years in a row to a Presbyterian Church in Greensboro. Rev. Dr. John R. Church, General Evangelist of the Methodist Church was a special inspiration to me. As an approved local preacher, I had preached in a number of revivals in churches of the Western North Carolina Conference, and had been a part of the musical talent at several camp meetings.

50

MULTIPLY YOUR AFFIRMATIVES

The more things in which you believe, the more positive your outlook on life. Also it broadens the perspective of things that enrich and ennoble. A list of things one can think about without question include honesty, justice, purity, faithfulness, loveliness, inclusiveness, kindness, hopefulness, neighborliness.

When I was wrestling with the call into the ministry, someone told me that I would have to love people. I loved my family, some of my relatives. But "people" was a concept that had not occurred to me. At the time I couldn't care less for people. Then, as I later traveled beyond the local area, I began to notice people struggling with the difficult issues of life—how to feed the family, work with a wayward son, keep the family together and survive hurtful losses, etc.—and my views and relationships with people began to take on a kinship to them. I wanted to be of help, to care, and even to love. I learned that people in America, even people I knew in foreign countries, responded to kindness and respect.

I was later confronted with a tendency among people to include things that traditionally were unacceptable, in which I did not believe. I put together a conference entitled, *Holding Fast to Our Affirmatives.* I believe it is best to eliminate as much of the "gray" as possible and leave pure black and white. Some disagree, but I stand pat.

Shakespeare once wrote, "Diseases desperate grown, by desperate remedies are relieved, or not at all." As a pastor, I was upset. I was hurting for what was happening to my church. The people of the state had voted and passed Proposition II about homosexuality. The lines of demarcation between those who opposed it and thought it was wrong, and those whose votes passed it, were so close and ambiguous that good people on both sides of the issue found little clarity or charity from those of "the other side."

It was a malady that had grown desperate and bid well to causing irreparable damage to the Annual Conference, unless a remedy was found soon. Regardless of the good intentions of the proponents of that Proposition, and irrespective of the well-meaning efforts of those who would overthrow or amend it, the damage was already done. Good people in our churches, and mine, voted what they believed, and were convinced that those who would undo their actions were, in essence, saying, "you poor ignorant people, don't you know that you've made a grave mistake? Now come along and we'll help you see the light."

People skilled in interpersonal relationships generally agree that when an issue results in a question of who is right and who is wrong, the issue becomes destructive and unproductive. The members of my church were saying, "Why do the leaders of our denomination fight against us? We'll not support anything 'they' want us to give to. Cut my over-and-above giving to the church. It's their church anyway, not ours."

During the first five years as pastor at one church, I had tried very hard to build confidence in the "Conception System," in Episcopal leadership, and in what the "Missional Covenant" meant. I had invited the bishop to come and, by dedicating a new cross on the church steeple, cement that bridge of confidence.

ADDENDUM

Ecclesiastical History of Philip's Life

- Granted a local License to Preach in the Greensboro, NC District, Western NC Conference of The Methodist Church, April 1934
- Admitted on Trial in that Conference in Salisbury, NC, Oct 1936
- Appointed pastor, Sandy Circuit, Leicester, NC (Buncombe Co) Asheville District, 1936-'40
- Appointed pastor, Franklin Circuit (Macon Co), Waynesville District, 1940-'43
- Special appointment as a military chaplain during WW II under the supervision of the Methodist Commission on Chaplains in Washington, DC, 1943-'63
- Transferred from the Western NC Conference to the Rocky Mountain Annual Conference, Jun 1963
- Appointed Minister of Outreach (Evangelism), First United Methodist Church, Colorado Springs, CO, Aug 1963
- As an additional duty, I was also appointed pastor of Edison-Leader UMC 1964-'67.
- Appointed Interim Senior Minister at First UMC, Nov 1966-Mar 1967 and Oct 1978-Jun 1979
- Appointed Minister of Pastoral Care at First UMC, 1968-'80
- Leave of Absence, March 1980 through March '81
- I was asked to become the Minister of Cultivation at First UMC, Colorado Springs, CO, Jan to June 1981.
- Appointed an approved Conference Evangelist of the Rocky Mountain Annual Conference, April 1, 1981
- In 1983, I was approved to be an evangelist for Christian Ashrams.
- Member of the National Assn. of United Methodist Evangelists, 1983-2011
- Retired from mandatory appointments, June 1983
- In retirement, I incorporated Special Care Ministries, Inc. and served as the Special Care Minister, 1983-'87.

- Founder of Wilson United Methodist Fellowship in Northwest Colorado Springs. It became Wilson UMC in 1987, Oct 1984-'86
- Member of "The Seventy," the United Methodist Foundation for Evangelism, Lake Junaluska, NC 1986-2008
- Regional Representative, United Methodist Foundation for Evangelism, Lake Junaluska, NC, 1986-'89
- I was invited to be the English-language pastor of Korean Christian (nondenominational) church until I was eighty-five, Jan-Oct 1988 and Aug 1996-Feb 2001
- Appointed the pastor of Avondale UMC, Avondale, CO, Nov 1988-Jun 1995
- In 2010, I completed seventy-four years as a United Methodist minister, active and retired.
- Except for one year, my residence has been in El Paso County between 1960 and 2011 (the present). I have spent the last 12 years attending First UMC in Colorado Springs.

Military Chaplain 1943-'63, Philip's Assignment, etc.

- Harvard Univ. Cambridge, MA, Army Chaplain School, July-Aug 1943
- Grand Central Air Terminal, LA, CA, 329th Fighter Group, Aug '43-Mar '44
- Ontario Army Airbase, Ontario, CA, 443rd Army Airbase Unit, Mar '44-Jun '44
- Avon Park AAF, Avon Park, FL, 325th AAF Base Unit, Jun '44-Aug '44
- Page Field, Fort Myers, FL, 338th AAF Base Unit, Aug '44-Sep '45
- MacDill Field, Tampa, FL, 326th AAFBU, 498th Bomb Gp, Sep '45-Aug '46, VIIITH Bomber Command
- Rhein-Main AAB, Frankfurt, Ger 831st Aviation Engineering Bn, Aug '46-Nov '46
- Hoersching, AAB, Linz, Austria, 79th Fighter Group (P-47s), Nov '46-Jun '47
- Bad Kissinger AAB, Germany, Hq XIIth Tacticl Air Command, Jun '47-Jan '48
- Wiesbaden, USAFE, 501st Air Sv. Gp, 150th AF Comp Wing, Jan '48-May '4
- Vance, AFB, Enid, OK, 3573rd Pilot Training Wing (AME), May '49-Apr '51
- Spence Air Base, Moultrie, GA, 3302d Training Sq, Apr '51-Jan '53
- Parks AFB, Pleasanton, CA, 3295th Military Training Wing, Jan '53-Aug '54
- HQ 16th Air Force, Madrid, Spain, Joint US Military Group, Aug '54-Sep '57
- Whiteman AFB, Knobnoster, MO, 340th Bomb Wing, Sep '57-Aug '60
- USAF Academy, Colo. Springs, CO, Hq USAF Academy, Aug '60-Jul '62
- Kincheloe AFB, Sault St. Marie, MI 507th Fighter Inter Wing, Jul '62-Aug '63
- Retired Aug 1, 1963 in the grade of Colonel

Military Awards, Medals, Citations, Commendations

American Campaign Medal, World War II Victory Medal, World War II Occupation Medal (Europe), Humane Action Medal (Berlin Air Lift 1948-'49), Ten-year Reserve Medal (with hourglass), National Defense Service Medal, Air Force Longevity Service Medal (with four oak-leaf clusters), Commendation Medal (Meritorious service as first Protestant chaplain in Spain 1954-'57), Air Force Commendation Medal (Meritorious service for International Relations at Kincheloe Air Force Base, Sault St. Marie, MI, 1962-'63).

Military Chaplains Association (MCA)

The professional organization for military chaplains began during World War II. It was later chartered by Congress. At first it was called the Army and Navy Military Chaplains Association. When the Air Force became autonomous it was added, as also was the Veterans Administration. When I was commissioned a first lieutenant in June of 1943 I knew nothing about the association.

In time, I became very active and was invited to chair the host committee for the national convention in 1968, again in 1978, and yet again in 1988 in Colorado Springs. I was highly pleased that my colleagues elected me as their president in 1970 and again in 1971. I was the first Air Force chaplain elected to that position

How could I be the associate pastor of the largest United Methodist Church in the entire Western Jurisdiction and, at the same time serve as the president of a national organization? It meant attending executive committee meetings in Washington, D.C. and presiding as president at two national conventions, one in Washington and another in California. But my senior minister and pastor-parish relations committee gave me short times away to do that. They seemed glad that their associate pastor was so honored. At times I was super busy.

Third Conference on Ministerial Excellence

"Dynamics of the Christian Life Today", July 21-Aug 2, 1974
Host church—First United Methodist Church, Colorado Springs, CO
Philip L. Green, Church Staff Coordinator

Invitations were sent on an interfaith basis to large multiple-staff churches, interdenominational, and inviting clergy and laity alike. From across America more than 140 professional church leaders enrolled. Some brought their spouses and families to the mountains for a vacation before and after this event. Those who wished lodging in homes at $3.00 per day were given that plan.

Eleven plenary sessions were given during the five days of this event. In addition to Dr. Seward Hiltner from Princeton University, the other distinguished speakers and panelists included:

Bishop Melvin E. Wheatley, Denver Area United Methodist
Fr. Rev. Dr. John M. Cassem, Regis College Denver
Rev. Dr. Lawrence L. Lacour, Host Church Senior. Minister
Rev. Dr. Thomas J. Shipp, Lovers Lane Methodist, Dallas, TX
Rev. Jack T. Slaughter, CPE Supervisor, Ft. Logan, Denver
Dr. John K. Sterrett, Int'l Committee for Space Research

Co-Sponsors:

Rev. Charles D. Whittle, Board of Discipleship, U. Meth. Church Nashville, TN, Assistant General Secretary.
Chaplain, Colonel, Charles R. Posey, President, Rocky Mountain Chapter of the Military Chaplains Association. (MCA)
Rev. James L. Barber, District Superintendent.
Rev. Dr. Terry L. Smith, Exec Director, the P. Peak Assn of Church

Plenary Session Topics:

"Protestant Spirituality" Dead, Dying or Beginning a New Birth?
Counseling for Commitment (two sessions)
Experience and the Christian Life
The Church and Counsel
Church Responsibility for Community Life
Can Pastoral Care Help the "Problem" of Theology in the Church?
The Caring Pulpit
Medical Serendipities from the Space Program
The Imperatives to Care

Small Group Topics

Reaction Groups to Plenary Session
Optional Small Groups
The Caring Process in Large Churches
Crisis Counseling
Lay Priesthood of Caring
Death and Dying
The Church and the Alcoholic, the Addicted and others.

How did the conferees react and respond to this in depth pastoral care conference? It is obvious that I had had broad and comprehensive assistance. Dean Seward Hiltner and other plenary session speakers were the best resource persons in putting it together. I was breathless until the evaluations came in. Nearly every conferee completed one, which was a minor miracle, as requests for evaluation go. The staff of the host church joined me in great happiness when the vast majority of evaluations were unusually high. Along with the remarks were helpful suggestions for the next such conference. Many expressed the hope that we would have another one soon.

My superior, Rev. Dr. Larry L. Lacour, was very complementary which made me glad for the painstaking care I had given to the project.

At the recap session with the principal leaders, they gave me pats on the back which I gladly share below.

Dr. Lacour commented at the recapitulation session with the leaders of this event: "Phil is better than he thinks he is."

Later Bishop Melvin E. Wheatley wrote, "Phil, I want to thank you for elevating the position of Associate Pastor to the level of distinctive and distinguished service where it properly belongs".

Rev. Dr. Charles Whittle, who represented the General Board of Discipleship in Nashville, referred to me later as, "A super hero, who never tried to be one".

A District Superintendent that attended this event asked me, at the end of my nine years of retirement, to consider going to a small church sixty miles from home as its pastor. At first, I referred her to any one of several retired ministers in Colorado Springs. She told me there were two retired clergy in Pueblo only sixteen miles from that church's cite, but that, she wanted me.

I told her that I already had a fixed itinerary that would take me out of the state for nine weeks and that it would be unfair to that congregation for me to begin in November and be gone after Christmas that long. She further kept after me by saying that she would ask someone else to fill in for me while I was gone. So I agreed to go and be interviewed by the Pastor-Parish Relations Committee, knowing that a 74-year old preacher would not be wanted. I was mistaken. I served there until I was eighty, because I was needed by that congregation and the D.S., who had heard me say at Annual Conference in June, "I ain't done yet".

No one could look back over the subsequent years with me and fail to begin to glow at the amazing results of that one week in July 1974. It meant very much to me.

Operation Southern Hospitality

In 1951, after duty at Vance Air Force Base, I was sent to a Contract Flying Base known as Spence Air Base near Moultrie, Georgia. The US Air Force was very short on pilots and chose to train young officers at a number of such bases. Ours was Hawthorne School of Aeronautics. There were four others in that company in North and South Carolina, and in Jacksonville, FL. In each five week class of trainees there were students from friendly countries in Europe. I was a member of the Moultrie Lions Club and invited the club to adopt a class and invite these young trainees into their club and into their homes. When I asked other service clubs, including the Rotarians and Kiwanis to do the same, "Operation Southern Hospitality" was born. I was asked by higher headquarters to tell how I did it so successfully at Spence Air Base.

That organization helped the trainee pilots from those foreign countries to get acquainted with the American way of life, as well as to build bridges of understanding between cultures.

Pastoral Care Evangelism

When I discovered "too late" that the rules of my denomination would not allow me to be appointed to the same duty as the one I had just finished as Conference Evangelist, I incorporated a similar ministry using the title shown above. To make the corporation legal I had to have an organization with specifically assigned duties and a description of the new organization that included a sponsoring board with a chairperson, a secretary and a treasurer. A brief description of that ministry included:

It is that kind of pastoral care that incorporates a skilled intentionality calculated to go beyond meeting the immediate needs of persons and makes the pastoral care event the beginning of a relationship that will,

'open to non-members who come for pastoral care, for counseling, and pastoral acts (weddings, funerals, baptisms, etc.) channels of communication for follow-on acts of caring and conversations which could lead to a commitment to Christian discipleship and church membership.'

'open doors of return to, and revive interest in inactive and withdrawn members who have strayed from the life of faith; been estranged because of real and imagined wrongs done to them by other leaders of the church; have misunderstood the polity, social principles, and/or the theology of the denomination; have been hurt by the church's neglect; have been crushed or bewildered by life's circumstances; or no longer have an interest in active church participation, for whatever reason.'

'lead church members to a greater reliance upon Christ, to a willingness to seek supportive relationships within the church, and to a more dedicated commitment to the vows of membership.'

'assimilate new and old members into worship, nurture, and faith-living within the church, in such a way as to make discipleship a joy and service a privilege.'

Grand Festival Of Faith Celebration

of the Bicentennial of the USA and the Centennial of the State of Colorado May 9, 1976, 4:00-6:00 p.m. Wasson Stadium, Colorado Springs, Colorado
Pikes Peak Region Coordinator, Philip L. Green
(with the help of all religious bodies of the region)

PROGRAM

Prelude music by the Colorado Springs 60-piece Orchestra
Proclamation, Mayor of Colorado Springs
Narrative, "The Right to Faith"
Three anthems by a six-hundred voice volunteer choir accompanied by the orchestra:
- "Hallelujah" from the Mount of Olives—Beethoven
- "Salvation is Created"—Teschesnokoff
- "Battle Hymn of the Republic"—Wilkowsky

Other music:
- "Horay Nirkoda"—Youth, Temple Shalom
- "Come, Come Ye saints"—choir of Church of Christ of Latter Day Saints
- "Fanfare"—Bell Ringers of First United Methodist Church
- Congregational music— "Our Father's God, to Thee"
  "America the Beautiful"
  "For All the Saints"
  "My Country, 'Tis of Thee"

Prayer of Penitence and Hope (see below)
Volunteer Offering
Keynote Address—"Almost a Chosen People"
Memorial Moments (see below)
Bicentennial Shout
Benediction

Memorial Moments

Early on the morning of February 3, 1943, the Army Transport "S.S. Dorchester" was torpedoed off the coast of

Greenland. With complete disregard for their own safety, they made their way on the deck and went among the confused fear-stricken men, encouraging them, praying with them, calming their fears, and assisting them into life boats and life jackets. They are credited with saving many persons by persuading them to go overboard where there was a chance of rescue. When the supply of life jackets became exhausted, each chaplain removed his own jacket and gave it to another person. The ship was sinking by the bow when the men in the water and in the lifeboats saw the chaplains with arms linked, moving their lips in prayer. They were still so when the ship made its final plunge.

The annals of our leaders of the faith hold no record of greater personal heroism and self-giving than that exemplified by these four chaplains; one Catholic, one Jewish, and two Protestant. Though free to save themselves they chose a greater freedom; to save others. In their memory, and in memory of all who have inspired us to goodness and nobleness, let us sing the words in our program entitled, For All the Saints.

Prayer of Contrition and Hope

In contrition, O God of our fathers, we come to you because we have not always been worthy of the religious liberty which has been guaranteed by our Constitution for two hundred years.

We are heartily sorry that we have not managed our corporate religious freedom to work together as people of faith in doing those things we need to do together. As religious bodies and power structures we have been tardy in espousing your requirement to do justly, love mercy and to walk humbly with our God. We have kept locked the treasury of our latent potential to change the things crying to be changed.

Instead of being facilitators and enablers, we often have been stumbling-blocks to the coming of your kingdom. Only haphazardly have we been a part of earth's cure. Most reluctantly and timidly have we been to declare the day of salvation; your transforming, redeeming love.

As individuals we are contrite because we have not valued our personal religious freedom very highly and therefore, have not become the persons we could have become. Instead of being sons and daughters in our house of freedom, we have been willing to be hired servants. We have been content with a half-hearted effort at being our brother's keeper, when we were free to be our brother's brother. We have been at liberty to wash away impurity in the sea of your forgetfulness, yet like Augustine we have said, "but not now."

"Getting and spending, getting and spending," we have laid waste our powers, when we could have been enriching our inner being by contemplating those things that are true, honest, just, pure, lovely, and of good report. We have been free to come to the source of cleansing and healing and forgiveness but have remained in the far country of estrangement and separation and sin. We have taken our freedom to spend our money as we please to rob you of your tithe, and have stopped our ears to the "thunder of bare feet" of the needy.

As we confess our sins, cleanse us from all unrighteousness.

Give us the hope of a better life and better use of our corporate and personal religious freedom in the remainder of our lives and in the beginning of our third century of religious freedom. Let your truth make us free. Let the words of Isaiah encourage us, "They that wait upon the Lord shall renew their strength, they shall mount up with wings as eagles, they shall run and not be weary, they shall walk and not faint."

May the words of our mouths and the meditations of our hearts be acceptable unto you, O Lord, our rock and our Redeemer. Amen.

Philip's Interesting'Firsts'

1. First US Air Force elected National President of the Military Chaplains Association.
2. First USAF Spiritual Life Conference Director, Baptist Assembly Ground, Ridgecrest, NC, 1953
3. First and only Protestant chaplain assigned to 16th Air Force, Madrid, Spain, 1954-'57
4. Initiated, Committee on the Chaplaincy, Rocky Mountain Conference and was its first coordinator, 1963-'69
5. First chaplain of the Pikes Peak Retired Officers Assoc. 1965-'67
6. First Associate Pastor of First UMC with 6,000+ members, 1963-'80, Colorado Springs.
7. Founder, Duo Church School Class, First UMC, 1963-still going in 2011, 7:30 a.m. chapel worship service.
8. First staff representative of First UMC Counseling Service, 1973-'77, Colorado Springs.
9. Founder, Colorado Interfaith Counseling Center and Pastoral Resource Institute, Inc. and board chair, 1977-'85, Colorado Springs.
10. Founder, Special Care Ministries, Inc., Colorado Springs, 1983-'88
11. Founder and Director, Aspen-Glow Camp for Senior United Methodists, Rocky Mountain Conference, Templed Hills Conference Camp, Woodland Park, CO 1981-'84
12. Founder, Wilson United Methodist Fellowship in NW Colorado Springs, CO 1984

Following are more pictures of how God used me

Pre-Military Pastor
1936-1943

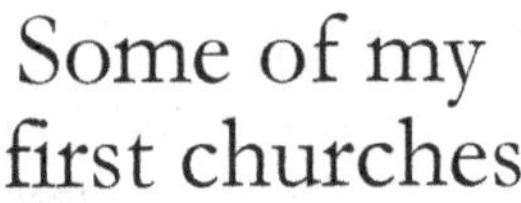

Some of my first churches

Snow Hill UMC

Louisa Chapel

Old Brick Church

Iotla Church

Clarks Chapel

In December 1948, the U.S. and allied personnel on duty in Wiesbaden, Germany, chose to sponsor Christmas parties for all the children in all the schools in that area (estimated 7,000 children). I was asked to be the one to organize those parties. To succeed at this gargantuan task, I had the enthusiastic help of a great number of people on occupation duty at United States Forces in Europe, including their spouses. This was just one of my humanitarian projects |
and these are just some of the children.

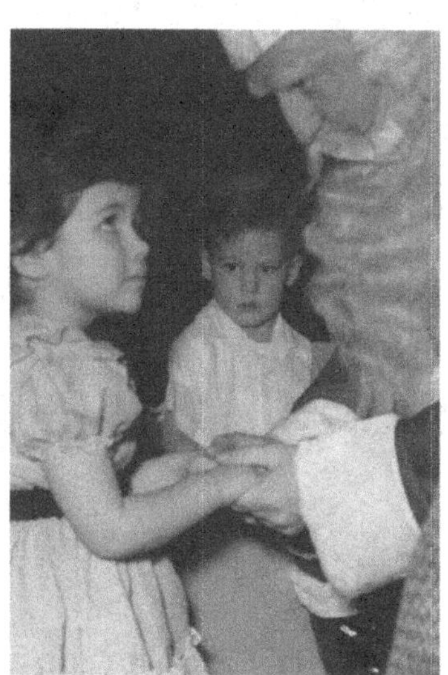

"Hello Santa"

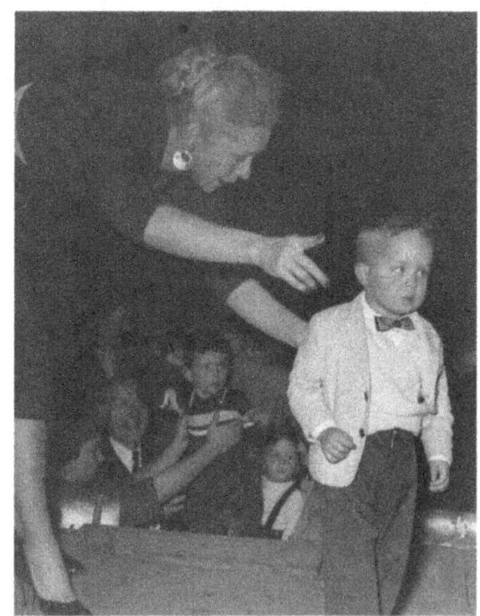

"Do I have to?"

Christmas party in Madrid, Spain, 1956
Some loved Santa Claus, some did not.

1943 Young Chaplain

1948 Career Chaplain

1963 Colonel Chaplain

2009 Retired Chaplian

Some of my worship sites during my military years.

Converted barracks
Wiesbaden, Germany 1948

Spence AFB Chapel, 1952

AF Academy Chapel, 1962

Eddison-Leader
1964-1967

Some of my post-retirement churches

Wilson UMC 1984-1986
Founder

Avondale UMC
1988-1995

Korean Church 1995-2000
English Language Pastor

Before my arrival as his Associate Pastor in 1963, the Rev. Dr. Ben F. Lehmberg had built the church up from 3,000 to more than 6,000 members. It was the largest church building in the city, the largest Methodist church in the Western Jurisdiction, and one of the ten largest in the country. I served for 17 years as the Associate Pastor and twice as Interim Senior Pastor. In 2011, I was honored by being named Associate Pastor Emeritus.

Some Public Relations pictures

My Commander on left
Spence Field, Moultrie, GA

I am a 32nd Degree Mason

Celebrating the 9th Anniversary of the
U.S. Air Training Command

Visiting Pastor Knodt, Schlangenbad, Germany

Me with Bevo Howard (right)
entertaining a guest

Interviewed by Harlan
Ochs for FUMC archives

Opening ceremony of
hobby shop 1951

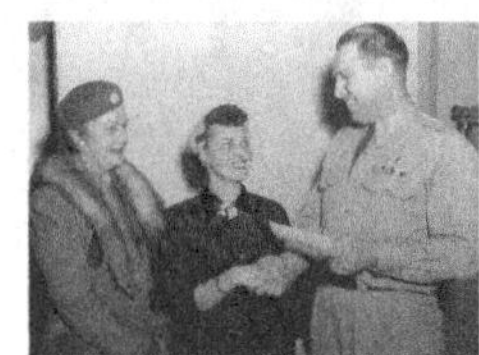

"So glad you came."

Planting a cross at Sunrise Service

The Offering

Vacation Bible School

Baptising a young convert Leicester, NC 1938

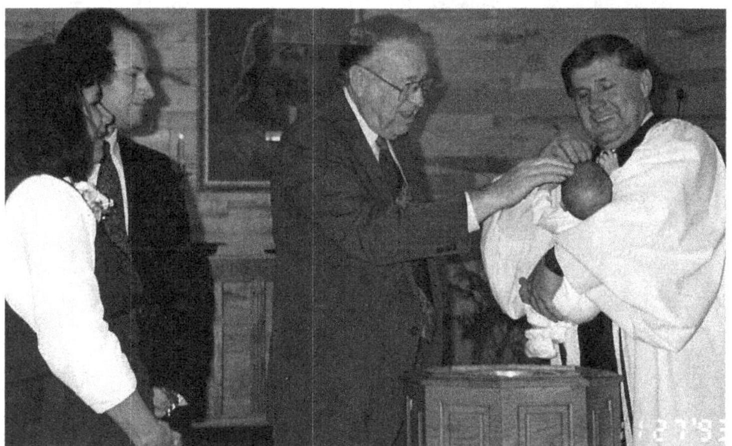

Baptising a great grandson 1994

Germany 1948

Moultrie GA 1952

Funeral of a friend
I conducted at age 95

Conducting a
military funeral

Bishop Arthur Moore receiving a
communion set, Germany 1947

Communion Service, Madrid, Spain 1956

SOURCES

- The Bible—Scripture quotations are from either the King James Version or the New International Version.
- Most of the photos in the book were taken by Phil. Some were donated by family members and professional associates. The military headshots are copies from military base photo shops.
- Pamphlet, *The Mayo Clinic Plan for Healthy Aging-How to find happiness and vitality as you age,* pamphlet.
- *Chief Center on Aging and Older Adult Ministries*
- *Learn to Grow Old* book by Paul Tournier
- *Death, the Final Stage of Growth* book by Elisabeth Kubler-Ross,
- *Aging Is Not for Sissies* book by Terry Schuchman
- *Too Young to Be Old* book by John Gilmore
- *The Purpose Driven Life* book by Rick Warren
- *The Mountains Are Happy* book by Philip L. Green
- *On Golden Pond* movie gave me some thoughts.
- The Reader's Digest article *Health Care for All* Nov. '08
- Time Magazine article *How Faith Can Heal* Feb. '09

MEET THE AUTHOR

Philip was born in September 15, 1914, the son of a United Methodist circuit-riding pastor in the Blue Ridge Mountains of Western North Carolina and was ordained a Deacon and Elder by 1940. He was appointed a pastor of Sandy Circuit of six churches in 1936 and of the Franklin Circuit in 1940.

In 1943 he became a military chaplain during World War II and served in the US Army Air Corps and the US Air Force for twenty years, retiring in the grade of colonel in 1963.

The chaplains of the Air Force, Army, Navy, and VA, elected him the first Air Force national president of the Military Chaplains Association in 1970. In this photo he presented that year's National Citizenship Award to Senator John C. Stennis of Mississippi.

Shortly after duty at the Air Force Academy, he was invited to become the Associate Pastor of a six thousand-member church in Colorado Springs, CO. During 17 years there he served twice as interim senior pastor. In November 2011, at age 97, the church honored him with the Associate Pastor Emeritus.

Following church retirement in 1983, he started a new congregation, began writing books, and helping God answer his lifelong 'prayer of dominant desire.'